Values and Ethics Series, Volume 9

The Burdens of Justice
in Families, Education, Health Care, and Law

James F. Smurl

Foreword by Douglas Sturm

Loyola University Press
Chicago

Loyola University Press
3441 North Ashland Avenue
Chicago, Illinois 60657

Cover design by Nancy Gruenke
Interior design by Mary O'Connor

Library of Congress Cataloging-in-Publication Data

Smurl, James F., 1934–
    The burdens of justice : social issues in crisis / by
James F. Smurl.
       p.   cm. — (Values and ethics series ; v. 9)
    Includes bibliographical references and index.
    ISBN 0-8294-0743-X
    1. Social justice—Case studies. 2. Social ethics—United
States—Case studies. 3. Distributive justice—Case studies.
4. United States—Social conditions—Case studies. I. Title
II. Series : Values & ethics series ; v. 9.
    HM216.S543   1994
    303.3'72—dc20

                                                92-36257
                                                    CIP

To Mary Hennigan Smurl, my best friend

Contents

Foreword
   by Douglas Sturm   *ix*

Acknowledgments   *xv*

Introduction   1

1. The Burdens of Justice   13

2. In Families   49

3. In Financing Public Education   77

4. In Basic Health Care   93

5. In Contract Law   117

Conclusion   143

Notes   149

References   185

Index   207

Foreword

"Let justice roll down like waters and righteousness like a mighty stream." These words of Amos, pronounced centuries ago against a society riven with covenantal infidelity and social antagonism, retain their powers of inspiration even yet. They provoke a vision that reaches far beyond what has ever been accomplished in human history. But they articulate a hope that encourages peoples, particularly peoples who have been and are still marginalized and deprived, to yearn for the kind of political community that may someday be. They give rise to movements for liberation from all the forces of delimitation and degradation that stifle the creativity of life. Moreover, they are directed toward a future that is, in some fashion, rooted in the present despite all appearances to the contrary.

As such, justice is far more than a moral principle, narrowly understood. It is far more too than a stipulated imperative imposed upon us to constrain our natural impulses and to sustain a modicum of order, thereby allowing each of us to pursue our respective self-interests protected by the artificial boundaries of law. Rather, justice is, in the philosophical language of the Western intellectual tradition, an ontologically grounded principle. It is a statement of our identity, both individually and collectively. It betokens something about our fundamental condition as denizens of a cosmos in which we all belong together. The obligatoriness of justice is grounded in the most basic character of our life. That, of course, was the burden of Plato's argument in the *Republic*. Justice is not alien to us. It is not an embellishment. It is not a heteronomous imperative. It is, in the old-fashioned sense of the term, a virtue, a quality of human excellence. To be ourselves, in the fullest and most complete sense, is to be just. In the presence of justice, we are all enriched; in the absence of justice, we are all deprived. Justice is a quality of human stature; injustice is indicative of human failure.

In this text on the "burdens of justice," James Smurl has performed the singular service of reminding us, once again, of the integral importance of justice in our lives together. We need to be reminded. That has been the genius of the work of political philosopher John Rawls, who, over the course of his career, has forced—at least those in professional life—to consider with deep seriousness the grounds, the meaning, and the implications of justice, which—as he not improperly claims—is the primary virtue of our governing institutions. That has also been the genius of the theologies of liberation, beginning with Gustavo Gutiérrez, that have emerged over the past three decades in many areas in the world and that proclaim, as a basic principle, a preferential option for the poor.

Smurl, in his own way, stands with other political philosophers at a point of confluence, where these two strains of thought and practice are brought together. His primary concern is distributive justice, and his primary focus is the United States. He is writing as an American to Americans. We are, as Smurl rightly notes, children of circumstance. We are born of particularity. We are progeny of the mythos and the ethos of time and place. That is our immediate and inescapable condition. We must speak within that context, but, given our critical powers, we must also speak to that context while comprehending all of its agonies and ambiguities. That is the function and responsibility of practical reason. While we cannot but be informed by the narratives of our time and place, we bear the burden of refining, if not radically rescripting, those narratives. Moral tales are not, in themselves, definitive. They are susceptible to critical scrutiny given all the resources we can muster to ascertain what they really mean and how they really affect the lives that we live together. America's moral tales stand in dire need of a radical rescripting, given the full meaning of justice and given the troubled character of our history.

Twenty-five years ago, Dr. Martin Luther King, Jr., asserted what had long been known by few but vigorously denied by many; namely, that, since its inception, America has suffered from a profound cultural and moral schizophrenia. In its liturgical expressions, America repeatedly touts itself as the model of a modern democratic society, a land of opportunity, a place of liberty and justice for all. But those declarations are belied by a powerful subtext, fixated in institutional form, of white racism and male dominance and accompanied by persistent poverty. As if that were not enough, our schizophrenic character is compounded by a constant struggle between two antithetical moral impulses: the appeal to utility and the urging of justice. The appeal to utility mandates that we test all of our activities and associations by a mythic bottom line, invested with the presumption of realism. In its international counterpart, the appeal to utility assumes the form of national security. The cry for justice, on the other hand, announces that rights are trump. Prosperity and security cannot be sought by any means; their pursuit must be constrained by and subordinated to a universal principle of human dignity (if not, indeed, the dignity of each and every creature, human and otherwise) with all the fundamental goods and rights that apply. In the struggle between these impulses, the appeal to utility is most often the victor and, in at least some of its forms, reinforces the stranglehold that oppressive structures have on many peoples in American culture. So, for instance, programs of affirmative action are resisted in the name of efficiency, and proposals for low-income housing are opposed in the name of economic survival. These complexities and confusions of the American story, once they are discerned with any clarity, should drive us to the kind of critical reconsideration that Smurl has so meticulously set out in his study.

Distributive justice is Smurl's topic, but he approaches it with an illuminating twist. In Harold Lasswell's felicitous phrasing, distributive justice has to do with who gets what, when, where, and how. We normally think of distributive justice as the allocation of goods and privileges. It is that. But with keen insight into the full dynamics of social interaction, Smurl would have us consider the other side of that process, namely, the allocation of burdens and pains. That is, in the distributive network that permeates any given social system, one of the more excruciating moral questions that must be posed is: who pays? If some must suffer in order for others to gain, according to what principles? With what kinds of safeguards are those pains to be spread across a population? This side of the distributive question has been largely ignored, except by the privileged who, when pressed, are all too quick to invoke either a jerry-rigged principle of entitlement or a flimsily argued apology that everyone benefits in the long haul from the maldistribution of power and wealth. But if such an invocation is, as it so obviously appears to be, not a considered judgment of practical reason but a thinly disguised form of rationalization, then what principles should prevail? And how might such principles be made effective in practice? We are indebted to Smurl for bringing this kind of moral question to the forefront of our reexamination of the American story.

Moreover, we are further indebted to Smurl for probing the meaning and implications of distributive justice in significantly divergent spheres of our common life—ranging from the subtle and oftentimes intimate interactions that distribute the burdens of family life to the more formal and deliberative kinds of exchange that characterize marketplace bargaining. The requirements of distributive justice, Smurl claims, following the lead of Michael Walzer, cannot be expected to be uniform across all these spheres. We are at risk should we oversimplify the imperatives of justice. Yet, we may also be at risk, I would suggest, if we assume the imperatives of justice are so complex—so context dependent—that they hold nothing in common or, alternatively, that they are held together by nothing in common. Perhaps—could it be?—that permeating all the several spheres of justice is a dominant and pervading affirmation, namely, that we belong together in the encompassing community of life, that we depend on each other for our sustenance and enhancement and that as we receive from so also we ought to give to that community what is necessary for its vitality and vibrancy. If that be the case, then justice, in all its multifariousness, is a function of the creativity and flourishing of our common life. Solidarity is the name of that affirmation, but a solidarity infused, as Smurl would have us admit, with mutuality of sacrifice. But, then, we must recapture the full depth of the meaning of sacrifice. Sacrifice, in both its ordinary and extraordinary instances, entails a giving. It is a gift, however much it may have the feeling of an imposition. It is manifest in assuming the burdens of life. Obversely, to sacrifice is, as the etymology of the word reveals, to make sacred. Sacrifice, in its appropriate form, instills the intentionality of sacrality in relationships. It is a giving that expands the quality of life. It is a loss whose intent and effect constitute, in principle at least, a gain in our solitary existence. In that sense, justice, even its distribution of burdens, is a quality of human stature.

From time to time, Smurl insists that, in contrast to Rawls's concentration on a full compliant society—that is, an imagined system wherein all parties are given, without quarrel or qualification, to do justice—his reflections are focused instead on the rough-and-tumble of everyday life as it is lived where not everyone is so inclined. That may be so. However much Smurl's normative nudgings seem to derive from the insights and principles of practical reason and however much he would have us deal with the world as it exists and not as it might be imagined, it must be admitted that he is reaching for a radical transformation in the habitual thought patterns and practices of American society. Yet, surely, that is as it must be, given the convoluted traditions we have inherited and the concomitant institutional pressures that seem to hold us captive. To place before us the imperatives of justice, however much they may be grounded in our most fundamental condition and however much they present to us a vision of the good life, is to rub against the grain of our customary understandings and expectations.

That is why Smurl is calling for nothing less than a new public philosophy, a radically revised American story, through which we acknowledge and respect our deep differences, yet are brought together in a community committed to walking in justice with one another and to sharing in the joys and to allocating the burdens of our common life in such a way that the lives of all are enriched with qualitative meaning.

Douglas Sturm
Bucknell University, Department of Religion
Lewisburg, Pennsylvania

Acknowledgments

Over the course of the twelve years this book has been in the making, Indiana University at Indianapolis has provided assistance in the form of two sabbaticals, agreeable and efficient support staff, technical support, and funding for manuscript preparation. For those contributions I am most grateful, but far more thankful still for the community of scholar-teachers the university has allowed to develop among members of the Department of Religious Studies. The content and form of every chapter in this book has been shaped and reshaped by those special people. Conrad Cherry, Tom Davis, William Jackson, E. Theodore Mullen, Jr., Rowland A. Sherrill, and Jan Shipps will always deserve my unwavering respect and heartfelt gratitude.

A longer list of benefactors will be evident in individual chapters. Chapter 1 has been shaped most by my foremost and most learned mentor, Bernard J. F. Lonergan, S.J. Mary, my faithful friend, wife, and mother to our four children; my deceased father, James Joseph Smurl; and my mother, Rita Gildea Smurl, have taught me more than I can put in writing regarding justice and common burdens in families. Professor Diane Yeager of Georgetown University was the talented editor of *The Annual of the Society of Christian Ethics* in which I first expressed my thoughts regarding the renegotiation of the burdens of justice in public education (Smurl 1987, 147–48). My colleagues at Indiana University's schools of medicine and nursing, and, in particular, those in the departments of genetics, obstetrics and gynecology, and community health nursing, and those at the Hastings Center and the Kennedy Institute helped me understand much of what I have learned about health care. My understanding of law and legal culture owes much to the faculty and library staff of the

School of Law at Indiana University in Indianapolis, the staff of the American Bar Association, and the archivists for the Brandeis Papers at the University of Louisville and at Harvard University's Law School, my time at which was made possible by a 1981 Lilly Endowment Open Faculty Fellowship (Smurl 1983).

Finally, there are those very special people who have read the entire manuscript and have offered wise counsel about its arguments and thoughtful advice about its style. Highest on the list of those persons are colleagues in my department; my wife, Mary; our son, Paul; Kristin O'Connell; and Rebecca Grenoble. I would also like to offer my appreciation to the editorial staff of Loyola University Press.

Introduction

This book is about distributive justice. It is concerned with the right provision of social goods, including the equitable allocation of common burdens, among members of social communities. Its subject matter is shaped particularly by my own experience during an important transitional period in life in the United States. During such times the continuities and breaks in the landscape of our social and cultural heritage become more apparent. Milestones of the past get recalled and trends liable to mark the future are imagined.

As the case studies described in the following chapters should demonstrate, these recollections and projections also suggest that our understanding of distributive justice is far from perfect. As a consequence, my investigations of contemporary cases of distributive justice in law, health care, education, and family life led to two additional lines of inquiry. One explored the shape of justice always and everywhere. This was theoretical and cross-cultural and is reported in chapter 1. The other examined historical patterns of justice intraculturally. This is introduced below and is recounted more fully in chapters 2 through 5.

Patterns of Justice in Human Lives

People in the United States, like all humans, spend most of their lives in familial and civil communities where moral qualities are critical to community well-being. Naturally, life in these groups will be better if people have opportunities for self-development in an atmosphere that promotes the best for all while harming none. Moral qualities conducive to such an atmosphere include beneficence, truth telling, promise keeping, and justice.

Of all the moral qualities that communities need and desire, justice, especially distributive justice, is the most urgent. In families, as well as in the civil spheres of education, health care, and law, distributive justice deserves priority since the common life created by social goods is shaped decisively by its harmful features. These are the central concerns of this book.

All the case studies are of the United States, as am I. In studying them, I have considered the moral, political, and cultural experiences of the people of the United States. Though shaped by those experiences, I have aimed to make my analysis self-critical as well as socially responsive. I acknowledge that scholars are nourished by and accept communities that shape the character of their scholarship and that they should take some responsibility for what these communities have done and may yet accomplish.

Because religious traditions in the United States have influenced interpretations of social justice, they deserve serious investigation. They have created some habitual, but not always helpful, ways of pursuing distributive justice. Especially in times of social and cultural transition—times of war, famine, natural disaster, technological advance, and migration, for example—we attend to these patterns of distributive justice. Regrettably, some patterns do not recognize that to solve problems of distributive justice, we need more than independent actions; we also need corporate and systemic approaches.

Patterns of Interpretation

The perplexing character of some American approaches to distributive justice becomes evident in the response to three questions: (1) What prompts people to call for greater distributive justice? (2) What form should any necessary adjustment take? (3) Who should make such adjustments?

Forms of Hume's Approach in the United States

Influenced by the eighteenth-century Scottish philosopher David Hume, answers in the United States to these three questions typically hold that (1) conflicts created by scarcity and competition cause people to call for distributive justice; (2) technical procedures, such as lotteries, can adjust those conflicts; (3) those with appropriate technical expertise should administer them.

These responses suppose that social life is held together not by passion for the public good but by a spirit of avarice and limited benevolence. Combined with two other eighteenth-century convictions—fostered by Adam Smith and James Madison—these responses left a deep imprint on America. Smith, in *The Wealth of Nations,* held that capitalism would vanquish scarcity. Madison deeply distrusted the use of power and its capacity to corrupt the people wielding it.[1]

Such convictions often had religious roots and found strong supporters among heirs of the Protestant Reformation. Henry Ward Beecher, for example, held that unfettered competition is one of history's most powerful forces for Christianizing a people. For him, tensions between egoism and altruism, justice and love, competition and cooperation are tensions rooted in a sinful human nature. This strongly individualistic position exhibited little sense of the public interest or of the role of public property. Thus, Beecher contended that success and morality go hand in hand and that poverty is either nonexistent or a product of vice (May 1967, 65, 69, 70). Indeed, he maintained that any move to equalize wages negated the "law of intelligence and skill" (ibid., 71).

At the turn of the century, public-interest progressives so favored these efficient strategies that they would entrust technical elites with responsibility for distributive justice. Today some claim that economic goals and plans ought to be achieved by national rescue boards of experts. Supposing that this economic model is applicable in all areas of national life, they hold that our problems are better solved by technical fixes than by the political imagination and public virtue endorsed, say, in Aristotelian modes of social and political life. Indeed, they find few moral constraints worth considering in programs of an efficiently administered society. In sum, a competitive twist in the account of distributive justice can prompt one to think that all situations involving distributive justice are conflictual and that they are to be regulated in terms of comparative justice.[2]

Approaches Focused on Property and Redistribution

In the United States, some other approaches contend that calls for distributive justice arise out of conflicts between the haves and the have-nots and that an appropriate response is reallocation by government or by philanthropists. For example, in the late nineteenth century some saw distributive justice in terms of labor-capital conflicts, pitting the indigent against the well-off. Even some of the more progressive social and religious reformers of the period seemed taken by the notion that calls for distributive justice are fundamentally summons to reallocate property. When Pope Leo XIII called for the rights of laborers in his encyclical "On the Condition of Labor," Henry George promptly dubbed it socialistic (George 1891). George insisted that there was a moral duty to earn a share of God's bounty through labor, but he was unalterably opposed to property owners' arguments that they were entitled to "unearned increments" accruing to properties simply because they owned them.[3] Similarly, Borden Parker Bowne favored legislation to protect the public from property-based rapacity and called for cooperation rather than competition to solve social and political conflicts. But he criticized those who laid all social ills at the doorstep of society and who failed to see that they often were attributable to the faults of individuals who misused property (Bowne 1892, 261–63).

By the 1930s, a quite different focus on property could be found in the far less progressive interpretations of Charles Coughlin, the popular radio priest. For him, the blame for early twentieth-century economic woes lay properly at the feet of communists, socialists, wealthy elites, and foreign financiers of Semitic origins—all of whom, he was convinced, had cornered holdings that should be redistributed (O'Brien 1968, 150ff.)

Shortly before Coughlin, the progressive Roman Catholic theologian John A. Ryan sought to redirect this tendency to depict the occasions for distributive justice in terms of polarized property holding. Ryan admired George but rebutted his position (1916, 21–47), countering that industrial incomes, not holdings, were the principal occasions for distributive justice.

> Distributive justice is primarily a problem of incomes rather than of possessions. It is not immediately con-

cerned with John Brown's railway stock, John White's house, or John Smith's automobile. It deals with the morality of such possessions only indirectly and under one aspect; that is, in so far as they have been acquired through income (ibid., xiii).

Ryan's comparisons were not as dialectical as were those of Bowne, George, and Coughlin, but neither did his views root deeply in culture in the United States. Ryan did not issue jeremiads about putative and intractable conflicts between the children of darkness and the children of light. He drew attention to practical resolutions of the moral issues created by a not totally unjust social system (ibid., preface) through policies and practices that might achieve a greater measure of justice.

With respect to property, for example, Ryan contrasted two conceptions. A traditional one, rooted in medieval notions, virtually equated property with an opportunity to work. Profit from property figured only slightly, if at all. A sharply divergent modern conception, however, tended to equate property with capital and made it the principal source of interest—indeed, of unlimited, indefinite, and sometimes excessive rates of interest (1931, 169–70).

Another influential social critic in the United States, Walter Rauschenbusch, also depicted distributive justice in terms of property but saw moral conflicts between egoism and altruism, between the interests of individuals and those of communities (1912, 436). In the first quarter of this century, this heir of the Protestant Reformation drew deeply from a theology emphasizing sin and egoism. From his perspective, social problems were battlefields on which the kingdoms of light and darkness conducted their cosmic struggles. It seems to follow that, since "the instinct of self-interest is stronger than that of devotion to the common interest. . . . If the two come into conflict, the common good suffers" (ibid., 272).

Contemporary works like Robert Nozick's *Anarchy, State, and Utopia* (1974) argue that legitimate acts of acquisition are the sole basis for entitlements. But that is historically naïve since it excludes consideration of the systemic effects of past actions and sufferings on contemporary interactions.[4] Alasdair MacIntyre's response to such a thesis is:

> But, if that is so, there are in fact very few, and in some
> large areas of the world *no*, legitimate entitlements. The
> Property-owners of the modern world are . . . the inheri-
> tors of those who, for example, stole, and used violence
> to steal the common lands of England from the common
> people, vast tracts of North America from the American
> Indian . . . [and so on] . . . (1981, 234).

Social criticism in the United States, including MacIntyre's,
has taken a dialectical bent because social and political
rhetoric generates more heat than light.[5] It can also be
ascribed to the prophetic narratives from which social interpreters in the United States have taken their clues,[6] and it
owes to some perduring images of self-sufficient farmers and
tradespeople. Even though one's capacity to earn a living has
become the most important contemporary form of property,
some religious or cultural convictions equating property with
real estate and other holdings have an uncanny staying power.
Points made by Ryan and George were overlooked in the late
nineteenth century when Henry Ward Beecher and others
employed red herrings to blame the moral vices of the indigent or of some alien and subversive ethnic and political
groups for the plight of the have-nots, thereby thwarting redistributive efforts afoot at the time. Henry George was more
astute, notwithstanding his account of economic disparities in
the moralistic terms of "sober and diligent thievery." He
rightly perceived that property, income, and holdings are
social products resulting from the efforts and achievements of
entire communities of persons. In his call for a single tax on
the unearned portion of wealth and income, however, he gave
a fundamentally redistributive response to the allocation issues
created by collaborative productivity.

Compared with those who overdrew the distinctions
between the good guys and the bad guys, Ryan used more
neutral economic characterizations. He emphasized that
incomes rather than possessions are the proper concern of
distributive justice, and that the titles to incomes were conditioned or modified by the rightful claims of other persons. For
example, titles to interest on capital are modified by the rights

of employees to equitable wages. To the extent that Ryan's position was more critical about the moral justifiability of titles by which holdings were acquired, it represented an improvement over George's position and was far more nuanced than those of Beecher then and Nozick now.[7] However, it was not so significant an improvement to maintain that distributive justice is more a matter of incomes than possessions since incomes are simply alternative forms of holdings. Ryan's position continued to affiliate distributive justice with what one acquires and ran the risk of suggesting that distributive justice is only a matter of redistribution identified too closely with economic orderings.

In sharp contrast with those who hold that distributive justice is a form of rights-based entitlement, Walter Rauschenbusch and his numerous religious and cultural heirs in the United States have contended that distributive (or social) justice is rather a form of love-based charity or altruistic giving in the form of "missionary activity to the needy." This takes the form of giving alms instead of paying a debt or according a benefit. It is not something to which people are entitled, but something bestowed in a socially conscientious fashion. Hence, it is more like relief or, in contemporary terms, welfare.

While this view was gaining strength in the United States, others, influenced by Pope Leo XIII's encyclical on the condition of labor, were moving toward an emphasis on justice in terms of legally ensured entitlements (Abell 1968; Lebacqz 1986, 67–71). Not until Reinhold Niebuhr promoted his form of Christian realism toward the middle of this century did a more realistic form of social justice appear in Protestant social thought in the United States (1932, 1945). However, while improving on previous understandings of love and justice, Niebuhr's account of these moral values contrasted them in such dialectical terms that it created a new set of conceptual problems. Like other tensions regularly invoked in United States culture (tensions between individuals and communities, freedom and justice, the right and the good), such distinctions sometimes become political emblems of contending camps of libertarians and communitarians.[8] But late twentieth-century liberation theology has highlighted a possible point of convergence between those factions by emphasizing that true justice requires love, that love and justice cannot be separated, and that to know the God of love requires one to do justice (Lebacqz 1986, 107, 114).[9]

However, a very conservative element in United States culture remains tenaciously attached to expressing distributive issues in terms of voluntary altruism, while progressive elements are attracted to potentially more coercive governmental measures to rectify injustices. Compared with those who view distributive justice as a form of love-based charity, progressives see it as a matter of justice in which governments assure equal opportunity in the style of welfare liberalism.[10] Popularized in the Roosevelt administration after the Great Depression and greatly expanded between the 1950s and 1970s, this response to distributive problems emphasizes that national harmony is attainable through sharing the benefits of economic growth as an essential element of the public good. But it overlooks how the burdens of that growth should be apportioned.[11]

Not unlike its neocapitalist counterpart of the last few decades, welfare liberalism supposes that the purpose of government is to give individuals the means to pursue their private ends. Thus, it too has a myopic notion of the public or common good. That good is surely the concern of government, but some past and present forms of welfare liberalism seem so bent on redistribution through legislation, judicial influence, and taxation that they rely too heavily on state power.[12]

In the neocapitalist position, the nation becomes one all-inclusive interest group, where government serves only to safeguard the peace and security that permit self-reliant individuals to pursue their largely economic aims in freedom, while leaving the problems of the poor and the suffering to private, voluntary associations (Bellah et al. 1985, 262–64). Ironically, to neocapitalism and its diametrically opposed counterpart, welfare liberalism, the aim of government is to provide physical security and material well-being, while maximizing individual choices so that citizens may pursue their private ends (ibid., 262, 265). The major differences are in the means to be used and in the selection of the agents to be entrusted with the task. Like welfare liberalism, neocapitalism suffers some illusions. These incline neocapitalists to believe that the links between private markets and government activity can be dissolved and that the private sector has no interest in governmentally granted privileges (ibid., 266).

That the neocapitalist position has considerable appeal for neoconservative, entrepreneurial forms of religious belief cannot be missed by anyone who has followed the news over the last decade (ibid., 264, 265). What might be missed is that, as in the case of the welfare liberal position, neocapitalism represents a variation on an enduring response to people's concerns about distributive justice. Whereas welfare liberalism seems continuous with the populist position of the early part of this century, neocapitalism has strong continuities with the establishment position elaborated in that same time period (ibid., 265). All these positions show a strong, if not always well-conceived, compassion for the disadvantaged.

Many people in the United States have long equated such compassion with distributive (or social) justice. They have long been persuaded that those better off are both charged with and are adept at redistributing wealth. These have become truisms to which no rejoinder is expected. They are the Establishment's basic tenets. That position holds that the financial and industrial elites assumed stewardship for the wealth of the nation by following the gospel of wealth[13] and that voluntary divestment is a form of public service and is the way to create a viable and morally decent society. This is a long-standing and often rejuvenated tradition in the United States. It takes the form of voluntarily associating with others in creating institutions that benefit the public, such as universities, hospitals, museums, symphonies, churches, and civic clubs.[14] At times in the last century, this position was expressed as a philanthropic altruism, but even then it remained a movement spearheaded by financial and industrial elites who understood stewardship as an activity of those better blessed or gifted on behalf of those less well endowed.[15] In almost all its forms, it has been characterized by the belief that this stewardship would foster cosmopolitan and flexible forms of noblesse oblige, reconcile peoples' differences, and heal wounds made by the competitive national quest for wealth.

More Adequate Interpretations of Distributive Justice

Each of the above-mentioned depictions of the nature of distributive justice has influenced our policies for allocating the benefits and burdens of social life in the United States. Each has its limitations as well as its assets. A more adequate interpretation of distributive justice recognizes that the very nature of social life and its constituent social goods is the principal reason for invoking distributive justice.

Unfortunately, this has not been commonly recognized in the United States. Those most influenced by the social and political thought of Aristotle, Aquinas, and Locke have noted it best, as did John A. Ryan. Among contemporaries whose perspectives and commitments bear the traces of this intellectual heritage are John Rawls (1971) and Alasdair MacIntyre (1981). But Rawls's theory of justice lacks sufficient historical and social concreteness; especially since it slights the fact that many human attributes belong, in some way, to the community as a whole (Sandel 1982, 78, 102, 174).[16] By comparison, the eminently concrete position of MacIntyre fails to determine why and how people select from the alternative narratives and practices he describes.

William Galston's approach is more historically and socially circumspect. It contends that appeals to distributive justice stem from the very nature of human existence in communities, the chief good of which can be had only through this form of justice (1980).[17] In addition to that, Michael Walzer in *Spheres of Justice* (1983) recognizes that this entails allocations of social and political power.[18] Analogous stances, like that of Karen Lebacqz, contend that, to be adequate, accounts of justice must be tripodal, attending to what it takes to have just persons and structures as well as just actions (Lebacqz 1986).[19]

More adequate accounts of distributive justice acknowledge that appropriate responses to injustice will depend not only upon a judgment about what has caused it but also on the purpose of any corrections. The actions to be taken will be of one sort if the aim is to harmonize relationships among a less than perfect and often conflictual people in a less-than-perfect world but will be of a distinctively different sort if the overarching goal is to prevent one sphere of social goods from extending its sway over other spheres.

The argument of this book is that the aim of distributive justice is both to design and to maintain just situations and social structures in communities and to promote justice in the people who encounter each other in these situations. Those forms of justice cannot be achieved in the same way for every sphere of life nor by creating utopias. The goals will differ from sphere to sphere, with different aims in families and in education than in the legal system or the economy. Moreover, one may be able only to approximate the ideal right ordering rather than to attain it fully.

This book also contends that the legitimate distributors of the resources in question, whoever they may be, should accept and be accountable for executing the responsibilities of distributive justice in communities. These distributors tend to be those most familiar with the details needed to do the job well. Only they help assure that matters will be handled at the most immediate level possible. In families, for example, these are the persons responsible for family well-being. In schools, they are teachers, administrators, and boards. In health care, the listing includes individual practitioners, their professional representatives, the administrators of health-care facilities, and, for some goods and services, governmental officials.

Among these people, the best suited are not necessarily those in power but those characterized by the wit, wisdom, and justice to use that power well. Control over the resources in question and the power to enforce specific forms of distribution are necessary, of course. In and of themselves, however, they do not create credentials sufficient for the task at hand. The distributors also need to be practiced in the area in question and to be committed to doing the job well.

There are several efficacious routes toward more adequate interpretations of distributive justice. The route taken in this study has been shaped by two experiences. One is a renewal of scholarly interest in distributive justice stimulated principally by Rawls (1971) and Nozick (1974) and carried forward in communitarian critiques of liberalism by MacIntyre (1981, 1988) and Sandel (1982). These studies prompted reconsideration of conventional understandings of justice, its relationship to other forms of the human good, and its application to allocating social goods and opportunities in a democratic society. The communitarian critique, in particular, occasioned a rethinking of the limits of the post-Enlightenment agenda in liberal, social, and political thought and highlighted some of the more common ties of life in the United States.

A second experience reflects that I have been a scholar and teacher in religious studies for more than twenty-five years, the last twenty in religious ethics at Indiana University in Indianapolis.[20] Throughout, I have been attentive, and sometimes indebted, to theological reflections in the United States on justice and to the intracultural similarities and differences in those forms of reasoning. But this is not a theological study. It is rather like investigations of the religious and other cultural beliefs and values embodied in cultural patterns of thinking and acting. I have examined these as an empathetic observer who adopts neither the perspective of a partisan insider in a particular community of belief nor an outlook completely divorced from such a community.

Working from such a stance, inquirers in each of the case studies in this book follow a route that includes factual, conceptual, and normative inquiries. Each, in turn, leads to metaethical inquiries—inquiries in which cultural suppositions, past and present, along with the patterns they take in understanding and practice, are scrutinized critically. Though concerned at every turn to portray the record accurately, this account of the thick ties among facts, meanings, and standards is more than simply factual, it also probes cultural premises for the concepts and standards used in the United States to seek a just ordering of social advantages and disadvantages.

1

The Burdens of Justice

The introduction outlined some habitual approaches to distributive justice in the United States. This chapter discusses norms. It studies conventional understandings in the light of moral principles, shifting attention to what might better guide the moral reasoning of people always and everywhere.

Where do these principles come from? They follow logically from close scrutiny of what people must do to rightly interact with others every day. If the principles thus obtained are rationally justifiable, then it is important to ask how people know what ought to be done or avoided and whether people have acted reasonably in doing right and avoiding moral wrong.

These social interactions are somewhat chaotic. As people seek to acquire social goods and avoid harms, they may experience trust and cooperation. If the way social goods are allocated is individualistic and idiosyncratic, their purposes cannot be accomplished very well (Walzer 1983, 7; Galston 1980, 110, 115). Social goods often directly affect the capacity of persons to achieve their individual and common human goods, and all social goods have negative aspects, which must be assigned to someone.

William Galston's distinction between internal and external social goods is helpful in understanding how basic human goods are at stake in our handling of social goods. Not only property and economic goods, but internal social goods are also distributed.[1] Consider, for example, the social goods in family life, education, health care, and leisure. Many of these are internal or bodily in that they help meet natural needs, the sustenance and development of human life (Galston 1980, 56–58, 112–16, 164). As such, they are much more important than external goods like prizes, honors, money, and commodities, which enable persons to achieve some but not most major levels of fulfillment (Galston 1980, 99). External social goods may be linked to internal social goods; for example, one's salary is the means of one's survival.

Both internal and external social goods have some distasteful or harmful features. They can be socially painful, generating long-lasting, cynical, and distrustful memories for entire communities, for example, the sufferings of people who have been wronged because of their ethnic background, sex, race, or religion, or of the weaker parties in economic exchanges who become more disadvantaged in each transaction.

Involuntary relationships are especially critical in communities (*Nicomachean Ethics* 8, 13, 1162b21–35 and 5, 3, 1130b30–1131a9; Donagan 1977, 101, 108).[2] Besides causing pain and humiliation to some, involuntary relationships can create entire weak classes that stand to be harmed over and over because they lack political power to break their chains. Most poignantly, people's basic needs go unmet, and the pain and suffering appear to be inflicted on them by persons who have duties to protect them.[3]

When power is exercised with an uneven hand, when privileges are not earned, when the basic needs of life are placed beyond the reach of the disadvantaged, and when people are persecuted because of their sex, race, religion, or habits, social and cultural conditions are out of joint. Most telling are the harms imposed on others not so much by some lottery of life but rather by persons seeking their own rather than the common interest. In the words of the pastoral letter of the United States Catholic bishops on economic life, "the moral test of any society is how it treats the weakest and most vulnerable in its midst" (Gannon 1987).

To such hard case scenarios, add the common experiences of unmet needs, pain, loss, and humiliation that are neither freely chosen nor bargained for. These burdens are often assigned by unknown persons who are unresponsive to complaints or who refuse to be held accountable.

Social goods are the currency of social relationships (Walzer 1983, 7) as well as the means communities devise for enabling members to attain some of the more important human goods (Galston 1980, 56, 110). As to the distribution of social goods,

Aristotle considered the central question of justice to be "equality in what sort of things, and inequality in what sort of things?" (*Politics* 3, 12, 1282b–121). More simply, who gets what and on what basis? (Galston 1980, 55). Since justice without some loss is an illusion (Held 1984, 79), the decisive questions are who will be required to bear the burdens and why. To answer such questions, one must examine the practical insights, judgments, and decisions which communities think should govern how social goods are distributed.

The worth we assign to justice is rooted in a commitment to the rational life (Galston 1980, 280). Making good on this commitment entails identifying the burdensome responsibilities of reasoning and choosing, such as interacting with others according to what Aristotelians call altruistic prudence (Galston 1980, 279–83; Engberg-Pedersen 1983) and the burden of asking whether people rightly understand the connections between people and social goods. This chapter is concerned with the ways people respond to their experiences of the burdens of justice.

Experience and Practical Insights

Until they are interpreted, our perceptions about justice are in themselves neither right or wrong. One must ask whether one's perceptions are correct. Do we rightly identify the relationships between social goods and persons? Are our practical insights reasonable? Have we rightly identified the alternatives? Did we consistently take the actions that we deemed were most reasonable and just?

Practical insights mediate between our experiences of social goods and our expressions about them. Because our understandings of social goods unfold historically and our practical insights develop subtiley, they may incorporate prejudices, mistaken ideas, and even nonsense. Therefore, practical insights call for critical scrutiny. They are the first, and often the last, reasons we give for our claims about right and wrong in allocating the advantages and disadvantages of life together. One must go beyond the supposition that our views of justice and injustice are wholly conditioned by the times and culture and the supposition that they are nothing more than effects of changing times and shifting social organization. One should also scrutinize how one arrives at insights to judge whether they are attentive, perceptive, and intelligent. To illustrate how such an inquiry might work, consider first the practical insights at the heart of several statements about justice.

Expressions of Practical Insights

One day while nailing shingles with a carpenter friend, I was treated to a fairly popular statement about justice. While we worked, he asked what I did for a living, probably noting that my roofing skills were not enough to keep food on my table. When told that my principal interests in teaching and scholarship centered on justice, he replied, "There's not much of that around, is there?"

Another friend, who has followed my interests for about two decades, sent me a cartoon of three fish, lined up according to size. Each of the two larger fish was devouring the next smaller one. The dialogue balloon at the mouth of the smallest fish declared, "There is no justice!" That of the medium-sized fish, about to consume the smallest one announced, "There is some justice!" and that of the largest fish, standing ready to eat both smaller fish, confidently proclaimed, "There is justice!"

These two expressions embody fairly widespread insights about the just allocation of advantages and disadvantages. In both individual and community expressions about justice, much is not spoken. Much more passes "beneath conscious prehension to a fiduciary hold on what [people] sense to be axiomatic" (Turner 1976, 156). These moorings become evident in the times when one's back is against the wall—times when a person "seizes roots, not straws" (ibid., 162). Among the mainstays in times of crisis are "certain consciously recognized (though not consciously grasped) cultural models" or "root-paradigms" that express shared "cultural goals, means, ideas, outlooks, currents of thought, [and] patterns of belief" and that help people to enter relationships with others, to interpret them, and to be disposed either toward alliances or toward conflict (ibid., 156).

These root-paradigms are not systems of univocal concepts, logically arrayed; they are not, so to speak, precision tools of thought. Nor are they stereotyped guidelines for ethical, esthetic, or conventional action. Indeed, they go beyond the cognitive and even the moral to the existential domain, and in so doing become clothed with allusiveness, implicitness, and metaphor—for in the stress of vital action, firm definitional outlines became blurred by the encounter of emotionally charged wills. Paradigms of this fundamental sort reach down to the irreducible life-stances of individuals . . . (ibid.).[4]

Because root-paradigms are effective in getting people through tight spots, they are not scrutinized. The moral standards they embody become normative for the decisions and actions of individuals and communities. These root paradigms and their expressions should not be taken lightly.

Practical insights often fall short in explaining experience and do not make for sound reasoning about moral values. The experiences that the insights interpret are but the raw material that classical philosophy terms *potency*. They are informed by insights that, in turn, are expressed in one's own thoughts, or in one's spoken or body language. Like the statements children employ when challenging their parents, for example, "fair is fair" or "I'm my own person," these statements express perceptions and seek to evoke agreement from others.

More artistic expressions of practical insights include media coverage of the funerals of John and Robert Kennedy and Dr. Martin Luther King, Jr., in which viewers participated emotionally in a kind of ritual; the traditional field songs and religious services of African-Americans; and Edward Hopper's paintings, which portray the "silent closeness of strangers in the city."[5] These artistic and musical expressions make experience intelligible for viewers and listeners. In "Art as a Cultural System," Clifford Geertz writes:

The capacity, variable among people as it is among individuals, to perceive meaning in pictures (or poems, melodies, buildings, pots, dramas, statues) is, like all other fully human capacities, a product of collective experience which far transcends it, as is the far rarer capacity to put it there in the first place. It is out of participation in the general system of symbolic forms we call culture that participation in the particular we call art, which is in fact but a sector of it, is possible. . . . It is, after all, not just statues (or paintings, or poems) that we have to do with but the factors that cause these things to seem important—that is, affected with import—to those who make or possess them, and these are as various as life itself. If there is any commonality among all the arts in all the places that one finds [them . . . it] lies in the fact that certain activities everywhere seem specifically designed to demonstrate that ideas are visible, audible, and—one needs to make a word up here—tactible, that they can be cast in forms where the senses, and through the senses, the emotions, can reflectively address them (1983, 108–9, 119–20).

Because most habits of heart and mind in our expressions of our practical insights are not conscious, they are considered elusive in formal ethical reflection. But a community's expressions are more conscious and the habits of heart and mind that create and communicate them are more accessible. Therefore, we shall examine mainly community expressions and the habits they rely upon.

Narratives and Normative Inferences

Narratives are stories that interpret experience. Some narratives merely imply an interpretation; for example, a criminal who meets adversity is said to get what he deserved. Other narratives deliberately present an interpretation, for example, biblical and other stories about paying one's debts.[6] Both may communicate how a society expects its members to act. These narratives are sometimes the only explanations most can muster for what they say and do—or avoid doing—in the name of justice, but they are as powerful as formal judgments and principles. A commitment to be rational in matters of justice requires, then, scrutinizing the practical insights in one's narratives and formal principles, as well as the purposes of those who promote the stories.

To take one example, consider the ideal of self-sufficiency. Is it true that a person can fend for herself or himself, can till the soil or ply a trade—or make a start elsewhere—if only others would not interfere and force this person to act against his or her will? The practical insights at the heart of narratives about self-sufficient farmers or merchants do not agree with the contemporary experience of persons who are unable to make a living other than by selling their labor. Similarly, Marxist narratives about spontaneously developed, nonalienating systems for the division of labor and eulogies about peasant families that produce their own life-necessities (Held 1980, 119, 212, 217–18) can be questioned. Inevitably, the insights and the narratives mask reality rather than interpret it.

Other examples of faulty insights will be found among narratives that aim to identify those to whom should we entrust the responsibility for making just distributions of social advantages and disadvantages. Many people in the United States in the late nineteenth and early twentieth century believed that the way to sustain a moral order in their newly industrialized society was to entrust the task to those privileged by divine grace or some other good fortune. In this view, philanthropists would create and maintain universities, hospitals, churches, and symphonies, which ameliorate the lot of those less fortunate. However, the practical insights that prop up such stories have long since been suspect. The same applies to insights at work in later narratives about national solidarity and the need to make the government responsible for administering welfare.[7] Equally dubious are insights in narratives employed by latter-day neoconservatives to assert that the private sector is now best suited to do what philanthropists used to do, not through voluntary associations but through for-profit corporations. These insights do not seem to follow from correct perceptions of social conditions or to explain correctly current social conditions.

However, the practical insights in prevalent cultural narratives in the United States about equality are the fundamental objects of critical inquiry, for, as Aristotle stated it, the central question of justice is how equality applies to some sorts of things and how inequality applies to others. For instance, Adam Smith's insights about productive and nonproductive labor in his tales about the so-called frivolous professions— clergy, law, medicine, and the arts—do not make relevant distinctions. His work *The Wealth of Nations* builds on the insight that humans cannot escape their propensity to barter for their own interest. Another problematic example is the intuition in John Rawls's theory of justice that people can be free and equal moral persons, able to set aside self-interest to agree with each other on principles of justice to govern a well-ordered society.[8] All these examples are brimming with beliefs as well as with insights and should not be uncritically accepted as foundations for judgments for making just decisions about social goods.

More perceptive are insights in narratives that distinguish between the simple equality of people and the complex equality to be taken into account when people make claims with differing foundations. Simple equality means that people are simply equal in worth or dignity ; individuals are to be respected independently of their differences in capacity or achievement. But some differences in people must be recognized. For example, while respecting persons equally, one may be required to accommodate their different needs according to some rule. We need narratives that recount more complex forms of equality, for what Aristotle called a *regime* (*Politics* 3, 7, 1279–a25) rests on its claim to help people live well or virtuously (*Politics* 3, 9, 1280a3–1,1280b39) or to represent the general good better than a mere assemblage of self-interests. Since regimes are warranted only if they contribute to the common good and commonweal (*Nicomachean Ethics* 4, 5, 1149a28; Engberg-Pedersen 1983, 48), the stories on which they rely should be scrutinized very closely.

The validity of narratives about social goods can be evaluated. As suggested above, one can test whether or not they accurately describe the community's experience and shared understanding. We also can evaluate them in terms of the habits of mind that generate and sustain them. Since the knowledge that guides living often lags behind the knowledge about getting on with life, the narratives and practical insights that would govern social goods may stem from a form of mythic consciousness in which one experiences, imagines, understands, and judges simultaneously, without distinguishing among these four different modes of knowing.

The worlds presented in these accounts may be so common, familiar, and domesticated that they may be taken as real, but the accounts may be little more than sagacious myths that sustain a pervading bias in common sense. Their narrators, as well as their hearers, may come to believe "that ideas are negligible unless they are reinforced by sensitive desires and fears" or that, to be taken seriously, they must arise from an "intense flow of sensitive representations, feelings, words, and actions" (Lonergan 1958, 538, 632).[9] They can captivate imaginations, whip up emotions, and urge hasty action. Then mythmaking should be called myth mongering (Lonergan 1958, 543; Smurl 1978, 73). The insights and narratives supporting schemes for creating and allocating social goods may become habitual (*hexeis*), but they may not be practices (*praxeis*). They may simply be techniques to get desirable social behaviors.

What kind of empirical knowledge do these stories express? Was it tested before it was made regulative? (Lonergan 1958; Habermas 1984, 301–4, 308–10, 333). For example, to decide whether the narratives correspond to reality, we should first consider what might have been overlooked or misread. In addition, we should consider whether our perceptions are accurate. One needs cognitive skills, including true memory, nimblewittedness, objectivity in unexpected situations, and open-mindedness about the true variety of things and situations (Engberg-Pedersen 1983, 208, 210; Pieper 1965, 15–17). Justice helps develop cognitive habits that take account of self as but one among others. Justice aims to order rightly the relations of others as well as ourselves to social goods (Engberg-Pedersen 1983, 44, 47–48, 56).

In a market-oriented society like the United States, people might perceive all goods as commodities. Can practical insights that regard police or fire protection, marriage and procreation rights, and other social goods as marketable commodities be correct? Besides the undesirable consequences of such insights, they represent serious misunderstandings. Clearly, open-mindedness about the fundamental differences between human beings and television sets, between police or fire protection and an airline trip, between procreation rights and sperm for sale would lead to quite different insights. A commitment to justice would yield practical insights and stories in which the market is part of the community, but not the whole of it.

Social goods, which affect people's worth and security, are not appropriately governed like commodities. For example, arguments favoring slavery and indiscriminate endorsements of surrogate parenting treat social goods as commodities. A more perceptive account of our shared understandings would apply the axiom that "the morality of the bazaar belongs in the bazaar." Similarly, it would foster the judgment that no particular social good—like procreation rights—should be distributed to men and women who possess another social good—say money—simply because they possess the latter and without regard to the meaning of the former (Walzer 1983, 109, 20). Practical insights about the sovereignty of separate spheres of social goods are not only more accurate, they also contradict insights (and corresponding narratives and practices) that hold that freedom of choice and action should govern all spheres of social goods (Walzer 1983, 100–3, 120).

For more correct insights about social goods, storytellers should practice the habit of impartially regarding "not only . . . the relation between an individual and an object of desire or aversion but also . . . the relation of other relevant individuals to that object or objects of that kind" (Galston 1980, 101). Then they will communicate practical insights about social goods in the light of a generalizable standard of common interests (Habermas 1984, 311, 325–26, 334, 336). Furthermore, such habits advance what Aristotle called the common advantage or the political good of justice (*Politics* 3, 12, 1282b16–21; see also *Nicomachean Ethics* 5, 3).

The practical insights that declare how social goods should be governed must be practices in the Aristotelian sense, that is, moral and political activities that fulfill the people performing them (*Nicomachean Ethics* 4, 4). Thus, the practices require and foster the "good and reasoned state of capacity to act with regard to the things that are good or bad for man" (*Nicomachean Ethics* 6, 5, 1140b5). They also require that the narrators be prudent and, above all, that narrators and listeners be just (*Nicomachean Ethics* 5, 1, 1129b30–1130a5; *Politics* 3, 13, 1283al38; Engberg-Pedersen 1983, 224). Aquinas declares that "among all the moral virtues it is justice wherein the use of right reason [that is, prudence] appears chiefly. . . . Hence the undue use of reason appears mostly in the vices opposed to justice, the greatest of which is covetousness [which leads to fraud and cunning and other vices]" (*Summa Theologiae* II–IIae, Q.56, a.8, c.; Pieper 1965, 21; MacIntyre 1981, 166–68). Prudence and justice, including respect for others and their goods, are essential requirements for those who fashion stories about social goods from practical insights. Accordingly, the governing scheme must be just and justice must characterize the actions and traits of the governors as well as those of the governed (Galston 1980, 100).

Bernard Lonergan suggested a short list of imperatives in the rational consciousness that foster practical insights: be attentive, be perceptive, and be intelligent (that is, be prudent and just). To meet these imperatives, experience and relationships may need to be reperceived and practical insights may need to be reinterpreted. An individual may be willing to extirpate practical insights and narratives but communities are not likely to be as courageous. Both the anguish of an individual swimming against the currents of public opinion and that of a community making a cultural divestment may be as wrenching as a religious conversion.

The carpenter mentioned earlier may have been disappointed with others who did not share his values. But the cartoon of the three fish manifests a desire to avoid the personal, social, and cultural responsibilities of testing practical insights, responsibilities such as cultivating the justice needed to see rightly, to correct one's mistaken insights, poor judgments, and inconsistent actions, and to reform conventional wisdom and undertakings in communities. Indeed, such reforms create cultural and social stress and threaten cherished cultural beliefs and values.

For those who communicate practical insights in a community, Habermas sets forth the criteria of competence (the responsibility to represent experience adequately), appropriateness (describing the relations of persons and social goods in ways that respect the general advantage as well as for one's own good), and authenticity (about one's intentions, interests, and goals). Those who communicate practical insights should be persuaded that the well-being of individuals coincides with the well-being of the community. Therefore, the recent emphasis on recovering and using cultural narratives and practices needs to be morally and socially accountable.[10]

To assure that the public understanding of social goods and their allocation will not serve any interest group,[11] social and political leaders need to balance power (Schmookler 1984; Harrington 1985). These procedures should follow the Aristotelian perspective on intellectual and communicative responsibility. The participants in public discussions about social goods must be able to work for common interests guided by the principle that the benefits and burdens of common life are to be arranged to achieve the political good of justice.

The participants will need to identify community habits that restrict their freedom.[12] Not all members of the community are equally well suited for the task of negotiating such impediments. For example, members of some cultural and religious communities may be unable to present clearly or discuss their beliefs about public policies for social goods. They may feel that discussing their beliefs is not appropriate. Some groups are more inclined to impose their standards on the community rather than help discover common standards, and some prefer not to participate. Thus, some may bear the burden of changing their habits to show that they stand for the public interest as well as for wanting their views to be respected.

What standards should the participants use to decide? Since the goal is the political good of justice, the criteria should include the general and impartial guidelines of morality and community beliefs that embody these principles. To be intelligible to all, they must be discoverable within the community, reiterated over time and across cultures, and verifiable through a consensual process (Walzer 1983, 9–10; 1977, xiii-xiv, 47, 64; and 1987). Only then should they be endorsed as standards in the pursuit of the community's chief good, justice. Philosopher Virginia Held and theologian James Sellers argue that public policies cannot be governed by appeals to norms that are extrinsic to the participants (Sellers 1970, 265, 269; Held 1984, 40–61).

Reasoning toward Principles and Habits of Justice

It is easy to be mistaken about what it takes to develop principles of justice or the guidelines that follow. It is easy to create practical insights and stories that declare what human relationships involving social goods should be but it is difficult to be certain that one's perceptions are correct. We must decide and act whether our perceptions are correct or not. Although most people would rather avoid it, reflecting on one's perceptions and practical insights is necessary to be rational and just.

It is even easier to make mistakes in reflections, by aiming to confirm that one's insights are true and using the insights to develop principles for evaluating similar cases. Mistakes in the principles are carried further when we apply the principles. Because we are not always clear about the source or the validity of our principles, we may give them too much weight or authority. Religious and other human commitments may cut reflection short if, for example, principles are invoked in terms that preclude critical reflection, as asserting that "the principle of autonomy (or beneficence or justice) requires . . ." In even the most formal and erudite treatises in ethics, what is critiqued and the way it is critiqued may not be fully reflective judgments.[13]

One must address the authority of one's moral principles if one is to be accountable as well as reasonable. Because one decides and acts on one's principles, one should conscientiously test them, for, although statements of principles are regarded as scientific or scholarly, practical insights and narratives may be easily dismissed as merely interesting stories or interpretations. Unless someone has acted hastily on practical insights, mistakes in practical insights and narratives are not as far-reaching as those made in reflections and judgments that achieve the status of accepted principles and are taught authoritatively by philosophers, theologians, and social and political scientists. Thus errors later in the process have more serious consequences because they support some enduring habits. For all of these reasons, each person regularly must ask whether his or her practical insights are correct and whether they should govern his or her actions.

Is the Practical Insight Correct?

To check our practical insights, first consider two positions, those of John Rawls (1971) and Robert Nozick (1974) on distributive justice. Then consider whether or not the insights are correct, reasonable, and fully considered. Do they explain how social goods are governed? Are the principles they propose to govern demonstrated rather than taken for granted? Are their authorities probed before being applied to social goods? After all, the principles to which one appeals may seem intuitive, self-evident, or otherwise established as authoritative but they can be only as solid as the practical insights and judgments supporting them.

In his widely acclaimed book *After Virtue*, Alasdair MacIntyre took us on what Amy Gutmann calls "an intriguing tour of moral history" at the end of which "we learn that the internal incoherence of liberalism forces us to choose 'Nietzsche or Aristotle,' a politics of the will to power or one of communally defined virtue" (MacIntyre 1981, 49, 103–13, 238–45; Gutmann 1985, 310). In her critical evaluation of this conclusion, Gutmann faults MacIntyre's critique of the post-Enlightenment project of a morality founded on rights. His critique is mistaken, says Gutmann, because "it invites us to see the moral universe in dualistic terms," dividing humans into the category of those who are naturally egoistic and those who are on the way to becoming altruistic (ibid., see MacIntyre 1981, 212–13). It so sharply distinguishes between liberal theories of rights and Aristotelian theories of virtue that they appear incompatible. MacIntyre equates liberal theories of rights with universalized notions of justice and correlates Aristotelian theories of virtue with the definitions of "the good" one finds in specific communities. In Gutmann's words, "either justice takes absolute priority over the good or the good takes the place of justice;

either justice must be independent of all historical and social particularities or virtue must depend completely on the particular social practices of each society" (1985, 316–17).

MacIntyre attributes the contemporary disagreement about justice to competing rationalities (1988) that may threaten society and block modern politics from achieving a genuine moral consensus (1981, 227, 236). MacIntyre perceives an irreconcilable conflict between the principles of distributive justice found in representative positions A and B, rather perfect mirror images of theories espoused by Robert Nozick and John Rawls (1981, 227ff.). Position A and Nozick's theory, which emphasize claims based on what one earns and are said to be favored by merchants and blue-collar workers, are meritarian. Position B and Rawls's theory, which represent liberal professionals, social workers, or those whose wealth is inherited, are defined as egalitarian. But MacIntyre describes egalitarianism as a position advanced by people who, impressed by the harm inequality creates, want to redress it through redistributive taxation. That is quite different than arguing that persons have equal worth or dignity and equal claims based on needs and achievements. MacIntyre declares both positions logically incompatible since the former "holds that principles of just acquisition and entitlement set limits to redistributive possibilities," while the latter "holds that principles of just distribution set limits to legitimate acquisition and entitlement" (ibid., 228). In other words, "how can a claim that gives priority to equality of needs be rationally weighed against one which gives priority to entitlements?" (ibid., 231).

To be reasonable we must ask whether or not these descriptions of positions A and B, Nozick and Rawls's, are accurate and whether or not they are so irreconcilable. MacIntyre may have overdrawn to make the case better for his own practical insights about some ill-defined, but purportedly traditional notion that only one's contributions to the tasks of communities warrant desert (ibid., 233).[14] Moreover, MacIntyre overlooks several key features in Nozick's and Rawls's principles that appear unreasonable and make their irreconcilability irrelevant and MacIntyre's alternative less convincing.

MacIntyre's discussion of principles of distributive justice contains five categories of mistakes in critical reflection. First, it grants too much to the terms in position *A* and Nozick's theory. Because both seem to equate distributive justice with redistributions, they arouse fears of appropriating and redistributing someone's possessions—say, by taxation. Presenting the terms this way is contrived. It alarms people and distracts them from investigating the validity of the titles they hold to their possessions. Despite what Nozick says, acquisitions are not always justifiable.

The second mistake is that MacIntyre does not probe Nozick's principle of just acquisition and entitlement. Nozick glosses over the issue of whether titles are just and ignores issues like whether rights are legal or moral titles and whether they derive from needs, efforts, or sacrifices. For example, the claims of workers to wages—based on their needs and efforts—are different from and stronger than the claims of investors to their profits. Because MacIntyre attributes position *A* (Nozick) to blue-collar workers, saying one has a right to what one has earned implies that the claims are based on efforts, sacrifices, and achievements. If so, then this position is partially compatible with the theory of distributive justice that applies several equally relevant criteria to the allocations of different social goods. In any case, it is a mistake to claim, as does MacIntyre, that position *A* (Nozick) makes no reference to the notion of desert (ibid., 232). It is a far graver error to fail to recognize that the ambiguous use of *earned* would treat all means of acquisition as equally valid and thus, for example, could not prohibit slavery on the grounds that according to a shared social understanding people are not and ought not to be treated as commodities.

In the third error, MacIntyre fails to recognize either that claims about needs and entitlements are not equally pertinent to all social goods or that some goods are inseparable. This common error seems to begin with not considering the variety of social goods and is propagated by seeking a single principle of justice to apply to all social goods.

MacIntyre's rhetorical question, "how can a claim that gives priority to equality of needs be rationally weighed against one which gives priority to entitlements?" (ibid., 231), deserves an answer. A short answer would say that need can be weighed against entitlements if the social goods are fundamentally different. A longer answer would examine different spheres of social goods, such as family, education, politics, religion, and health care. In the sphere of basic provisions and securities, whose social goods include food, water, health care, and police and fire protection, it is reasonable to hold that equal needs should have priority. In the spheres of work and commodities, claims based on efforts, sacrifices, or achievements should have priority. It is not impossible to weigh competing claims based on these two different principles, as we shall see shortly in the case of titles and food. One needs to reflect and occasionally to set aside one's professional world of logical arguments and reenter the world where people know the difference between food as a basic necessity and food as a market commodity.[15]

Lest we seek a single, philosophically sound criterion to guide the distribution of all social goods, Michael Walzer has pointed out that the quest seems quixotic because a "need generates a particular distributive sphere, within which it is itself the appropriate distributive principle." For example, desert appropriately rules the sphere of awards, and free exchange appropriately rules the sphere of commodities, though because money is used everywhere, criteria may cross the boundaries between spheres (1983, 3–30). Rawls's theory, which uses two principles, liberty and equality, is more attuned than Nozick's to the necessity of using more than one criterion. But in MacIntyre's rendering of Rawls's theory, all relevant criteria are reduced to the principle of desert (1981, 234). The distinctions between spheres of social goods reveal the fatal omission in practical insights that declare that there is but one kind of social good and but one criterion that should govern them.

A fourth slip is taking the apparent irreconcilability of needs and entitlements far too seriously and authoritatively. To say one is entitled to something is to stake a claim, perhaps even to assert that one has a stronger claim to it than others similarly situated. It is not unreasonable to claim one has greater need for something, like food when starving, and thus has a more pressing claim to any available food than do others who are well fed. That someone has bought the food, and thus has moral and legal rights to it, may or may not override the claims of the starving person, who points out that its owner does not need it as much. Whether the starving may help themselves to others' food or whether the well-fed should share would be settled by prudent exceptions to principles.[16] Need and entitlement (assuming a just means of acquisition) often are so intertwined that they are distinguishable in concept, but not in reality. Reflections that treat them as unalterably opposed concepts are inadequate foundations for reasonable decisions and practices.

Finally, the fifth mistake is MacIntyre's application of the Aristotelian tradition. Persuaded that contemporary accounts of distributive justice are both hopelessly polarized and wrongheaded, he suggests "an older, more traditional, more Aristotelian and Christian view of justice," founded on community-defined concepts of virtue that exist alongside more modern moral concepts of rights and that "can be restated in a way that restores intelligibility and rationality to our moral and social attitudes and commitments" (ibid., 234–35, 241). Though he acknowledges that his rendering of the Aristotelian tradition is open to criticism and dispute, his claim that this tradition upholds desert as the criterion for distributive justice is riddled with inaccuracies and ambiguities.

Compare MacIntyre's account, for instance, with William Galston's equally Aristotelian, but more nuanced and reflective account. Relying on Aristotelian premises regarding the human end (*telos*) and its basic goods of life, development, and happiness and the hypothesis that "the full development of each individual is equal in moral weight to that of every other," Galston considers desert as what benefits individuals, and on that basis develops some principles of entitlement. He demonstrates that desert must be based upon some fact about the deserving individual, that not all facts about individuals are relevant, that the relevant facts need be neither moral characteristics nor themselves meritorious, and that there are distinct classes of desert, for example, prizes, grades, compensations, reparations, praise or blame, approvals, and punishments (1980, 92–93, 159, 170, n.47, 176, 297). Significantly, income—or what one earns—may be a prize or a reward rather than a compensation. How one classifies a desert substantively affects one's theory of distributive justice.

MacIntyre may have targeted correctly some of the cultural culprits responsible for our confusions about justice, but he missed some. Neither position *A* or *B* says enough about the facts that make people either undeserving of their poverty (as in position *B*'s claim) or deserving of what one accrues through a life of hard work (as in position *A*'s claim). Neither position *A* nor *B* tells us why the facts they highlight about people are stronger grounds for desert than, say, facts about what people acquire in the form of prizes, rewards, or the unearned income generated by stock market fluctuations, which is surely not entirely attributable to personal efforts. The most dubious claim of all, finally, is MacIntyre's contention that position *A* and *B* hark back to an older, more traditional, Aristotelian and Christian tradition (1981, 234). Galston's examples are more Aristotelian, more judicious, and not so driven to oversimplify social realities. Galston also seems to recognize that political as well as scholarly reasons may motivate recovering traditions and applying them to contemporary problems. Thus the process may entail personal and social responsibilities.

MacIntyre's approach benefits from the pedagogical advantage of pitting one position against another. The moral and social choices facing us are simply and clearly delineated and we are prodded to debate them and settle on one or the other. Perhaps its most serious flaw is that he does not sufficiently inquire whether his practical insights and narratives, which are the foundation of his principles of justice, are true.

Practical insights about social goods (as in family life, education, health care, and law) not only aim to explain how they are distributed, they also set norms for their distribution. That is, by explaining how things are, they also suggest how they should be. Some of the most important questions about practical insights ask whether the insights about principles governing social goods should be put into practice.

Our reflection on practical insights must attend to motives and alternative courses of action as well as to the truth of insights. As one moves closer to decision and action, one begins to focus more intently on just what is to be done, the steps to be taken, and its consequences. One also becomes increasingly concerned with knowing whether an action is egoistic or other-regarding, revisionist or conservative, rational or irrational.[17]

To be accountable for our motives and actions, we reflect on the habits of mind and heart that shape our decisions. We need recourse to moral guidelines regarding the good of others and ourselves, especially for decisions and actions that allocate social goods, which by definition should be based on the practical insights of the society.

To reflect adequately on one's practical insights requires a tripodal theory of morality and justice. Criteria for moral habits or *virtues* constitute the first leg. Criteria for moral *standards* (principles, rules, and rankings) for creating and allocating social goods is the second leg. Principles for morally justifiable social situations or arrangements constitute the third leg.[18]

Just Persons

From the Aristotelian perspective, applied in some Jewish, Christian, and Islamic traditions to interpret their moral beliefs systematically, attaining one's personal long-term good and realizing the same for others are essentially similar; that is, both aim to satisfy natural human needs. The human good is more than one's personal long-term good; it includes the good of others. Prudential reasoning about the personal long-term good of an individual and altruistic reasoning, which concerns the good of others, are essentially similar, for they are concerned with the greater good (*Politics* 1, 2, 1253a–18; Engberg-Pedersen 1983, 56). In this moral reasoning, one must take one's moral bearings from what is good or bad for humans rather than one's personal interests. Seeking one's own interest can turn logic into cunning and unleash immoderate appetites and drives for personal importance and status.[19]

The prudence that both philosophical and theological Aristotelians have dubbed altruistic requires a general justice, a state of rectitude within individuals and of rightly ordered cooperative endeavors. Justice represents the whole of human moral good and virtue, and all other moral virtues are but forms of justice.[20] Compared with other cardinal virtues, justice is, in the words of William Galston, "essentially comparative"; it looks "not only at the relation between an individual and a particular object of desire or aversion—as do temperance and fortitude, for example—but also at the relation of other relevant individuals to that object or objects of that kind" (Galston 1980, 101). Hence, justice that prudently regards the good of others represents right relationships for persons and communities.

Disagreeable or strenuous work, such as the dangerous work of soldiering and the sometimes degrading and stigmatizing work of garbage collection, is undeniably necessary in communities (Walzer 1983, 165ff.). Because such tasks occur in so many spheres of social goods, they are fit illustrations of the virtues persons need to be just. People who assign them and decide the compensation or reward for them must be aware of their motives. Performing menial or physical labor may damage some people's senses of personal status for such work is customarily assigned to slaves rather than to free citizens, in other words, to socially vulnerable racial, ethnic, and sexual groups. (Conversely, performing such tasks may stigmatize the workers or their group as untouchable or degraded.) Those who perform this work are vulnerable to those who assign it. Decisions about who must do this work turn not so much on the ability, industry, drive, or preference of the worker but rather on the resources and alternatives and, more importantly, on the perception and habits of the decision makers. Persons who lack personal justice are unlikely to reflect rationally about how to equitably assign hard work so that it does not degrade the worker.

Selecting Principles for Just Actions

To approximate the preeminent moral good of a community, namely, distributive justice, its policymakers must rationally choose their actions in the light of some criteria for distributive justice. To single-mindedly apply a standard, say, freedom or promise keeping, would not discharge their responsibility because both these standards suppose the social situations that distributive justice establishes. Only when allocators attend to distributive justice can they rightly arrange the benefits and harms of common endeavors. Above all, only then can the members of a community be assured that the burdens are assigned rationally and equitably.

Consider, then, how reflection on a matter like allocating hard work might proceed. What tests the justice of the allocations? I propose the following: The way a community allocates its burdens is the decisive test of whether it is approximating its chief moral good, distributive justice. For example, cleaning the kitchen after a meal is a measurable responsibility even though some member of a family either may have a facility for doing it or may enjoy it. When responsibilities are estimable and verifiable by some rational standard, they are burdens. They become harms when they damage the fundamental human goods of persons in some rationally verifiable way. For example, some burdens generate long-lasting disadvantages for all persons in certain, racial, ethnic, sexual, religious, and socioeconomic groups by either limiting their freedom or by handicapping them in competition for rewards.

Burdens are inevitable in every sphere of social goods. Some are unavoidably harmful. Which are justifiable? The harms of levies on wealth and income, for example, do not compare to the loss of a person's life or damage to one's physical or mental abilities through invasive medical treatment or substandard education. The harms that taxation works may be justifiable provided they are allotted according to relevant differences between people, that is, according to complex equality. For example, tax rates may be linked to one's capacity to pay, but not to one's race or sex. Damages to one's life or physical and mental capacities are rarely if ever justifiable because they create systematic harms. Similarly, assigning the dangerous business of military service exclusively to certain classes of persons or locking generations of children in certain categories into schools that do not prepare them adequately for adult life are difficult to justify. Harms to entire classes of persons should be judged unwarranted and barred in much the same way as slavery was abolished.

The overarching moral principle is beneficence, which respects others as persons and obliges persons to promote the well-being of others by actions that are themselves permissible and do not disproportionately harming themselves. The complementary principle, nonmaleficence, proscribes harming others without justification. Both of these principles of respect for persons are prominent in most of the world's religions and are widely shared cultural understandings.

A derived principle specifies which harms are justifiable. The principle of degree of harm to fundamental goods declares harms that deprive persons of intrinsic and fundamental goods like life itself as almost always unjustifiable, harms that are detrimental to intermediate and instrumental goods like physical and mental health possibly justifiable, and harms that damage purely extrinsic goods not essential for life more readily justifiable. The hard work associated with family life, for example, would fall in the last category, unless it works less justifiable harms, as it would if it were assigned to the children alone. Depriving persons of opportunities to develop physically and mentally or depriving them of social status and importance by imposing, say, hospital bedpan duty on only one group, nurses, is almost never justifiable. Not only does it fail to respect the principle of simple equality, but it also seems to fail the test of complex equality by assigning hard work on the basis of irrelevant characteristics that seem unjustifiably discriminatory. Similarly, the wide discrepancies between expenditures per pupil in wealthy and in poor school districts is also discriminatory because the pupils suffer systematic harms.

The third principle, proportionate harm, which derives from the principle of beneficence, states that even less serious harms must be commensurate with the ability of classes of persons to sustain and to recover from them. While no one really can afford to lose his or her life, reasonably healthy persons can be required to endure some discomfort, for example, in the course of their jobs. Persons can be required to pay taxes proportioned to their net worth and income but the penniless should be held exempt. When it comes to allocating combat duty there is no reason to select only Blacks, or Chicanos, or, for that matter, men. (Claims that all men are physically better endowed for such work than are all women, for instance, are essentially insupportable.) A historical example is assigning the harshest, most unpleasant, and riskiest jobs in coal mines to certain ethnic groups.

The similarly derived principle of systemic harm states that if harms—especially the more serious harms to fundamental human goods—affect entire classes of persons across generations they are even harder to justify. Some cannot be justified and should be banned outright, for example, unjust situations that force persons into one-sided transactions that assign them responsibilities that they are not able to discharge. These situations give rise to entire classes of weaker parties who stand to be repeatedly harmed because they are not effectively free and lack political power. Such unjust situations often result from voluntary negligence, if not deliberate choice, by public officials, as under some caste systems, when officials have, even if without malice, assigned hard work to socially vulnerable classes.

Besides the principles of simple and complex equality, beneficence, and nonmaleficence, principles of justice for specific situations are needed. The only known sources of such principles are rightly thinking persons who habitually act well in the particular sphere of social goods (Engberg-Pedersen 1983, 230–32). Even if they are unable to explain how they decide or are incapable of teaching others how to decide, they instinctively choose the right action. For example, some parents allow their children to exercise appropriate responsibility for their age; some physicians and nurses know how to break bad news to their patients; and some political leaders distinguish between public and private interests in public policies. These skillful persons take account of self as but one among others, perceive the ways in which other persons are equal or not, and understand how others might be helped or harmed. Only such persons can find the common ground to allocate social goods justly in a particular sphere. The conclusions of such persons are truly appropriate, that is, in the common interest, and authentic, that is, wary of how one's own interest influences one's deliberations (Lonergan 1958, 610–11; Habermas 1984, 301–4, 308–311, 325–26, 333–34, 336).[21]

From our example about assigning hard work, we may draw three conclusions. First, no one who is not practiced in the particular sphere should presume to or be permitted to assign its burdens and harms. Second, even among experienced persons, only those who are just persons themselves should presume to or be allowed to assign burdens and harms. Third, the just, experienced persons need to acknowledge that, in a less than perfect world populated by less than perfect persons, progress toward justice may be the best one can hope for—as long as we remain ready to revise social arrangements that have become unjust.[22]

One may have to measure the world not from perfection downward but from chaos upward. While not relinquishing ideals, one should not strive to refashion too quickly this less than perfect world and its less than perfect persons. Striving for improvements is akin to making the tempered steel of contingency somewhat more pliable. If we are to be even modestly effective, however, we must give pain and suffering greater weight; indeed, they must determine the just allocations of advantages and disadvantages of social goods. Consider, for example, the considerable wisdom in the following national proposal for allocating hard work.

> We can share (and partially transform) hard work through some sort of national service; we can reward it with money or leisure; we can make it more rewarding by connecting it to other sorts of activity—political, managerial, and professional in character. We can conscript, rotate, cooperate, and compensate; we can reorganize the work and rectify its names. We can do all of these things, but we will not have abolished hard work; nor will we have abolished the class of hard workers. . . . The measures that I have proposed are at best partial and incomplete. They have an end appropriate to a negative good: a distribution of hard work that doesn't corrupt the distributive spheres with which it overlaps, carrying poverty into the sphere of money, degradation into the sphere of honor, weakness and resignation into the sphere of power. To rule out negative dominance . . . is the purpose of . . . the politics of hard work . . . [but its] outcomes . . . are indeterminate . . . Walzer 1983, 183).

Walzer thus outlines a partial-compliance theory of justice, as contrasted, say, with a strict-compliance theory such as the one espoused by Rawls (1971). But partial compliance may be the best we can hope for if I am right about the problem of liberating the human consciousness and correct in my conviction that how a community assigns the burdens, pains, harms, and sufferings in its spheres of social goods is the decisive measure of its justice. Real situations and practices are made up of insights, expressions, reflections, decisions, and actions. Nonetheless, if one is interested in what could be, one must consider the principles for creating and renewing just situations.

Just Situations and Practices

To attain a measure of justice in the creation and allocation of either the benefits or the burdens of social goods, we need to know more than can be derived from considerations of virtues and principles that guide action. We need to know what situations and practices will either foster or subvert those virtues and principles. We need to determine whether the distributions can achieve the common advantage that Aristotle termed the political good of justice, which assigns advantages and disadvantages according to the complex equality of the members of the community (*Politics* 3, 12, 1282b121; and *Nicomachean Ethics* 5, 5, 1134a1–15).

Some will argue for meeting other requirements, such as freedom from interference, telling the truth, or keeping promises. Because in our mercantilist culture contracts and other promises are freely made, these arguments overlook that all these promises purport to be made under fair and voluntary conditions. But most of our important obligations are not freely bargained for. Some are simply imposed. That we must accept them makes creating and sustaining just social conditions even more important.

The conditions and practices associated with hard work in families as well as in civil communities of work, law, education, and health care are excellent case studies for investigating whether a community has created just situations. What should worry a community more than the unjust distribution of hard work, however, are the institutionalized and systemic forms such practices can take. Entire classes of people can be deprived of social and cultural advantages for generations if situations are legally sanctioned, as when a hard-work caste is established.

Consider, for example, how such systemically disadvantaging practices threaten the much-prized value of liberty. If liberty is preserved—even in its negative version, freedom from interference—it will be because those who prize liberty have helped create and maintain social settings that assure others can become equally free. The freedom anyone enjoys depends on these social and cultural settings, for disadvantaged persons may not be inclined, even if they might be able, to communicate truthfully, to keep their promises, and to refrain from otherwise harming people. A steadfast dedication to equal liberty is, therefore, in the interest of all.

In addition, we have intergenerational responsibilities. As we are responsible to future generations for our natural environment, we are responsible for our social and cultural environments. Some professions look to the training of new practitioners and some practitioners willingly create practices that will benefit the next generation more than their own, but we infrequently allocate the burdens of hard work with future generations in mind. Instead of benefitting the whole community or empowering future generations, all too often we let young men and women grow up with little opportunity to develop and use their talents. Some persons accept a diminished lot in life and perceive harsh and unpleasant work as their destiny. However, the song lyric from Jerome Kern's *Showboat*, "body all achin' and racked with pain," barely suggests the long-term and systematic social and cultural disadvantaging of Black Americans and many other minorities in a nation that professes to reward citizens for their achievements.

Decisions and Actions

We have reflected on our practical insights about social goods in the light of the tripodal theory of justice and considered the principles required for justice in persons, for just interactions between persons and social goods, and for just situations and practices. We have traced the patterns of consciousness in persons from practical insights and their expressions to reflection and judgment. What remain are decisions and actions. After describing the habits of heart and mind that shape decisions and actions, we discuss the moral imperatives.

Habits of Consciousness

Practical insights, reflections, and decisions function legislatively, but only decisions have a truly executive function. By deciding to do what one knows is reasonable, one acknowledges an obligation to act. One can avoid reflection or refuse to act as reflection advises, or renounce responsibility altogether and choose to do what one prefers. As Bernard Lonergan observed, "decisions are right, not because they are the pronouncements of the individual conscience, nor because they proceed from this or that type of social mechanism for reaching common decisions, but because they are in the concrete situation intelligent and reasonable. Again, in both cases, decisions are wrong, not because of their private or public origin, but because they diverge from the dictates of intelligence and reasonableness" (1958, 628).

In making decisions, persons are not only concerned with how things are or ought to be. They also are concerned with themselves as effective agents. Their effective freedom in choosing subjects influences their accountability for specific choices (Lonergan 1958, 617–24, 627).

The four factors that determine effective freedom are the available resources and alternative courses of action, one's perceptive habits, one's intellectual habits, and one's willingness to reflect and act consistently. One's willingness, though shaped by one's perceptive and intellectual habits, is most critical. For example, one may not really be open to one or another alternative even when it appears necessary or one may not be able to persuade oneself to select it. One simply may settle for fewer or more familiar options, especially when one habitually decides by considering one's personal or one's interest group advantage rather than what benefits each of us because it benefits others (Pieper 1965, 17–21; see also Engberg-Pedersen 1983, 53–57). Thus one's lack of habitual justice limits one's willingness and of freedom of choice.

Some Protestant traditions of moral philosophy treat human willingness as if it were independent of knowledge and regard bad will as the root of all evils. By so emphasizing acts of will that immediately precede action, one may overlook the steps that led up to the choice. Faulty choices are more often based on failures of understanding than on bad will.[23]

To accept uncritically the hypothesis that will is the key to morality is to accept both the unreasonable actions and the common biases that corrupt consciousness but that will alone cannot vanquish. Willingness is not only a matter of willpower. One's willingness to make the intelligent and reasonable choice also depends on how attentive and perceptive one's insights have been, how considered one's reflections and judgments were, how familiar and masterful one is at deciding, and how risky the choices are. There are always many routes to avoid the decisions and actions that may bring burdens.

By exaggerating the role of will in morality, religious and other communities can diminish the ability of their members to reflect. Loyalties to the community may outweigh the public advantage. Overemphasis on will can foster decisions and actions that favor self. Some communities that lean heavily on authority and discourage critical reflection about moral norms invite members to avoid the burdensome responsibilities of determining whether one's insights are correct.

The ethical narratives of these communities may seriously undermine rational decision making. As noted earlier, narratives contain not only symbols but their interpretations. They arise from a mythic consciousness that perceives no distinction between experiencing, imagining, understanding, and judging. Because of the emotional power of words, actions, and rituals, the world created by mythic consciousness is impressively convincing.

But these worlds and the decision making they foster do not always represent reality well, and they sometimes unwittingly promote a form of moral infantilism. No matter how impressive the presentation, it is only as intelligent as the insights it communicates. Furthermore, these narratives are restricted to the familiar, to understanding things as they relate to us. They are not sufficiently disinterested to understand how things are related to others. While disinterestedness is required to cultivate the prudence and justice necessary for just persons, principles, and situations, mythic consciousness and narrative forms of ethics seem little interested in disinterestedness. More seriously, following mythic metaphors blindly in making decisions may substitute the community's world of sense and value, its stories, and its own idiosyncratic standards for rational consciousness (Lonergan 1958, 532, 533, 538–40, 542).

Moral consciences formed by mythic metaphors are vulnerable to manipulation by what one writer calls "speculative gnostics and practical magicians" who take advantage of people's poorly considered insights. Because most people have more life skills than intellectual skills, mythmakers more easily capture their imaginations and rouse them to action. Examples of such leaders are some television evangelists as well as some earnestly antireligious, seemingly gnostic humanists preaching dialectical creeds. Merchants of fanatic nationalism, such as Hitler, of totalitarian socialism, such as Stalin, and a host of other effective storytellers dissuade listeners from critical reflection to promote their simple-minded solution to social problems.

Whether civil or religious, such cultural and social traditions use mythic consciousness to prod people to act, irrespective of their understanding. As the most effective way to communicate these traditions, the story can make a reasonable decision appear pointless. Root paradigms can have the same effect on people in crisis. Victor Turner's analysis of root paradigms may have been insufficiently critical of this effect. Saying that root paradigms are neither logically arrayed systems of univocal concepts nor precise tools of thought nor, most certainly, stereotyped guidelines for ethical, esthetic, or conventional action is not claiming that they are beyond the grasp of cognitive and moral consciousness and belong instead to the realm of emotionally charged wills and people's unalterable postures in life (Turner 1976, 156). Saying so is tantamount to saying that, right or wrong, the postures people take and the decisions they make in crises need not be intelligent or reasonable. Even root paradigms, I contend, rest on insights that need to be tested. Otherwise the acts of will that put them into practice can be arbitrary, irrational, and mistaken.

Consider the decisions and actions in allocating hard work. If a person is assigned hard work by someone who does not seem to respect him or her, the person may lose the sense of self-worth and dignity. Hard work may put life or health at risk or rob one of opportunities for a developed, reasonably happy, and intellectually satisfying life, or create systemic and transgenerational disadvantages for classes of persons. Thus, in deciding whether or not to volunteer for or otherwise accept such work, or in deciding whether or not to assign it to others, the decisive considerations are the possible harms and one's willingness to risk them. The harms include harms to self as well as to others, because we owe respect to ourselves as persons. To choose hard work that is likely to create harms to one's fundamental goods, just as to impose the same on others, cannot be considered a fully reasonable decision, but to create social conditions that make harms almost inevitable for one's progeny or for whole classes of persons in a society would be even more unreasonable.

Creating such conditions may appear, at first glance and in good faith, rationally necessary or obligatory, but reflection will show the conditions are unjustifiable. Often they appear obligatory mainly because individuals and communities lack justice themselves or are unwilling to revise their practical insights and judgments. Alternatives may be few; people may not be aware of the harms. The decisive question, nonetheless, is whether they are willing to choose otherwise or at least willing to be persuaded to do so.

It is said that the wife of Mohandas K. Gandhi refused to take her share of cleaning the latrines in their ashram. Although she was convinced that while such hard work might be a caste duty for some, it was unfitting for one of her caste, eventually she accepted her turn. Many stories recount such changes in mind and heart that enable persons to decide and act to alleviate unjust allocations of harms.

Like Mrs. Gandhi, people may be unwilling to accept their share of burdens both because of their religious and cultural convictions and because custom has allowed them to pass the burdens on to others. But I rather think that, even when power is a factor, people are acting on dimly sensed worries that changing a practice threatens their status and sense of importance. Were it not for these or other such attachments, people might be more willing to regard and to treat others as equal in worth and dignity.

The harms created by institutionalized and systemic forms of enslavement need not be recounted here. We should note, however, that the persons responsible for these harms are not always morally accountable. Although their moral consciousness may have been essentially free, the available alternatives and resources and the widely shared but mistaken common sense of their times may have limited their freedom. Common biases enchain the consciences of the keepers as well as of the kept. Revising them requires more than simply being consistent in what one knows should be done. It also requires a willingness to set aside, to modify, or at least to renegotiate some cultural paradigms.

Imperatives for Making Decisions

It is clear that a rightly guided act of will requires effective freedom or willingness, which relies upon habits of sensitivity, perceptiveness, and attentiveness, and intelligent practical insights and reasonable judgments. Thus, the first imperatives for making decisions are similar to those for reflecting on practical insights, namely, be attentive, be intelligent, and be reasonable.

In addition, decisions and actions require that we be consistent, be responsible, and be free. When an act of will follows a rationally acknowledged obligation, one becomes a rational doer. Becoming one requires that one maintain consistency between what is known and what is done, thus, consistency and responsibility are imperative.[24] As we have also seen, rational consciousness frequently needs to be liberated. We are always renegotiating and surmounting ourselves as moral agents, so that to be free may be the most global imperative.

As individuals need sensitivity and attentiveness, intelligence, reasonableness, willingness, and responsibility to make decisions, communities must abandon commonsense biases in favor of a common faith in pursuit of truth, with a sustaining hope, mutual regard, and sensitivity to human needs and sufferings.[25]

To make decisions and act on them, we need symbols that enlarge our effective freedom. The humor that laughs with rather than at another is one such symbol (Lonergan 1958, 626). So too are images which leaders such as Gandhi and Dr. Martin Luther King, Jr., used to unsettle and rearrange conventional perceptions and to expand human willingness. Whatever the symbol used, our willingness increases with our sensitivity to the pain and suffering of others. Humor and compassionate understanding help sustain appropriate habits of justice and prudence.

Because the responsibilities of changing one's mind and heart and personal habits, of revising community practices and traditions, and of coping with partial success are heavy, the enduring difficulty is to persuade one's self and others to accept the burdens of both personal and social justice.

What resources are available to achieve justice? Some religious traditions invite people to act unilaterally, to value exchange forms of justice, and to witness to their beliefs in ways that resemble interest group politics (Tracy 1986, 119, 121, 127). Some philosophical and theological theories of justice fail to identify just persons, just principles, and just situations as essentials.

Religious traditions can be helpful if marshalled carefully. Like all cultural resources, they embody beliefs about the world, about human beings and their social bonds, and about government and politics, but not all their beliefs can be easily explained to outsiders. Neither do these beliefs treat common human bonds, sufferings, and sense of community. Like the writings of some cultural communities and the classics of the neo-Platonic traditions, classic religious writings do not much treat these topics. Instead, they emphasize individual rights to freedom but do not cite other pertinent moral values to appropriately channel that liberty. Thus, they lead uncritical believers toward an ideology of a minimalist state corresponding to the Christian concept of pre-Constantinian social organization with little or no responsibility for public affairs. Some religious communities may be inclined to wait for outside intervention rather than to act with hope and patience (Hauerwas 1981, 128), and thus neglect duties to future generations.

However, some cultural and religious resources, such as the world-affirming classics of religions and philosophies in the Aristotelian lineage, are helpful. They draw attention to the political good of justice and how this good is understood as a form of distributive justice (*Politics* 3, 12, 1282b16-21; *Nicomachean Ethics* 5, 3).[26] These traditions provide reasons for respecting the earth and its creatures, for establishing social institutions to alleviate human sufferings, and for showing compassion to "the poor of Jahweh," whose suffering for the sake of justice is especially blessed. These views about the world, its history, and the bonds between peoples inculcate a sense of responsibility for maintaining public order and well-being.

We need criteria to identify more appropriate solutions to the problems of human decision making and action. As Michael Walzer emphasizes, one should begin with one's values and everyday practices, using the social criticism of some Hebrew prophets (1987, 69ff). Michael Ignatieff in his *The Needs of Strangers* (1985) contends that, without a public language to express our needs, we risk becoming strangers to our better selves. According to Ignatieff, the central issue is how to express our human needs in ways that respect our individuality and liberty, while at the same time affirming our solidarity. Michael Harrington, wary of the influence of statism and technocracy on scholarship in the social sciences, searched for models of just communities among trade unions (especially in France) and among persons who seemed to possess greater cultural stability than middle-class persons (1985, 204ff.; see also Bellah et al. 1985, 152–53, 211–12; and Barber 1985, 15). In the lower socioeconomic classes, Harrington finds appropriate narratives and practices of justice and social movements that seek to apply ethics to public power. He argues that in such communities one finds a moral vocabulary and practical reasoning that recognize that the common good and justice in the community are essential for a good moral life.

The above suggestions are in accord with the conviction that the decisive measure of justice in a community is the way it assigns the burdens, pains, harms, and sufferings of social goods. Even so, the best we can hope for seems to be an approximate justice, which will require searching for common ground. In the United States, the search lies principally in our culture, which is marked by revolt against extrinsic authority and a thirst for participation (Sellers 1970, 264). James Sellers has argued that these marks suggest building on moral standards that are within persons rather than imposed. Thus, liberating rational consciousness includes working with others to shape a common moral life (Sellers 1970, 265, 269; see also Bellah et al. 1985, 38, 75–81). Religious communities may foster working with others but not if they stand on only the leg of authority for their moral guidance. Other communities, such as families, neighborhoods, workplaces, and voluntary associations, offer opportunities for such cooperation.

Conclusion

Understanding justice requires reflecting on how humans have attempted to understand their experiences of social goods. In this chapter we trace patterns from experiences of social goods through practical insights and reflection to decisions and actions. We attend to the way people interpret experiences, express their insights, and then reason, decide, and act. We consider habits of heart and mind that direct the process and make some inferences about norms. The responsibilities of creating just persons, just principles, and just situations seem to require a transformation of the habits of individuals and communities.

The central theses in this chapter are, first, that justice is the chief personal and social moral virtue and that persons and communities bear the burden of cultivating it; second, that a just allocation of the advantages and disavantages of social goods is the chief virtue of communities and that striving to achieve distributive justice is one of the burdens that fall primarily on community leaders; and, third, that the decisive test of distributive justice is how the disdvantages and burdens are arranged. Undoubtedly the heaviest burden is guiding the community toward distributive justice because of the harms some persons will unavoidably suffer to their fundamental human goods.

The carpenter's remark about justice mentioned earlier in this chapter may reflect disappointment that others did not share his commitment to justice. The cartoon of fish devouring each other may reflect the cultural, social, and personal burden of reworking our practical insights and narratives regarding justice. Not only must one personally strive toward the justice to interpret, express, and act on one's convictions, but one must face one's mistaken insights, poor judgments, and indecisive or inconsistent actions and take corrective measures. Furthermore, as difficult as refashioning one's habits is, it is still more difficult to rework habitual mistakes in the insights, decisions, and actions of communities.

The following chapters examine the burdens of justice in several categories of social goods. These chapters suggest that, to meet the tripodal responsibilities, individuals and communities must address their culture and that thay may profit from knowing how social goods have been distributed in such spheres as families, schools, health care, and law. In so doing, one realizes that, while the distributive problems experienced in several spheres are often analogous, only prudent persons, practiced in those spheres, can settle what needs to be done.

In Families

Contemporary literature on the family is riddled with contradictory claims and interpretations. Some, mainly from politically and religiously conservative perspectives, find the family an imperiled refuge, shrinking in importance in modern times. Others, mainly from politically and religiously liberal viewpoints, contend that the family was never quite that important and often has been either a prison or a source of violence and inequality. The family, they declare, is surely in flux, but it needs to be. Some claim that dramatic sea-changes have occurred in family life over the last fifty years—perhaps more in some socioeconomic groups than others. Others, appealing to studies such as the 1970s reiteration of the Lynds's famous 1920s Middletown study, claim there has been little change in families over the last half-century (Caplow et al. 1982).[1] Others believe the family has become overburdened with functions that civic and religious institutions have either abandoned or neglected. Still others find that family members spend little time together and often delegate child care to institutions and to the mass media. In addition to these contradictory claims of fact there are equally conflicting interpretations of family life. Some see the family as a commune, as an encounter group, or as a refuge from work and politics. Such images clash with most family experiences, which fall somewhere between newer and traditional images of the family (Stannard 1979, 93).

Even the hardiest inquirer can scarcely be impartial when writing about the family. Inevitably, one thinks and writes about one's own family. Yet think and write about it one must since the family is an important symbol of human interdependence, solidarity, and separateness, what Levi-Strauss called a tribal totem. Because families are interrelated with their society and culture, reflecting on families involves law, politics, and economy. The family is no more a private institution than it is a purely public one. It is not a living area sharply separate from a working area. It is not a civil institution, but it interacts with civil institutions. Some of its social goods are more properly associated with economics, education, health care, and politics.[2]

The family represents the first and the most important set of social relations that people experience. Family life trains us for community life. As Allan Bloom puts it, the family is the only common good we know by nature and the only one naturally available to modern humans (1986, 76, 78). By living in a family, people learn their first lessons about justice in the allocation of the benefits and burdens of life in common. The habits of justice created through family experiences shape one's later relationships.

Though difficult to study, the family is unavoidable in ethical reflections about justice. The family is the first of the case studies in this book on the burdens of justice because it is such an important instance of shared lives dedicated to the good of its members. The family is the first place where people create and allocate social goods and their burdens. Susan Moller Okin noted that one cannot grow up in an unjust family and later think rightly about justice and promote it in society (1989). Whether the family is a prison or a refuge, an encounter group or a commune, it should be a just community. How a family shares its human and social goods undoubtedly affects its moral character and consequently that of its culture and society as well.

Our first goal is to consider how opportunities for development, economic goods, and political goods (Galston 1980, 193ff.) are found in families. We are interested in determining which distributions might work harms to family members, which harms are justifiable, and which are not. As in chapter 1, we shall draw on religious and other sources for practical insights, reflections, and decisions about a just distribution of advantages and disadvantages. How the burdens are assigned is more decisive than how the benefits, such as equal opportunities, are assigned. Finally, drawing on the tripodal theory developed in chapter 1, we shall evaluate the justice of the family members, of their operating principles, and of their family situations.

The definition of *family* has been shifting because of shifts in society and culture and the influence of, for example, the feminist and sexual liberation movements.[3] The term *conjugal family* commonly refers to two adults of opposite sex and their children. This is the kind of family I have in mind. This is not to say that there are no other groupings in society nor that we fully understand which moral norms to use in evaluating them. It is rather to say that I am persuaded that, at least in the United States, we should limit the term *family* to those that are *conjugal* lest it apply so broadly that it has no useful meaning. In this chapter, we shall consider the burdens of justice in conjugal families. Of course, some relationships lack children, but the partners still work for common ends. Thus, there is still much to be learned from Rousseau's attempt to rescue the meaning of family from an exaggerated individualism that would make consent and freedom from interference the only criteria for lives lived in common. One need not concur fully with this view or with his claim that marital and family relations are determined by nature (Bloom 1986, 70, 78). Neither need one accede to post-eighteenth-century views that marital and familial relationships are nothing more than products of choice or purely procedural limited partnerships.

We should also note at the outset that some suppositions about justice in families are unwarranted, for example, the supposition that families generate inequalities because they favor their members over other persons (Fiskin 1983, 1–2; Walzer 1983, 229). Disparities occur in all communities and families do not create more inequalities than other communities. Similarly, the supposition that kinship ties and sexual relations are beyond the reach of distributive justice is also unwarranted. Michael Walzer's contention that freedom is the most appropriate distributive rule for allocating respect, love, affection (as well as dowries, gifts, inheritances, and mutual aid) within families seems both unwarranted and harmful (1983, 227–42).[4] Equally unwarranted and harmful is supposing that tensions between justice and generosity are inevitable, and that affording some persons more than they deserve is love. As Wojciech Sadurski points out: "Justice requires good moral reasons for a proposed distribution: generosity does without them" (1984, 345). Suppose, says Sadurski, a parent punished one of his or her children and forgives another for the same misbehavior. "No one has *lost* anything, but injustice was committed because the proportion of guilt and punishment was not respected" (1984, 344). From my perspective, however, something may have been lost by the one punishing as well as by the one punished.

This chapter concurs with Sadurski and discusses the burdens of justice among families consisting of adults and children and the burdens of justice among families of more than one generation. It examines harms that can be done to persons in families. We shall draw upon criteria developed in chapter 1 to argue that (*a*) harms to fundamental human goods, (*b*) disproportionate harms, and (*c*) systemic harms are not morally justifiable in families.

Burdens of Justice in Couples

Were we to take all of our clues about distributive justice in conjugal families from those few contemporary works that mention it, we would study troubled marriages or the domestic division of labor (which may benefit or burden some members disproportionately). Only a handful of commentators urge more careful study of the social relationships that make homes habitable and foster the education of children, in addition to the psychological examination of the couples' "internal worlds" (Flax 1982, 223).[5] Fewer still address the morality of disproportionate benefits and burdens in families.

Such an inquiry is the task of this chapter. To accomplish it, we need not consider all the problems just mentioned nor need we develop a moral theory of the family—even though one may be sorely needed (ibid., 252). Our first task is to determine whether the heavy psychological and social responsibilities of married people (as in other forms of common life) are harmful to fundamental human goods, whether they are disproportionate to a spouse's ability to carry or recover from them, and whether they can be transmitted to later generations.

The first responsibility of married persons is to respect themselves and each other. In marriage, one is responsible for developing one's self and for helping the other to develop as well. In conjugal friendships, one's friend becomes, as Cicero put it, "half of one's soul." Therefore, one can learn in marriage, as in few other relationships, that the good of others and one's own good are similar. Married persons need separate experiences and activities but one's personal good cannot be achieved by living as if one's life is strictly one's own or that "being one's own person" is a solo venture. One must respect the person one's spouse is or is becoming. After respecting oneself, the second responsibility of married persons is *beneficence,* promoting the well-being of the other without disproportionately harming oneself. Beneficence embraces the more stringent obligation of *nonmaleficence,* which forbids actions that harm others without justification. Thus marriage affords not only special opportunities for self-development but also special opportunities to benefit (or at least not harm) one's "other half."

This chapter focuses on the responsibilities of married persons not to harm their partners. Married persons must apportion these burdens between them. Because the steps toward benefiting one's loved one are not always clear, the maxim to follow should be "above all do no harm." In this chapter, we shall consider how married partners should allocate burdens justly and whether the allocation has a decisive effect on their moral character and their life together.

As in chapter 1, harms will be evaluated in light of three principles that are derived from respect for self and respect for others. According to the principle of degree of harm to fundamental goods, some harms adversely affect intrinsic and essential goods; some are detrimental to intermediate and instrumental goods; and some damage extrinsic goods. Harms to intrinsic and essential goods are almost always unjustifiable. Those in the intermediate range might sometimes be justifiable. Those that damage purely extrinsic goods are more readily justifiable. The principle of proportionate harm states that harms should be evaluated according to the ability of the harmed persons to sustain or recover from them. The principle of systemic harm states that harms that affect entire classes of persons for generations are rarely, if ever, justifiable.

Degree of Harm to Fundamental Goods

In marriages, threats to one's most fundamental human goods, like one's life, or to one's intermediate goods, like physical and mental well-being, have historically been grounds for separation and divorce and for entrusting children to others. Recently, however, critics have pointed out that in traditional married life-styles one's personal and professional development, say, through continuing education, may be denied to one or the other partner. One is being harmed, but the other may refuse to change the life-style. To the degree that the harming partner is effectively free, he or she is an accomplice in an unjust practice that denies the other the opportunity to develop his or her abilities. Of course, when children are denied the opportunity to develop their physical and mental capabilities, the injustice is more serious because children are more vulnerable and less able to sustain such harm.

Besides the desire to develop one's capabilities (Galston 1980, 262), one needs leisure in the Aristotelian sense of opportunity for contemplative practices (*praxis*) that attain their fulfillment within the agent performing them, as opposed to purely instrumental activities (*technis*) that attain their ends only outside the agent performing them (Galston 1980, 261; Pieper 1965; MacIntyre 1981). What this leisure, together with the material conditions for it, can do for the spouses as individuals and as a couple pursuing a common good is much more important than how it could make them more productive.

Because each partner has his own talents, should the one with the greater potential be given priority? There does not seem to be a compelling reason to do so. Conversely, however, it does not seem that those with lesser potential should always be given priority unless they are more vulnerable. For example, if resources and opportunities are limited, it would be more reasonable to give greater weight to developing the more capable party, provided both will benefit. In general, resources should be allocated so that each will have roughly the same opportunity for self-development.

Should someone object that, to have the same opportunities for each, couples might consent to arrangements that provide each with less opportunity than when each pursues individual interests, a short response would be that, while couples should be free to choose their own arrangements, their arrangements may not be correct. A better response is that in a morally good marriage, benefits or opportunities and burdens or responsibilities must be justly allocated. Consent does not make an arrangement just. To consent to an unjust apportioning of opportunities is to consent to what is morally wrong. Furthermore, frequently consent is not mutual because both partners are not equally competent and free. One may be more vulnerable or reliant on the other, and the arrangements to which they consent may so distribute the burdens of life together that either one's life or its development is seriously jeopardized.

What should trouble us more, I believe, are families in which one partner is given the development opportunities and the other partner is given the burdens of assuring them or families in which opportunities are provided for the children and none for the parents. How unjust this division of opportunity and responsibility is depends on how profoundly the burden-bearer is affected in his or her fundamental goods. If it involves the loss of life or physical or mental health, then the allocation is unjust. But the injustice of less serious harms can be mitigated by alternating risks or shortening the time of one's exposure to them.

I do not mean to suggest that self-development in a marriage is nothing more than individual fulfillment. Some forms of self-development cannot be achieved without the commitment of a marriage.

Proportionate Harms

Contemporary discussions emphasize the unequal division of labor in marriage. This emphasis may stem, in part, from an awareness created by the increased number of employed married women who try to meet customary responsibilities to spouses and children.[6] In part, it may arise from a confused notion of sharing responsibilities equally when marriages are in crisis. How labor is divided during times of crisis is not as morally decisive as how they are divided over the life of the marriage, creating practices that may endure for generations.

Harms that endure for generations are the subject of the next section. Here we hope to clarify popular complaints about inequitable burdens in marriage in the light of my theory about the burdens of justice. Assigning housekeeping and nurturing solely to women is unjust, we are told, because women do not receive equal pay for equal work, equal insurance and retirement benefits, or equal opportunity for consumer credit. Furthermore, assigning household tasks to women perpetuates the oppression of women in marriage (Hite 1987; Flax 1982).

These complaints employ ambiguous notions of equality, and are far less nuanced than the forms of simple and complex equality described in chapter 1. These complaints emphasize results more than opportunities and equal bargaining power more than cooperation. Those who would liberalize married life seem overconfident about knowing which social relationships are critical in marriage and which forms of marriage must be eliminated or changed (Flax 1982, 223–53).

Contemporary treatments of decision making in marriages either try to quantify the balance, say, as a 50/50 division of both power and responsibility, or, appealing to Machiavellian ideas, claim no equality is possible. Some treatments stridently unmask sexism, including plots to oppress one sex or the other. Although some note that to victimize either women or men is not necessarily a sexist plot but rather only a "set of social structures and arrangements that disproportionately distribute burdens and benefits" (Elshtain 1982, 296), they frequently fail to define the correct proportion. One is led to think that the key issue is raw, morally unconstrained, coercive political power. Power allocations are, of course, fit subjects for moral inquiries about justice, but many contemporary statements seem little interested in such moral inquiries and focus instead on how to reform marital power. However, deciding on these reforms requires understanding the moral issues in distributing the benefits and burdens, as well as a concept of equality that addresses differences in ability, need, and achievement. The principle of proportionate harm is a surer guide in making these reforms.

In a marriage, some of the burdens are objectively verifiable and some are merely perceived. We have seen that these burdens become harms, for example, when they seriously damage a partner's fundamental goods. Burdens can also become harms if they are disproportionate to a person's ability to sustain or recover from them. A spouse may be justified in risking his or her life and health or sacrificing self-development on behalf of the family, but a spouse cannot justly impose such burdens on the other. Furthermore, enslavement, physical violence, and harassment, even insisting on having more children than one's spouse can care for or support, are completely unjustifiable.

Keeping in mind that because the well-being of each coincides with the common good they should be fostering together, only the partners can decide whether a burden is disproportionate. The needs of one may need to be balanced against what harms the other might be called upon to endure. For example, illness or disability of one spouse may justify, say, a risk of bankruptcy to the other. Furthermore, a disproportionate distribution of benefits and burdens may be temporary or long-term, and thus more or less justifiable.

The principle of proportionate harm applies even more stringently in marriages with children because children have greater needs, are less able to sustain and recover from harms to their basic human goods, and are vulnerable to adults. The burdens of being just to children fall on their parents. Parents must alter both family arrangements that harm children disproportionately and life-styles that, by harming one spouse disproportionately, indirectly harm children. Because the parents' relationship is linked to their children's moral and social development, disproportionate harms to children should be averted whenever possible.[7]

Family members may not be aware of some disproportionate harms. They may uncritically follow the traditional practice of their cultures or the recommendations of movements that seek greater opportunities for one sex or the other or for parents or children and not notice other disproportionate harms because they have not been publicized by popular media.[8]

To avoid the distortions of political rhetoric, which impairs the ability of the partners to make just and intelligent decisions, I suggest a tripodal theory of the just distribution of benefits and burdens of common life. One base of this tripod is a concept of just persons. Another is an understanding of the principles of justice that guide the allocation of advantages and disadvantages. The third is an understanding of how people can create just arrangements in their marriages and how those arrangements may influence later generations.

Systemic Harms

Damage to the fundamental human goods of an entire class of persons, such as married males, married females, or children, may endure to the next generation. Because they become incorporated into custom and legal practice, systemic harms also damage the affected classes of persons socially and culturally. They spread through the society, depriving generations of people of opportunities for achievement and reinforcing their sense of powerlessness. Because they become customary, persons in the community can fail to see that the resulting inequitable status of some classes of persons is immoral.

Systemic harms in marriage should be studied because society counts on its stability and continuity. In intimate life, where spouses may be more vulnerable to disproportionate harms and to harms to fundamental goods, they may come to accept these harms as part of married life. For example, if a family accepts the cultural notion that declares it inappropriate for males to excel in cooking, housekeeping, or rearing children, the males may suffer harm to a fundamental good because they are not permitted to develop all their talents. Or, if a couple limits a married man's roles to disciplinarian, mechanic, handyman, and breadwinner, the harms can be disproportionate to his capacity to bear or recover from them, especially if he becomes the legal bearer of debts incurred by the couple and minors of the family.

In addition to being exposed to harms within the family that correspond to the harms married men risk, women often are exposed to harms outside the family. For example, women may be considered ineligible for full membership in the political community, ill-suited for positions of leadership, and not in need of the full protection of the laws. Despite the advances achieved by the feminist movement, many women are denied suitable employment, credit, and retirement benefits. Although in contemporary society one's chief asset is the ability to earn a living, women are not perceived as needing to develop job skills.[9]

Disproportionate harms that occur in the family are even more serious burdens because, besides affecting the couple and the children, they may be adopted as de rigueur by the children and later perpetuated in their own families.

Some recent notions stand to work systemic harms, for example, that marriage is a temporary alliance or unified partnership of two individuals who should maintain separate identities, be self-sufficient, and invest in their own personal and professional development rather than investing in each other and their marriage. By excessively valuing the self-cultivation of each spouse, they seem unable to imagine marriage as a form of support that promotes the personal and professional growth of each spouse more effectively than each could independently or that they could achieve together in a temporary alliance. Accepting uncritically some recent sexual practices, such as unrestricted sexual relations, also stand to work long-term harms disproportionate to a couple's ability to bear them. Sexually transmitted diseases can harm the other partner and the children in such fundamental goods as life, health, or developed life.[10]

More commonplace are the risks and harms of either infertility or overreproductivity. Family, religious, and ethnic assumptions may insist that couples have children even when one may not be able to meet the responsibilities of raising them or supporting them, or when one is infertile (and must incur extraordinary medical and legal expenses). Furthermore, the risk of harm from childbearing and childrearing to fundamental goods such as life and developed life fall disproportionately on the female partner. Hence, allocating these burdens justly requires considering both her abilities to carry the burden and how systemic is the presumption that she should do so without counting the cost.[11]

Some contend that harm is inevitable in marriages. They claim that inequities are attributable to social forces such as the law and the economy. They say far too little, however, about how married couples unwittingly transmit these harms to future generations. Even more than the law and the economy, social and cultural practices influence couples to accept the burdens and transmit them, by means of their children, to future married couples. Thus the burdens become systemic and the duty to carry them becomes part of the community's shared understanding.

This line of reasoning will be explored further in the next section when considering intergenerational ties, obligations, and equities. Two points should be underscored here, however. First, the harms mentioned above (both the harms to a couple's fundamental human goods and disproportionate harms) are transmitted through cultural practices and beliefs even though the principles they embody are frequently mistaken, contain little more than conventional wisdom, and have not always been successful. Second, these principles are so idiosyncratic that to transmit them as applicable to all humans, and, perhaps more importantly, to use them in forging public policy regarding marriage and families is a form of communal negligence.

A strong case can be made for such a strong judgment. For example, applying the conventional wisdom of a dominant ethnic group to families of a minority ethnic group can be a form of cultural domination. Even within an ethnic group, families in lower socioeconomic classes may be vulnerable to this harm, as shown in a recent study by William Julius Wilson (1987).

Wilson contends that the victories of the civil rights movement, affirmative action, and the Great Society in the 1960s have disproportionately benefited better educated and better motivated Black Americans. Not only were the less well prepared left behind by the upwardly mobile, they were also adversely affected when employment in the United States shifted from heavy industry to the service sector and urban jobs requiring less than a high school education became scarce. The better-paying jobs were captured by new waves of baby boomers and white women entering the work force. Unemployment and poverty among Blacks, especially for single-parent families headed by women, worsened, thus contributing to a cycle of disadvantages that will continue to future generations.[12]

Two other, more damaging cultural consequences follow. One is that these very disadvantaged families no longer have the more motivated Blacks as role models. The other is that public policy holds these families to the standards of other ethnic groups in ways that may be harmful to future generations.

As this discussion of couples and families contends, some of the most serious burdens of justice are associated with harms that can be devastating to fundamental goods, that adversely affect life and health, and that narrow the possibilities for a developed human existence. Furthermore, contemporary understanding of these harms may be clouded by the political, psychological, and social assumptions of conventional wisdom. If we pay more attention to the harmful consequences of these assumptions for marriage and family life, I believe our communities will be able to find better remedies for some contemporary injustices. The solutions may include, as I have suggested, revising the understandings and practices that mislead decisions about allocating the burdens of family life.

Burdens of Justice Between Generations

Responsibilities between generations are too numerous and complex to treat fully. One must be selective, as I am here.[13] The just allocation of responsibilities and harms between parents and children seemed to me especially useful because of current interest in proximate generations[14] and because I expected the topic to yield results applicable to other problems of justice in families and across generations outside families.

Some of the responsibilities between proximate generations are caring for children and elderly adults and educating youth, but in the United States today younger age groups are being hurt or will be hurt substantially by the debts of older age groups. Some calculations predict that, over the next thirty years, taxpayers will pay more than $20 in interest for every dollar of the federal deficit. Other inequities faced by the younger generation are the following: the percentage of younger families who own their homes has declined since 1980 because of high interest rates; yearly earnings for workers under age thirty-five have declined 15% (adjusted for inflation) since 1973, making payroll taxes for social security a greater hardship for younger workers; and the percentage of children living in poverty has risen 50% since 1980.[15]

Elderly persons in the United States, especially poor ones, are also disadvantaged, but as the population ages, federal spending for programs that benefit the elderly have risen at the expense of programs that benefit younger persons. Some see public resources being consumed to satisfy present gratifications like retirement programs rather than being invested in education or research to create human and material capital wealth (Moody 1985). Others call this allocation of resources stealing from the future and urge that the unearned portion of these resources be taxed to equalize the burdens better (Greenhouse 1986).

Besides carrying unjust economic burdens, entire classes of persons can also suffer social and cultural disadvantages. For example, the rates of illegitimacy and divorce and the number of single-parent households indicate that many children are being neglected (Preston 1984, 44, 46–47). Marriage and death used to transfer family property; divorce now plays a major role. The standard of living for women and minor children declines sharply after divorce, while it rises for men. Usually the home is sold and the couple divide the proceeds equally, but the husband retains his income and business or professional career assets, that is, his potential for future earnings, while the wife and children receive only a lump sum.[16] Divorced fathers commonly default on child support payments, and divorced mothers with children find they have no effective legal remedy. In many states, divorced fathers need not support children over age eighteen, an age at which many are entering college and need financial help. "Minors (are) sentenced to a period of financial hardship" and women and children are the disadvantaged in an emerging "two-tier society" (Weitzman 1985, xv, 355, 367, 372). Couples in our society are reluctant to have children. Spouses invest in their own careers rather than in nurturing children. They seek to maintain separate and self-sufficient identities, as well as checkbooks, in a "limited partnership" rather than a lifetime commitment (ibid., xvi, 368, 374–75).

That school districts in retirement communities and inner cities are underfunded points to another disturbing trend:

middle-aged and elderly persons without children are less willing to pay taxes for schools.[17] Because contraception and
abortion are legally private matters, taxpayers do not feel
responsible for educating other people's children.

The early literature of intergenerational equity may have
fostered an atmosphere of intergenerational conflict, according to Daniel Callahan (1986, 265–66). This conflict made
older persons common targets in political conflicts, and pitted
one vulnerable group against another. In addition, there are
also conflicts within a single age group (such as those between
the affluent elderly and the impoverished elderly) and conflicts between women and children in families broken by
divorce and those in stable marriages. Hence, there are intragenerational as well as intergenerational responsibilities.

In analyzing obligations between generations we should
note that they are not simply au courant but are addressed by
Confucian and Jewish traditions. And we should focus not only
on the plight of the elderly or on that of the young, although
the young bear most of the disadvantages of poverty, inferior
education, and debt.[18] Our concerns here are whether differ-
ential treatment of age groups is warranted, why responsibilities
between generations are important, and why persons of all age
groups should cooperate.[19] A special concern of this chapter is
how harms, burdens, and resources are allocated to the generations in families.

The moral issues in allocating resources between generations are considered using a theory that holds that justice can
be had only when people and their principles and social situations are rightly ordered. We first consider some cultural
notions and the concepts of justice they embody as well as
some practices that create intergenerational injustices. Then
we discuss pertinent moral principles for alleviating intergenerational injustice.

Concepts and Theories in Cultural Practices

A culture's notions about familial and intergenerational ties
and the practices they sustain are powerful instructors. Those
that suggest each member of a family must be independent
reinforce the notion that self-interest should be the norm.
Those that suggest family members should subordinate

personal interests to the family's interest bolster the notion that family members should be bound by mutual trust and solidarity in sharing risks and burdens.

When cultural concepts are transmitted, they communicate the practical insights that inform even the least reflective theories of justice that people use in acting and deciding. But many of the cultural notions are incorrect or inadequate. Consider some traditions that do not promote justice between generations in families today.

Our popular concept of equality is often expressed as equity or a strict proportionality between what one party puts into a venture (burdens) and what another takes out (benefits). Such a concept motivates many affirmative action rules[20] and policies that mathematically balance fiscal benefits and burdens between generations. Many persons perceive injustice or discrimination in these quantitative terms.

Equity is not always a helpful concept. For example, the physical discomfort of being pregnant need not somehow be borne proportionately by husbands. It is discriminatory, but not unjustifiably so, to allot most of the benefits of public education and the burdens of compulsory military service to youth, while assigning most of the tax burden to older, wage-earning citizens. The differences in sex and age group may be reasonable grounds for the inequities just mentioned, unlike the irrelevant differences invoked to rationalize paying women lower salaries than men for the same job or to give children excessive benefits while placing excessive burdens on older folks. Beyond embracing the principle of simple equality, which declares that all persons are equal in respect and dignity, one must acknowledge that their differences in needs, capacities, and achievements require that they be treated according to the principle of complex equality.

Probably few would apply a principle of equal rights to family and intergenerational discrimination. They recognize that we should treat different persons differently according to their important, verifiable differences. Some benefits cannot be correctly understood in terms of equal entitlements to what people deserve or have earned. For example, people in the United States often complain that many people are getting much more out of social security than they have paid into it. Social security seeks to meet the needs of persons while paying benefits proportionate to their contributions. The Social Security Administration establishes levels of need and makes payments to persons in proportion to their contributions over their working lives. Thus, the system applies a form of complex equality not found in United States cultural concepts. As Sen. Daniel Patrick Moynihan of New York said recently, the social security system is not a pension plan but is rather a way of meeting our intergenerational obligations.[21]

The inadequate notions of justice found in our cultural notions can be woven together into theories of justice that are honored as intellectually superior and authoritative. But these theories are problematic. Consider, for example, the following theories of justice that build on intuitively appealing beliefs, that is, beliefs found in cultural practices. Because these theories are regularly cited, they mislead discussions about justice between generations in families.

Probably no belief is more appealing than that in negative freedom or freedom from interference, including freedom from being coerced to do what, arguably, one should. The weaknesses of some social and political philosophies that rely on this concept of freedom are underscored in the discussion of equal liberty in chapter 1. Their failings are even more pronounced when they are applied to the problems of justice between generations in families. For example, it would be foolish to claim that parents have no obligations other than those to which they have consented. The major commitments people make—marriage, the decision to have children—contain unbargained-for responsibilities, as we acknowledge in a common formula for marriage rites, "for better or for worse." But recalling one's unconditional marriage vows is little consolation when burdened with serious illness or financial disaster. One's responsibilities to other generations of the family cannot be understood in terms of freedom from interference and meeting only those obligations to which one has consented explicitly. In family life, implied responsibilities and the burdens and harms they bring are to be accepted. If possible, they should be apportioned according to reasonable criteria comparable to the harm principles proposed later in this chapter.

Theories that make self-interest and competition essential in guiding a family toward justice are also deficient. Prompted by experiences of human selfishness or sinfulness, they suppose that in the family each generational group is bent on attaining its own interest, irrespective of the common good. In a Hobbesian war of all against all, each family member seeks all advantages for himself and does his best to assign all the disadvantages to the others. Most public policymaking seems motivated by this theory. For example, policy makers seem to think that dealing separately with the aging or with youth is better for each interest group. Similarly portrayed are relationships between generations.

Although theories based on self-interest seem realistic about human nature, they overlook positive human qualities. Didactic tales about filial duty, parental sacrifice, and responsibility to descendants also offer praiseworthy models.[22] Next to the human generosity demonstrated in these stories, talk of exact equity sounds hollow.

To oppose theories based on self-interest, several post-Enlightenment theories of justice have emphasized principles that they believe disinterested parties would endorse and that interested parties would be expected to follow. These ideal theories of justice expect that persons will strictly comply because they desire to behave rationally. One of the most complete contemporary expressions of an ideal theory of justice is the work of John Rawls (1971, 1975, 1981, 1985).

Strict-compliance theories fail at least partially. Harry R. Moody (1985) best summarized the reasons strict-compliance theories of justice are inadequate to resolve conflicts between generations in families. He claims they offer little guidance for making family decisions because they do not acknowledge that families live in nonideal historical and cultural conditions. People need a theory of justice that is sensitive to the realities of family life. As noted in chapter 1, a partial-compliance rather than a full-compliance theory of justice seems more helpful. Partial-compliance theories cannot claim to simplify the task as much as full-compliance theories seem to promise, but neither do they extirpate families from their times and places or expect family members to be uninfluenced by life stages.

An equally devastating theory of justice is expounded by Robert Nozick (1974). Nozick and others rely on a concept of putatively earned entitlements to property, disregarding how the property was acquired. They counterpose these entitlements to claims based on need, which they consider generally invalid. Thus, they treat all rights and entitlements as if they were property rights and they suppose that legitimately acquired property is the fruit of the owner's individual effort, rather than capital created by cooperative labor or the foresight of ancestors.[23] Nozick, in particular, fails to recognize that the incremental increases in property values are not earned exclusively by the individuals who hold title to them. Because of these shortcomings, entitlement theories of justice are particularly inept when applied to families and their generations.

Some other theories of distributive justice seem plausible but focus too much on redistribution. They stem from the belief that the right results are achieved by the redistribution of benefits and burdens, chiefly through taxation, between older and younger persons in the United States. Questions about promises and other commitments, about the extent of harms done by redistribution, and about the capacity of people to sustain or recover from harms are irrelevant to theories that focus on results or strictly proportioned equities. They overlook moral values pertinent to nurturing trust between generations of family members.

Moral Principles for Apportioning Burdens of Justice Between Generations

The justice of a family's practices toward its generations is shown by how it assigns advantages and disadvantages. Respect for persons, self-cultivation, beneficence and nonmaleficence will now be considered in terms of our three derived principles of harms to human goods and what they suggest are the most urgent obligations of justice between the generations in a family. The following examples are selective but illustrative.

The life, health, happiness, and well-being of parents and children can be jeopardized by how families and communities allocate risks and harms. People may not create hazards knowingly, but they often uncritically accept cultural notions that advise them unwisely, either about extreme harms, such as abandoning the elderly or abusing children, or about commonplace burdens, like lawnmowing assigned solely to parents, although teenagers are capable. Neither is it appropriate, for example, to exaggerate the minor risks to the health of older persons who might be asked to travel in bad weather to teach the illiterate or feed the hungry.

Customs that privilege certain categories of persons can place unwarranted burdens on others. How persons suffer in their life, health, happiness, and opportunities for self-cultivation is of major concern but so, too, are the uncritically accepted practices that cause these harms. While it may be justifiable for an employer to favor the younger and putatively more productive workers, it would not be justifiable if this favoritism denied qualified older persons employment. But when public policy makes basic human goods like food, housing, and health care inaccessible to senior citizens, particularly females without partners and the elderly poor, the harm is more serious. Conversely, it seems equally unjust when social security disproportionately advantages the more affluent elderly but the government does not ask them to accept, say, heavier taxes on behalf of their poorer peers, but places a greater burden on the younger citizens.[24]

Among the problematic contemporary practices that generate harm to the fundamental goods of one generation is incurring debt to meet college expenses. It is said that the way higher education is financed in the United States indentures the future of a generation. Edward B. Fiske, in a 1986 article titled "Student Debt Reshaping Colleges and Careers" in *The New York Times,* noted that, as tuition soars and more young people go to college, parents are unable or unwilling to pay for their children's education from savings and current income (1986, 34ff.). Having few realistic alternatives, an overwhelming majority of young people take on heavy debts to pay for their college educations.[25] This practice seems founded on a cultural notion that each generation should pay for its own education, at least after high school.[26] Michael S. McPherson, an economist at Williams College, seemed to have this notion in mind when he asked, "Is it right that a couple whose parents paid for their educations may now want their children to pay for their own?" (ibid., 41).

One proposal to relieve indebtedness for college expenses is selling "education futures" (like IRAs) to parents of prospective college students. Features of this plan are a federal loan bank, a repayment ceiling of 150%, longer repayment periods, payment schedules set according to the borrower's taxable income and payments made through the borrower's federal income tax return.[27] Education futures would invite parents and their contemporaries to share the risks and costs of their children's education, but the plan still bespeaks the conviction that each generation should pay for its own education (ibid., 36, 40–41).

Consider the case of Ann Van Cott and Mike Usman, sophomores at Valhalla Medical College in New York state in 1986. They married in 1986 with $66,000 of combined debts for their college and medical school loans. When they graduated from medical school, they owed $234,000 and when they finished their residencies, in 1992, they owed $334,000. They will pay more than $1 million of their joint income to retire the debt by the year 2008, when they will be forty-five years old (ibid., 34).

Four different, but equally significant, sets of burdens are created by expecting young people to incur heavy debts for their higher education. First, since one third to one half of all college graduates in the 1980s owed as much as $10,000 ($30,000 for graduate students), the magnitude of the indebtedness denies poor and minority students a higher education. Second, young people are deterred from training for lower-paying but socially desirable and fulfilling careers in, say, social service or education. They are shunted away from liberal studies into business, engineering, law, and medicine, which promise them higher incomes to repay their debts. Third, many students miss out on the educational benefits of extracurricular activities either because they work part-time jobs or because they work full-time jobs while attending evening and weekend classes. Fourth, the Reagan administration, faced with deficit federal spending and a billion dollars annually in student loan defaults, called for self-help on the part of students and their families, reduced federal funding for higher education, and moved funds from grant programs to loan programs (ibid., 34–35).

Some of these undesirable effects will be considered later for their systemic harms to younger generations and their children. I emphasize now direct harm to fundamental goods of some individuals. Practices that deter the poor and minorities from entering college, that turn young people away from socially desirable careers, and that prevent students from taking advantage of extracurricular learning opportunities in college life arguably impose unjust allocations of burdens because they can harm these persons' fundamental human goods, even more than government policies can.

Because these financing practices discourage minorities from attending college, they also block already sorely disadvantaged persons from attaining the fundamental good of a developed human existence. Furthermore, these people are deprived of the competitive edge needed in our merit-based society to progress toward both happiness and greater material goods. No one deliberately arranged it, but our method of financing higher education is a blunt instrument for dealing with the poor and minorities.

As for choosing college programs and careers, we have become morally jaded if we think such decisions are simply personal matters of selecting the best means to acquire property and possessions. Several writers have recently taken issue with this view and have reaffirmed the importance of planning a career that employs and further develops one's abilities and interests, not for the sake of making one feel good or comfortable but for the sake of those habits of heart and mind that find their fulfillment within a person, fulfilling that person and his associates (Bellah et al. 1985; May 1983). Persons of all ages need the kind of leisure mentioned in discussing the development of married persons. If contemporary practices of financing college education prevent persons from obtaining education and personal development, they harm both these persons and their intimates.

These examples raise important questions. Do these anticipated effects actually occur? If so, on what standards (such as the degree of harm or disproportionate harm) should we evaluate them? Only the persons affected can answer these questions. They alone may perceive the disadvantages as acceptable sacrifices made to obtain a greater good. However, if the harmful effects are both verifiable and grave, few can find legitimate moral excuses. Those affected should respect themselves as persons and not fail to develop their capacities on the grounds that they did so voluntarily. Those who tolerate this practice bear some of the responsibilities for the social costs created when generations of citizens are denied opportunities for self-development.

All the disadvantages mentioned in the discussion of the present method of financing higher education can be evaluated by the principle of disproportionate harms. It is difficult to apply because of the uniqueness of persons and because their capacity to sustain harms varies over their lifetime but there is no question that the very young and the very old are especially vulnerable. This reasonable presumption urges prudence in assigning burdens to these groups, but also those assigned to parents of any age. No generation is immune from harms that exceed their capacity to bear or recover from them, but in our discussion of disproportionate harms, as in the discussion of harms to fundamental goods, we shall use the harms done by the debt race between older and younger persons.

The poor generally and women and members of ethnic groups (like Asians and Hispanics today) are less able than others to sustain and recover from economic hardships. Because they cannot incur as much debt, they are deterred from obtaining higher education and therefore may be further disadvantaged. These people are clustered in urban areas, work in low-paying, service-sector jobs, have a high proportion of families headed by women, and suffer the social ills of crime, drugs, high rates of HIV infection, and generally poor health. William Julius Wilson argued that the causes are often as much economic as they are cultural, such as changes in employment patterns that affect people's ability to rear children and that deprive them of role models who might inspire them to strive for a better life (1987). Under these social conditions, customs, like financing higher education with student loans, that place educational opportunities out of reach of these persons, work unsustainable harms to them.

The potential for harm disproportionate to one's ability to sustain and recover from it seems far less serious for those who can select and prepare for well-paying careers, even if they are harmed by not being free to choose fulfilling but not financially rewarding careers. Yet, if motivated to continue developing themselves, better-paid persons may have greater opportunities to change to more fulfilling careers later.

All the previously noted harms to fundamental goods can become systemic. When they do, they are nearly as ineradicable as inherited disabilities. They are like the latter because the social notions that support them and endanger fundamental human goods for many persons can prevail across generations, and, because they are widespread, they become accepted as unalterable, natural reality.[28]

Some examples of systemic harms were mentioned in the discussion of systemic harms in conjugal families. The plight of younger generations, who will pay for present indulgences, is an example of systemic harm. So are the straitened circumstances of older divorced women with poor job skills. These women have already suffered from the persistent idea that women do not need higher education as much as men, and now find employers unwilling to hire or retrain older employees. The reluctance of some older persons to pay taxes for the schooling of children other than their own contributes to other systemic harms. The disincentives divorce settlements create for having children or investing in their nurturing further illustrate the impact of systemic harms on successive generations.

The principal illustration here is the harm done when financing higher education through student borrowing makes educational opportunities less accessible to the poor. The systemic harms that result can scarcely be justified, if at all. The intellectual and economic capacities of parents to rear their children will be constrained. Families cannot encourage or help a child to be able to say, "I'm the first in my family to graduate from college." For most people in poverty, no amount of self-help will enable them to shake off their social and cultural disadvantages.

Even advantaged couples, such as Ann Van Cott and Mike Usman, who will each be forty-five years old before they retire their educational loans, probably will not be able to afford children or, if they have them, to create an adequate college fund before their children will need it. Nor will they have many personal or other resources to commit to serving their communities. Thus, these harms become far-reaching, affecting not only the parents and children, but also the community. Furthermore, suppose that during their medical residencies they discover that they are not really content with medical careers and that one of them is a talented musician and the other a gifted teacher. They most likely would have felt obligated to continue working in the more remunerative field of medicine to repay their debts. This decision could be harmful indeed to the patients they treat but also to students or music lovers who might have benefitted from their pedagogical or musical talents. Such consequences would be prima facie evidence that systemic harms are created by the way higher education is financed in the United States today.

The systemic harms to families and across generations are attributable not only to mistaken cultural notions transmitted by custom, but also to academic theories, texts, and lectures about justice and equality in families. As can others, so can the academy accept and propagate mistaken cultural notions. Regarding, for example, how higher education is financed, some observe that "it is un-American not to be in debt," but it is not amusing to the borrowers. An attitude of amusement and acceptance reinforces what Fiske calls privatist, instrumental values by engendering in students a sense that they are in college for themselves because their studies are purely a means to a job and an income that will permit them to pay their debts (1986, 38).

Although unwarranted exemptions sometimes inappropriately privilege the young, I argue that some privileges granted the elderly are also unwarranted. For example, the elderly lobby against proposed bond issues for school districts. While it is true that the lower to middle income groups of elderly can ill afford further erosion of their fixed incomes, those in higher income groups can. Under the regressive federal tax system, affluent persons pay the lowest tax rates. For example, in 1987 persons with incomes over $100,000 paid 6%, whereas those with incomes of $30,000 to $100,000 paid 9.4% and those with incomes under $3,000 paid 15.4%. (Furthermore, the affluent elderly paid less in sales and property taxes, which seem to be the dominant way of distributing tax burdens [Papke 1987, v].) Although social security checks received by these elders may be modest, they are much less heavily taxed than other income. Affluent seniors surely can bear a greater share of the burdens of the justice that allocates educational opportunities heavily in favor of youth.

The United States property tax system (see the next chapter) transmits and reinforces mistaken cultural concepts (for example, equity) and theories of justice (based on property) considered earlier in this chapter. Sales and property taxes generally are not equitable because they are not adjusted to one's capacity to pay them (but can be made more equitable by applying the concept of complex equity). That everyone pays a flat 9% tax on the amount of sale certainly appears equitable, but since "everyone" includes the poor and the affluent alike, sales taxes are not always just.

Theories of justice that liken every entitlement to a property are also based on mistaken notions of equity. For example, the moral consciences of youth are corrupted by the popular contention that younger workers will never get out of social security as much as they will pay into it. The younger generation may not be able to change how education is financed in the near future, but they might support changes in social security when they become the next major group of taxpayers. Popular wisdom does not recognize that social security is designed to meet the basic needs of persons in the United States, regardless of what they have paid into the system themselves. Persons who have paid into social security larger amounts during their working lives may receive larger social security checks, but that is an adjustment; the purpose of the system is to assure that no elderly or disabled citizen has to do without basic provisions. Furthermore, popular wisdom fails to acknowledge that social security is a means for younger citizens to meet their responsibility to their seniors, if not to their own elderly relatives, then to others of their parents' and grandparents' generation. If young people feel no social responsibility toward their elders, they will not develop habits of justice that would later lead them to accept responsibility toward younger generations.

Theories that so emphasize consent and negative liberty (freedom *from*) overlook the importance of honoring obligations that arise from major commitments. These theories stress human competitiveness and self-interestedness rather than cooperation and generosity. They portray the ethical as an unattainable ideal rather than a concept that motivates actual people and communities. I contend that the errors of these theories are revealed by scrutinizing how the allocations of harms under our intergenerational compact determine the sense of moral community within families and between generations.

Conclusion

This chapter emphasizes some everyday difficulties in justly allocating the benefits and burdens of family life. The most stringent obligations in families are those that proscribe harms to family members' fundamental human goods. Some harms are radical and systemic, causing damages that cannot be offset by whatever benefit was achieved. Therefore, the way the burdens of life together are apportioned is a decisive measure of the justice of couples, families, and generations.

When relationships between these persons are unjust, it is time for a renegotiation. As indicated in the introduction to this chapter, the recent literature on couples and families in the United States is replete with suggestions that just such a time is at hand. The growing body of commentaries on the relationships between generations expresses a similar conviction. For example, Michael McPherson observed that "we need to renegotiate the terms of the social contract between generations to fit a markedly changed world" (Fiske 1986, 34).

I agree with McPherson that we need to renegotiate our social arrangements, but I prefer the less contractual metaphor of renavigation. Hazards lie on all sides of the way we seek, for there are dangers in the relationships between couples, within families, and between generations. Rather than come to a bargaining table prepared to negotiate a contract, we need to make gradual and sensitive course corrections.[29]

Competitive, contractual negotiations may be needed, of course, but they are not—and should not be—the norm. By comparison, in this chapter I emphasize the ordinary problems of justice in families, stressing the importance of building on common ground. I emphasize the solidarity based on continuous relationships which presumes that renegotiations will be more like delicate adjustments to our present systems rather than crudely contractual reworkings offered by reformers who question the legitimacy of these systems and stand ready to replace them with untried inventions. I highlight those areas where a common ground is more likely to be found, namely, the simple and complex equality of the persons in families and communities. I emphasize uncovering common ground in public policies regarding taxation and social security, in the plight of poor women and children, and in justice between the affluent elderly and the poor elderly.

Throughout I suggest that we search for some common moral grounds for responsibilities between couples, within families, and between generations. Those grounds are, as I have argued, most readily discernible in the commitments of marriage and family life. Thus, if our ties to those outside our conjugal family are to be understood and honored, the lessons provided by the burdens of justice within the family need to be learned well.[30]

In Financing Public Education

We now turn from the private matters of the family to civil and public issues. Education, health care, and the legal system will be considered in turn. This chapter will consider how the financial burdens of public education are apportioned. I begin with public education because some of the demographic, social, and cultural factors and some of the moral principles in our consideration of the family are relevant to our reflections on contemporary public education, which prepares so many to deal with health care and the law.

In the education of children, individual, private, and parental responsibilities intersect. Persons from the public, civil, and political realms are responsible for "the child as a whole . . . in all its possibilities, [and] not only in its immediate needs" (Jonas 1984, 101, 103)[1] and they bind people in fiduciary responsibilities across generations.

Public and private domains, freedom and justice, religion and culture interact more closely in education than in other spheres. In public education everyone's children become our own. Religion, politics, and culture come together and sometimes collide. But I contend here that the overriding moral duty in public education is a just allocation of its burdens.

As early as the Golden Age of Athens, public education has presented moral issues. We focus on the following questions: Who should pay for public education? How? Who should carry the other burdens? When and how should financial policies be reviewed?[2]

To see why the burdens of justice in public education need to be reviewed, we consider the *Rodriguez* case, decided by the United States Supreme Court in 1973, as an example of the human harms worked on some classes of persons by unjust methods of financing public education.[3] I argue that the way the burdens are apportioned measures the distributive justice of public school systems and consider procedures that can ensure justice in public education.[4] Throughout I give special attention to the role of religion in important public matters and suggest how renegotiation can promote public agreement about the burdens of public education.

I hope to show why justice should override freedom in forming policies for public education. I further argue that attaining justice in education depends less on realizing specific benefits than on how the burdens are apportioned. I contend that how the burdens are apportioned measures the moral goodness of a community. Thus, to achieve justice by renegotiating its policies in public education, a community must primarily address how the burdens are apportioned. This should be every citizen's principal concern, whether he or she is religious or not. Whatever resources we bring to bear on discussions of public education must yield accessible and common human reasons for acting one way or the other (Tracy 1986).

The *Rodriguez* Case

Over the last few decades, except perhaps for state aid to and regulation of private schools, the principal issues in public education have been matters of freedom and equality in educational opportunity or questions about curriculum or the character of teachers and textbooks, often separate from funding questions. Recent court cases have focused on freedom (especially religious freedom)[5] and on measuring the results of education rather than on how education is financed, although all parties recognize that the other issues are influenced by how fairly and reliably education is financed.

While not minimizing the significant moral stakes in educational opportunities, other moral matters are arguably more critical and decisive. The most disadvantaged pupils in the public school system today are in property-poor districts faced with sharply reduced federal assistance and substandard facilities, curricula, and teachers. They score extremely low on achievement tests and have poor attendance and high drop-out rates. The efforts to reform public schools inspired by the report *A Nation at Risk* (President's Commission 1986) have focused on upgrading curricula and personnel more than on improving the financing that could make these upgrades possible.[6] Ironically and, in some ways, tragically, recent efforts to promote religious and cultural freedom in public education come while demographic, social, and cultural factors are eroding an already weakened collective sense of responsibility for children other than one's own. The family is less able to meet its responsibilities toward its children and an aging, overwhelmingly white voting public is less willing to support urban public schools with large minority enrollments.[7]

The fiscal burdens of public education need to be renegotiated. One of the best known cases to contest school financing was *San Antonio Independent School District et al. v. Rodriguez et al.* (411 US 1–137), argued before the United States Supreme Court in 1973.

In the middle of this century, the Court had applied the equal protection clause of the Fourteenth Amendment to segregation in public schools and the establishment clause of the First Amendment to public aid for private schools. We have more to say about these two amendments in our discussion of *Rodriguez.* Here, however, we note only that the liberties guaranteed by the First Amendment can be understood in the light of the equality protected by the Fourteenth[8] and that equal liberty seems to have been an issue in some of the decisions immediately before *Rodriguez.*

Asked to determine which forms of state aid to private schools were permissible under the First Amendment, which prohibits Congress from establishing a religion, the Court found release-time programs (releasing students during part of the school day for religious education), the use of public buildings by private schools, and loans of public school textbooks to private schools acceptable. It declared grants for maintenance, tax credits for tuition, and partial payment of teachers' salaries unconstitutional. Most presaging was the *Nyquist* case, decided the year before *Rodriguez,* in which the Court struck down several programs in New York State that provided direct maintenance grants to private schools in low-income districts and tuition reimbursements for low-income parents of children in private schools.[9]

Most of these cases arose in the 1970s as parochial schools were experiencing unusual financial problems when the federal share of government spending for education declined, as states attempted to assist, among others, private schools in low-income areas, and as evangelical Protestants, who previously had been strong supporters of public schools, began establishing more of their own private elementary and secondary schools. These trends helped fuel the growth of the new religious right amid complaints that religion had been purged from public schools after Supreme Court decisions in the 1960s. With other church-related private schools (especially Catholic) that sought state aid, the religious right raised a public outcry for reform in financing public education.

Although *Rodriguez* decided rather narrow constitutional questions, both the dissenting opinions and the majority opinion reflect tension between the moral values of education and how they are addressed in public life, and how religion in the public schools (under the First Amendment) relates to equal protection (under the Fourteenth Amendment). The principal concern here is not so much the role of religion in the public schools or how it influences curriculum and pupils, but rather the role religious bodies play in deciding public school financing. To be sure, our public schools seem to be unconscionably silent regarding the religious dimensions of human life, and we truly need to rethink the role of religion in the curriculum. But insisting on prayer and rituals in public schools or expunging textbooks that offend hypersensitive people are unlikely remedies. An intelligible principle for everyone is to insist, as do some contemporary educators, that whenever the religious dimensions of subjects in the curriculum is pertinent, it should be addressed by teachers and textbook writers who are empathetic observers. But I argue that it is even more urgent to change those religious and civil paradigms that place distributive justice alongside transactional justice and sometimes subordinate it to the latter.[10] The *Rodriguez* case draws attention to the failures of these paradigms and suggests alternatives.

⎧ In 1968, a group of Mexican-American parents of children enrolled in the urban elementary and secondary schools of the Edgewood Independent School District of San Antonio, Texas, brought a class-action suit against several Texas governmental bodies. The plaintiff class was composed of poor and minority schoolchildren who resided in school districts with a low property tax base.⎭ ⎧Texas school systems received some state revenues and the proceeds from an ad valorem tax on property in each school district. The plaintiffs argued that this practice favored the more affluent, property-rich districts and violated the equal protection clause of the Fourteenth Amendment because it resulted in substantial disparities in per-pupil expenditures between affluent and poor districts. ⸲

A Texas District Court impaneled in 1969 delayed its decision until 1971 to investigate the case fully and to allow the Texas legislature to study how its schools were financed.⸲In 1971, however, after giving Texas an opportunity to remedy inequities in its school system, the district court found the state system unconstitutional under the equal protection clause of the Fourteenth Amendment. It declared that wealth was a suspect classification, that this classification created and disadvantaged a class of poor people, and could be upheld only if the state were able to show a compelling state interest for retaining the system⸲(ibid., 1–6, 1–18, esp. nn. 4–5).

On appeal to the United States Supreme Court in 1973, the decision of the Texas District Court was reversed on the grounds that it had not been demonstrated that the Texas system discriminated against any definable class of poor people nor that it discriminated on the basis of differences in individual incomes or the wealth of the families in any district. What had been demonstrated, the court said, was only that it disadvantaged those who lived in comparatively poor school districts, a fact that the majority argued did not make the resulting classification suspect under the Fourteenth Amendment. ⸲

Interpreting the case this way, the majority of the justices were not obliged to apply the test of strict judicial scrutiny employed in equal protection cases where the classification is suspect. Though judging education one of the most important state services, they did not find it among the constitutional rights recognized by the Court (ibid., 28, 29–39, 54, 115, n. 74).[11]

Hence, applying the less stringent standard of rationality, the Court found the Texas system imperfect, but rational. Although the Court was unwilling to interfere in state and local taxation and finance, the majority, in a postscript to their opinion, argued for "reform in tax systems which may well have relied too long and too heavily on the local property tax" (ibid., 18–53, 56–58, 62).[12]

The postscript implies a negative evaluation of the ad valorem property tax most states use in financing public education. In his concurring opinion, Justice Stewart contended that the method used in Texas, which is roughly the same one used across the United States, was chaotic and unjust. In a dissenting opinion that occupies nearly half the court record, Justice Marshall left no room for doubt about the nature and extent of the harms he thought such financing caused (ibid., 59, 70–133).

Since this case was decided, at least three district courts have concurred with the 1980 Wyoming court claim that it is "nothing more than an illusion to believe that the extensive disparity in financial resources does not relate directly to the quality of education" or with the more recent claim of the Arkansas Supreme Court that "[property] wealth is what primarily dictates the amount of revenue each district received and the quality of education in that district" *(Washakie County School District No. 1* v. *Herschler,* 606 Pac2d 310 [Ore 1980] and *Dupree* v. *Alma School District,* 651 SW2d 90 [Ark 1983]). *Rodriguez* and these related cases involve much more than equal justice for the economically disadvantaged and the special claims they make upon us all. *Rodriguez* is about the central issues in public education, a case that suggests that how we allocate the fiscal and other burdens of the system shapes the benefits our children receive. Therefore, the case highlights some enduring, intergenerational, and systemic problems in the education of youth in the United States.

Moral Issues and Harmful Policies in *Rodriguez*

The *Rodriguez* case reveals some gaps in the fundamental moral concepts that shape public policy in the United States. For instance, to apportion the advantages and disadvantages of liberty equally, we should have a concept of equal liberty that would suggest that public policy be fashioned by comparing the First and Fourteenth amendments of the Constitution.[13] That courts are not likely, for the moment at least, to so interpret these amendments abets a double misfortune. On the one hand, though the courts are frequently invoked, conventional legal wisdom lacks a concept of equal liberty sufficient for the cases presented. On the other hand, a concept of equal liberty would illuminate the rights that some religious plaintiffs seek to enforce. To preserve even their own negative liberty (freedom from interference), plaintiffs must establish a concept of equal liberty for all that includes some of the entitlement rights the less fortunate need to sustain equality. To maintain equal liberty in public life requires a tripodal theory of justice with special emphasis on the way the burdens of enterprises like public education are apportioned. Communities need more than rules and principles of justice; they also need just persons in public affairs, persons who are disinterested enough to consider others as well as themselves and who value the political good of justice more than freedom from interference. How they allocate advantages and disadvantages reveals the moral character of their communities, because the arrangements they make will not only promote or diminish distributive justice but also because they establish the extent of freedom and trustworthiness among citizens.

If communities must err in these allocations, they should err on the side of doing the least amount of harm possible, because the responsibility not to harm others (even by neglect) is one of the most stringent of moral obligations. The measure of a community's character is the extent to which its public policies harm those least able to bear further disadvantages. To do so persons in communities may have to overcome past habits as well as reform long-standing ways of conducting public affairs. For a community to base its public policies on moral values and the common interest, they must focus on how to minimize the harms in public education and how to approximate justice in allocating its burdens.

To see how the allocation of harms in public education is sanctioned in court decisions like *Rodriguez*, we must make three types of inquiries: (*a*) empirical inquiries or fact-finding, like the Texas legislature's investigations of public school financing in Texas; (*b*) conceptual inquiries, such as about the meaning of social goods like liberty and equality, and, most importantly, (*c*) normative inquiries, such as about the legal and moral standards employed by a community to govern the social goods in a sphere such as education. As noted in chapter 2, these standards are incorporated in the cultural notions and practices of a community. As in allocating other social goods, the decisions based on these cultural notions need to be reworked. Thus, we need to consider the customary, legal, and moral standards more fully, particularly the principle of no-harm.

As described in chapter 1, the most relevant moral principle is that of respect for others as persons in the form of beneficence—promoting their well-being by permissible actions that do not disproportionately harm oneself. The negative form of beneficence is nonmaleficence—avoiding unjustifiable harm to others. Some burdens are unavoidably harmful, leaving room only for asking which ones are justifiable. School levies on wealth and income, for example, harm the taxpayer, but do not compare to the injury done to a child's fundamental goods by an inferior education. Taxes are justifiable when they are levied according to relevant differences between people. Income taxes generally are progressive, that is, the rate increases with net income, and therefore are more justly proportioned to one's ability to pay, whereas property taxes generally are not so well proportioned. Locking generations of youth into schools that do not prepare them for life is such a great harm that it can scarcely, if ever, be justified. Practices that disadvantage whole classes of persons should be judged unwarranted and should be abolished like slavery was. To determine which harms associated with financing public education are justifiable and which are not, recall the following principles from chapter 1:

1. The principle of degree of harm to fundamental goods declares harms that deprive persons of intrinsic goods, such as life itself, a developed existence, and happiness, unjustifiable. Harms to intermediate and instrumental goods like physical and mental health may be justifiable. Harms to goods that are not fundamental, such as one's possessions, are more readily justifiable. The fiscal burdens of public education, for example, fall in the latter category. But textbooks and curricula that prevent pupils from developing maturity and a sense of responsibility deprive them of the fundamental good of a developed existence.

2. The principle of proportionate harm states that even if the harms are less detrimental, they may be unjustifiable because the persons affected are less able to sustain them. Persons of reasonable means can be required to pay taxes proportioned to their wealth and income, but the penniless should be exempt. A regressive tax, one that applies a higher rate to lower incomes and a lower rate to higher incomes, is generally not justifiable.[14] The principle of proportionate harms advises that harms be proportioned to a person's capacities to sustain or recover from them. Thus, false news stories or false reports made by governments to the public are proportionately less harmful to adults than to youngsters, who are less able to discern the truth on their own.

3. The principle of systemic harm states that harms that affect entire classes of persons or affect them for generations, especially if they are also the more serious harms to fundamental human goods, are extremely hard to justify. Some of these harms should be prohibited in principle. Forcing persons into one-sided contracts or involuntary transactions is a serious instance of systemic harm.

Rodriguez and all the school financing cases adjudicated by the United States Supreme Court complain of these three types of harm. For example, property-poor school districts have demonstrably less qualified teachers and less adequate facilities, and, predictably, endanger the mental and physical well-being of their pupils. Because they are children, and because they live in impoverished districts and are probably already economically disadvantaged, the pupils are vulnerable to harms to their fundamental human goods, such as developing their capacities or learning job skills. The results of reading and writing tests administered in the Edgewood school district of San Antonio in 1988 show that 50% of the pupils fell below national norms. The children may be so seriously harmed that they cannot recover. It may be that the children cannot even be fairly compensated for the life long consequences of poor instruction such as weak job skills or inability to support themselves or manage their affairs. But state fiscal policies make these serious harms systemic. States control how local school districts may raise revenue and set limits on total expenditures. Therefore, the most serious effect of the *Rodriguez* case and the cases that followed is not that taxable property values remain the principal determinant of how much a district can spend on its schools. More ominous is that state legislatures and courts perpetuate these systemic harms. The *Rodriguez* case can be read as a primer in the obstacles faced by communities seeking to allocate burdens justly in education.

While the harms done to the children are very serious, current fiscal policies have less serious, more readily renegotiable burdens. For instance, the way tax burdens fall on individual citizens does not always respect the principle of proportionate harm and can be reformed. The higher expenditures per pupil in wealthy districts is disproportionate and unjustifiable. One remedy is to replace the local tax on commercial, industrial, and mineral property with a statewide tax and direct the revenue to local school districts using a formula that compensates for any remaining unevenness in local school revenues. Neither tax inequities nor unequal opportunities would be decisive tests of the justice of the school system. But they are decisive when coupled with more serious harms, such as poisoning the well of social and cultural opportunities for youth, preventing them from acquiring competitive job skills, and encouraging adults to neglect their responsibilities toward present and future generations.

Some of these harms can be averted by reforming the tax structure. However, neither fiscal nor curricular reform can be truly effective without improving the sense of responsibility families and older generations have toward youth. "An increasingly old, overwhelmingly white voting public" and the school boards that represent them are unwilling to "support increasingly minority schools" but these attitudes can be changed.[15]

We must change the cultural paradigms that prompt us to continue these mistakes. One paradigm is a view of justice that sees contractual justice, following formal, written agreements, as distinct from distributive justice and suggests it is the only form of justice. Influenced by this paradigm, taxpayers and legislators overlook who gets hurt and how much when we carry out our agreed-upon financing for public schools. When public school finances are publicly debated, most often people speak of justice in terms of an agreement or contract. That suggests our cultural paradigm does not comprehend that contractual justice is part of distributive justice, but leads us to suppose that a contract, because both parties have agreed to it, must make a just distribution.

Our cultural paradigms fail us when we discuss how to finance the education of our children. To correct that failure, this moral analysis of public school financing focuses on duties and emphasizes the harms worked by the current method of financing. Were we to be consequentialist and look to the future, we could say, as do many others, that the critical choice in the United States today is whether to invest now in educating our children or to spend tomorrow for welfare programs to support them (Johnson 1985). This decision is even more urgent when one considers the shocking number of children who live below the poverty level and the poor job skills of adults who live in property-poor districts (ibid.).

The *Rodriguez* case reveals several kinds of harm perpetuated in nearly all of United States public school systems. It demonstrates how the courts and legislatures lock entire classes of persons for generations into systematically disadvantaged positions. Thus, we come to one of the questions raised at the beginning of this chapter, namely, when should decisions about education be revised? The next and concluding sections of this chapter give some answers to related questions: Who should bear the responsibilities for these reforms? On what standards should they make their decisions? Using what procedures?

Renegotiating the Burdens of Justice in Public Education

This chapter discusses reworking American notions and practices about education but not in the sense of renegotiating the social contract. Rather the concern is about procedures to assure justice in the culturally and religiously pluralistic public schools in the United States.[16]

Those who make decisions about education should recognize that what is best for pupils is also best for the community. They should be guided by what is good for human beings generally as well as how to develop the capacities of children and empower future generations. Public discussions about reforming education should be open to all members of the community. All should offer reasons and evidence for their proposals.[17] They should keep an open mind because they may have to overcome long-standing attitudes. No special interest groups should be allowed to dominate the discussions. Because some members of school boards and state legislatures may be loyal to powerful interest groups in their constituencies, some elected officials may need to be removed.

The goal of this public dialog is the political good of justice. In gauging or building consensus about public education, a community should consider not only the general guidelines of morality, but also its shared beliefs. A community may have to rethink its moral principles. The philosopher Virginia Held and the theologian James Sellers argue that appealing to principles not shared by community members is not an effective way to change public policy and that imposing moral values on people is not necessary because people can discover their own values (Held 1984; Sellers 1970). Norms shared by all the participants in this public dialog grow out of universal human experience.[18]

State legislatures, city councils, and local school boards, if they are truly representative forms of government, rather than merely administrative units, are generally the best arenas for public discussion to uncover a community's understandings about public education. The courts are generally not as useful because they reflect rather than scrutinize community beliefs, and work in an adversarial rather than a consensual mode. Courts therefore may impose norms on a community rather than articulate its intrinsic norms.[19] Other arenas are even less likely to lead to public consensus. Administrative law is too bureaucratic to renegotiate public policies. Political action committees, though effective at manipulating mass media, represent much too narrow a range of interests.

Whatever the arena, communities need procedures that ensure that all persons can participate. Some cultural and religious groups would rather impose their standards than contribute to the discovery of the common interest. Others prefer to withdraw from public dialog, refusing to promote a public climate appropriate for renegotiating the burdens of public education. Participants from special interest groups should recognize that public education promotes liberty and tolerance for all groups and should be interested in demonstrating to others that they support public education. If persons committed to a religious or cultural worldview feel aggrieved by public education or wish the community to understand their sense of being wronged and the contributions they can make to the public good, they should participate in the discussion. (The curriculum could include literature that recounts the struggles of some religious and cultural groups to be accepted and appreciated.)[20] Even persons who have no children in public schools depend on other members of society and therefore benefit if the other members have been adequately educated in job skills and habits of justice.

In the public schools of the United States young people from many backgrounds encounter one another and find common ground. The principal decisions about financing public education are about whether we are willing to accept the burdens for continuing these experiences. If we do, the task is to renegotiate the way those burdens are understood as well as apportioned.

Conclusion

As noted in the discussion of *Rodriguez,* ethical reflections on how public education is financed in the United States address three kinds of questions: factual, conceptual, and normative. The facts in the case, the court's legal concepts, and the historical record were factual matters. Our analysis of the harms worked by the current method of financing brought conceptual and normative issues to the fore.

Rodriguez is an example of responding to a social dilemma by bringing suit. However, the inequalities demonstrated between Anglo-American and Mexican-American school districts in Texas reflect larger demographic and cultural changes.[21] In the final analysis, however, the *Rodriguez* case highlights some beliefs and values that might guide both groups to common ground.

Some of the significant conceptual reflections in this chapter are about tensions between the meaning of freedom and equality and the moral concept of equal liberty, which lies at the intersection of the First and Fourteenth Amendments to the Constitution.[22] Another concept is the meaning of *indigent,* which plays a role in discussions about meeting basic needs, such as health care and legal aid, for all.[23] A principal concept in *Rodriguez* that needs more scrutiny is that of "adequate" or "enough" education as used by Justice Powell when he claimed that Texas provided adequate or enough education through its Minimum Foundation Program and that it was optional for districts to exceed this minimum (411 US 24, 37, 47).[24]

In this study, the most important meanings are those of benefits and burdens, burdening or harming persons who are unable to bear harms to their fundamental human goods, and burdening them so grievously that they are systematically disadvantaged.[25] Considering these normative concepts in the light of the principle of no-harm leads to examining some cultural habits. But correcting the injustice caused by present methods of financing public education may call for personal and community reform.

Finally, this chapter considers the persons who participate in changing public policy, the appropriate arenas, and appropriate procedures. It seems clear that renegotiating the burdens of public education will require the participants to correct personal attitudes and social habits, as well as select the best arenas and procedures. Above all, however, they will need to regard justice as the pivot on which they either succeed or fail in meeting the needs of the public's children.

4

In Basic Health Care

Is health care a commodity or a basic provision? Are United States citizens entitled to some minimum health care? This chapter clarifies the nature, the basis, and the extent of such entitlements and shows that guarantees of access to basic health care depend on how communities allocate the burdens associated with the entitlements. Purtilo and Sorrell defined the problem succinctly in the mid-1980s:

> Probably no issue in health care today commands more attention and elicits more despair than the topic of how to distribute health care resources equitably. Although the 1983 report of the President's Commission [for the Study of Ethical Problems in Medicine and Biomedical and Behavioral Research], *Securing Access to Health Care,* concluded that society has a moral obligation to assure equitable access to medical care, a dominant movement today is to redefine medical care as another economic commodity (1986, 26).[1]

Purtilo and Sorrell note a "growing consternation that some persons in need of basic health care services will be unable to receive them because of federal, state, and private insurer constraints which, in turn, have a constraining effect on hospital and provider policies" (ibid., 27). As health care economist Rashi Fein contends, to provide everyone with health care and contain the cost, a federally funded, universal, comprehensive health care program must be established. To those who object that the federal budget is already strained, Fein replies that the federal budget is as much a social document as it is an economic one (1986).

In 1986, the American College of Healthcare Executives, of whom 80% are hospital administrators, published a startling fact sheet titled "Access to Care." Concerned that many people seemed to postpone health care because of its expense, the association reported that an estimated thirty-three million persons in the United States do not have health insurance—an increase of 4 million since 1979. At least one member in each uninsured family needed but could not obtain medical care for financial reasons. Even among the insured many delayed seeking needed care because of the expense of deductibles and copayments.[2]

A survey of the association members reported that 96% believed that health care executives must demonstrate a commitment to affordable health care; 80% said that health care providers must strive to provide services for everyone; and 92% asserted that everyone in the United States is entitled to minimum health care.[3] The majority said that most of the cost of charity care should be paid from general revenues because these burdens are broadly shared.[4]

The opinion that health care is a basic life security and that access to primary health care is something an advanced industrialized society like ours should be able to assure all its citizens is widespread in the United States.[5] This chapter argues that a major reason the United States has not guaranteed all its citizens primary health care is that we have no proportionate and representative way of assigning the cost.[6] Because of late twentieth-century efforts to contain or shift costs, health care is perceived as a commodity.

Although nonmoral values like efficiency are pertinent in providing health care, so are moral values, like humaneness, generosity, and justice.[7] This chapter seeks to determine whether the justice of a health care system depends on how the burdens of health care are allocated. After a case study of claims about a right to health care, the factual or empirical bases for these claims and their conceptual and normative meanings are analyzed. Finally the chapter considers how the burdens of justice in primary health care might be renegotiated.

A Right to Health Care?

Some information about how the health-care industry developed in the United States can clarify the present moral dilemmas.[8] When medical science was only marginally effective, health care was a small industry. Low demand for services may have been one reason why the medical profession was organized like a guild of skilled craftsmen interested in protecting their autonomy (Walzer 1983, 86). In the early twentieth century, medical care improved, demand increased, and voluntary associations like unions, inspired by the new federal income tax, sought to have health care supported through taxes on industry or through general revenues. During the same period, developments in tort law provided for paying for injury or damage by insurance rather than by bringing suit to assign negligence.[9]

Since the 1930s, most health care costs have been paid by private insurance, such as the hospital insurance introduced by the insurance industry, led by Blue Cross, and by limited federal programs created by amending the Social Security Act.[10] Thus, except for HMOs, private insurers have reinforced fee-for-service medical practice, promoted for-profit systems of health care, and strengthened the perception of health care as a commodity.[11] The cost of health care now falls more heavily on the sick, the disadvantaged, and those unskilled in dealing with health care bureaucracies.

One of the more balanced arguments for a right to health care, presented by Edmund Pellegrino and David Thomasma, declares that health care is "fundamentally a form of personal security."[12] Since everyone at some time will need treatment for a curable disorder, relief of symptoms, counseling, reassurance, or health education, to promote developed life, an industrialized nation like ours must assure everyone first-contact care (Pellegrino and Thomasma 1981, 233, 235, 237, 242–43).

In *A Philosophical Basis of Medical Practice*, Pellegrino and Thomasma argue that in the United States in the late twentieth century access to first-contact care is a relative rather than an absolute right[13] but that access to first-contact care is "imperative." They propose the following priorities for health care: (1) primary care, especially first-contact care, (2) treatment to cure or prevent recurrence of illness, (3) containment of incurable diseases, (4) expensive, high-technology treatment of dubious value, and (5) treatment for disorders that are not incapacitating and require only relief of symptoms or self-care (ibid., 237–38, 242).

Facts, Concepts, and Norms

Although the position of Pellegrino and Thomasma is circumspect and intuitively appealing, it suggests that the authors may not have considered all the influences on human health. As noted in the discussion of practical insights in chapter 1, the correlations one finds in data may be a function of one's practical insights, and some insights may have fatal flaws. According to well-established theory, the major influences on human health, in order of impact, are (1) natural and social environments, (2) life-style, (3) heredity, and (4) curative health care (Blum 1976; Carlson and Cunningham 1978).

Pellegrino and Thomasma rely too much on data gathered by the medical establishment. They assume that humans are universally vulnerable to illness, overlooking the link between illness and environment and the roles of sanitation and vaccination. They seem to slight heredity and life-style, which have greater influence on health than health care does. Several commentators have asked why anyone would want health care when it is such an insignificant factor in a person's health. That Pellegrino and Thomasma's data were gathered by the medical establishment may account for their cavalier attitude toward prevention, which is emphasized more by public health professionals than those in private practice (ibid., 240).

Far more serious flaws appear in arguments about access to health care that seem based on ideology rather than facts. Few even mention all four major influences on health and fewer still rank them.[14] Most address only environment or only personal habits or whatever is in vogue. Some arguments labor under the illusion of scarcity. Impressed with advanced medical technology, which actually has limited impact on health, many people perceive health care as a scarce commodity. They see extreme measures, like transplanting organs and identifying which victims to treat first in a mass disaster (a priority process called triage designed to maximize the number of survivors), and conclude that health care is a scarce resource and must be rationed.[15] In addition, some scholarly observers hold that the distribution of medical resources is governed by competition and endless conflict between consumers.[16] But scarcity can be created by guilds seeking to manipulate competitive markets.

A widely used text, *Principles of Biomedical Ethics* by Tom L. Beauchamp and James F. Childress, inquires about "existing practices, institutions, and policies to determine their underlying principles and values . . . [and to] use these . . . to illuminate priorities" (1979, 257). This text draws analogies from common law, without noting that common law reflects our common errors as well as our wisdom.[17] Beauchamp and Childress thus endorse current health care policies and tend to validate dubious cultural notions. If cultural notions embrace some mistaken convictions, then moral reflection that takes these traditions too seriously—and calls for adherence and commitment to them—is uncritical and may compound the errors.[18]

Pellegrino and Thomasma make sensible distinctions between first-contact care and the costly, infrequently needed, and often optional secondary and tertiary care. They argue that everyone has a relative right to first-contact care and referrals for secondary and tertiary care, but do not argue for guarantees to the higher levels. Pellegrino and Thomasma propose realistic priorities for health care. They distinguish levels of care and levels of people's needs. Their concepts are more concrete and more realistic than those that call for a minimum of adequate health care and they are more specific than the definitions of primary health care used by the World Health Organization (WHO), but, influenced by the definition of the Institute of Medicine (1981, 234), they do not consider the influence of heredity or natural and social environment on health.[19]

The definition of primary health care used by the Alma-Ata Conference of WHO is broader, including first-level diagnostic, therapeutic, educational, and referral services by physicians in general and family practice (Lee and Emmott 1978, 613). In Titles VI and VII, the Declaration of Alma-Ata defines primary health care as "essential health care based on practical, scientifically sound and socially acceptable methods and technology made universally accessible to individuals and families . . . at a cost the community can afford." Primary care "reflects and evolves from the economic, sociocultural and political characteristics of the country and its communities." It addresses the community's main health problems and tailors "promotive, preventative, curative, and rehabilitative services accordingly." It includes plans for education, nutrition, sanitation, immunization, and essential pharmaceuticals, as well as for family planning and maternal and child health care. It coordinates with agriculture, industry, education, housing, and communication. Its operations are controlled by community groups, including local governments (World Health Organization 1978).

The Alma-Ata definition names the major influences on health. It emphasizes that health care should be designed to meet health needs, and that medical technologies should be suited to the community. It understands the term *health care providers* more broadly than we currently use it. By comparison, though Pellegrino and Thomasma's concept of primary care includes health education, it expects established providers to supply it, implying that what patients need to learn is the conventional wisdom of the health care profession. The Alma-Ata concept, however, suggests that such wisdom is not always sufficient for people's needs, since conventional health care is the least important of the four major influences on health.

Pellegrino and Thomasma, influenced, as noted, by medical professionals, anticipate formidable political obstacles to their proposals for improving health care. They seem to imagine future health care systems centered in established professions and institutions, while the Alma-Ata conference envisions community-based health care that recognizes all the major influences on health and how to use political power to meet a community's health needs.

Just as examining these definitions of health care shows that health care cannot be understood as a commodity, so does applying concepts of fundamental human goods. William

Galston understands health care as a social good because it is instrumental in maintaining fundamental human goods, such as existence, developed existence, and happiness. Unlike a commodity, health care is not an optional purchase. On the contrary, says Galston, one must first determine what benefits or harms human beings and then what helps them achieve basic human goods or prevents them from doing so (1980).

Human existence, developed human existence, and happiness benefit individuals and are, therefore, the goods on which a theory of justice rests (Galston 1980, 55ff., 92–96).[20] To obtain these goods, we come together in communities, since we "literally cannot live apart" (Walzer 1983, 65). Our survival and well-being require us to cooperate with others to create and allocate social goods that help us obtain our basic human goods. Thus, social goods are called instrumental goods. For example, the health care available in a community helps the members of the community promote their health. Therefore, health care is a social good and health is a basic human good.

Galston calls some basic goods urgent because (1) there is no ready substitute for them or they are essential; for example, developed life is not possible without life itself; (2) they represent the individual's needs, arising, for example, from his or her mental or physical capacities; and (3) they are necessary to obtain other goods; for example, to develop as a human person, one must first have intelligence and free choice. Social goods like nutritious food, potable water, shelter, and protection from threats to life and health, health itself, and whatever maintains and promotes health are the instruments to continue existence and attain developed existence (Galston 1980, 96).

The claims persons make to urgent social goods are favored by a prima facie presumption and cannot be overridden except for compelling reasons. Claims to property and commodities are not compelling. Meeting the needs of human persons is so powerful a demand that the priority of urgent human goods and social goods is one of the major underpinnings of a substantive principle of distributive justice. Valid claims for a just distribution of the social goods that help one obtain basic human goods are founded on this priority (ibid., 97, 143, 162).[21]

Examples of social goods that communities provide to help their members obtain urgent human goods are food and water, shelter, and sanitation (Walzer 1983, 66). These social goods bring costs and other burdens, of course. I argue that how the costs and burdens are assigned determines which goods are provided and how readily they are available. Because health care is an instrumental, or social, good used to obtain basic human goods, describing it as a commodity is a mistake.

Pellegrino and Thomasma do not treat primary health care as a commodity but as a social good used to obtain urgent human goods. They recognize that claims based on human needs for basic human goods have priority, that is, they acknowledge that need is a basis for entitlement to a social good like health care. However, they do not identify who has a duty to provide the care that they claim is a relative right.[22] Furthermore, they do not mention claims to health care based on a person's merits (1981, 241). Still, their concept of justice is more defensible than concepts that inflate merit and depreciate need.

Beauchamp and Childress declare that in ordinary discourse "the single word most closely linked to the general meaning of 'justice' is 'desert,'" and that what is "due or owed" a person is a function of what the person "deserves or can legitimately claim" on the basis of, say, "being productive or being in need" or as arising from "rewardable productivity."[23] They prefer being productive to being in need because they judge it a widespread intuitive conviction that "what a person deserves is a function of performance" and that a "scoundrel" (whose faults they do not specify) about to inherit a fortune "does not deserve the wealth" (1979, 169, 185).

Because Beauchamp and Childress take a view of health care that emphasizes curative medicine and is based on competition for scarce resources, they naturally emphasize the notion of justice as desert, but it seems unwarranted to give desert priority over need in allocating health care. They employ words with emotional connotations, like "rewardable productivity" and "scoundrels,"[24] and they rhetorically ask "why need is a more fundamental principle, for example, than ability to pay," overlooking that need and ability are not analogous and ability to pay is not ability to bear burdens (ibid., 192). Why need is the fundamental consideration in allocating health care was amply demonstrated by Pellegrino and Thomasma. In a puzzling correlation, Beauchamp and Childress link need and health care benefits with Marxist perspectives, but link the burdens of health care and ability to pay to libertarian viewpoints (ibid., 173).[25] To that unmistakably political point, they add that there is little altruism in humans, thereby making distributive justice a matter of "balancing . . . competing claims" to what they seem to think is a scarce resource by its nature rather than by design (ibid., 169–70). They expect competition for health care, like competition for consumer goods in a free market, to make the allocations. Just as they take an economic model as normative for allocating health care resources, they seem to take legal models as normative in creating a just society, as in the claim of a "close link between the lawful society and the just society" (ibid., 170).[26]

The concepts writers use to interpret the allocation of health care as a social good are only as good as the writer's practical insights. It is not difficult to agree with Pellegrino and Thomasma that basic physical and mental needs should govern access to primary health care. It is much more difficult to agree with Beauchamp and Childress that ability to pay may be as fundamental a principle as need. Neither Pellegrino and Thomasma nor Beauchamp and Childress, or most writers mentioned, regard health care as a commodity to be bought and sold in a competitive market. Most writers mentioned and, I believe, most persons in our culture, understand primary health care as a social good, an instrument to obtain urgent human goods. Thus, a wholly commercial view of health care must be rejected.[27] My minor disagreements with Pellegrino and Thomasma and my serious disagreements with Beauchamp and Childress are based on their underlying concepts. Intelligent and reasonable judgments are indispensable for setting policies for such an important social good as health care, but they first require adequate concepts of health care.

Three kinds of norms allocate health care: customary norms, including economic and professional norms; legal norms; and moral norms. Pellegrino and Thomasma acknowledge customary norms, but they argue for the priority of a moral entitlement to primary health care and would make it a legal right.[28] They recognize formidable political opposition, but contend that it can be overcome by recognizing human need and the welfare of human communities as the overriding consideration. Pellegrino and Thomasma note that we seem to be stymied by a "collective inability as yet to define the acceptable conditions of social justice" (1981, 240, 242), but they substantially contribute to a definition when they point out that socially just health care respects needs for urgent human goods. However, Pellegrino and Thomasma address the distribution of social goods, not the burdens, and therefore their argument can be criticized for promoting a welfare concept of distributive justice.

By comparison, Beauchamp and Childress acknowledge that customary, legal, and moral norms apply to health care, but their approach—examining contemporary practices to discover the norms in use—leads them to value customary and legal norms as much as moral ones. Their argument, in which a competitive market allocates the scarce resources of health care, concludes that distribution should be procedurally impartial but cannot guarantee persons substantive justice or equal freedom. In effect, they slight substantive moral standards of justice.

A procedurally impartial and competitive market for health care could be unjust if the competitors are not on equal footing. As William Frankena explains, some may have had poorer opportunities to compete effectively. Frankena argues that a system of distribution that gives priority to liberty but rewards only those who have made measurable and rewardable achievements cannot be justified (1976, 98–99). Thus, in Frankena's argument, as in Aristotle's theory of justice, competitions which do not assign advantages and disadvantages justly to all parties cannot be fair. The distribution of goods is fundamentally unjust because it does not assure the competitors equal liberty.

This fundamental injustice is missed by those who accept the customary practices in health care as empirically unassailable in moral inquiries. Contracts, promises, and sales are so familiar to us that they mislead our decisions.[29] Lacking a concept of the common good and hobbled by incomplete concepts of liberty and equality, some positions lean heavily on limited concepts like a formal principle of impartiality (similars should be treated similarly) rather than material principles like need and achievement to assure just allocation. For example, some arguments in favor of guaranteed primary health care use the language of contracts, claiming that publicly subsidizing the medical profession creates a quid pro quo relationship that implicitly establishes rights (Camenisch 1976, 8–9).[30] All such approaches to allocation based on entitlements, contracts, or fair play fail to address how the burdens and possible harms should be distributed. What then would be appropriate norms for the just allocation of health care?

Categories of Health Care Resources

The first step toward justice in the allocation of health care is to reexamine the facts and concepts neglected in conventional wisdom, namely, the major influences on human health, their relative impact on urgent human goods, and the social goods that are instruments for obtaining urgent human goods. The facts and concepts of allocating health care are discussed in the first part of this chapter. In this section, and in the conclusion to this chapter, I focus on the moral standards that need to be renegotiated, on how justice can be assured, and on the personal and social conventions required for a just allocation of the benefits and burdens of primary health care. The most pertinent questions are as follows: What is to be allocated? By whom? For what purposes? Using what criteria? With what personal changes in the participants?

I begin by examining the major health care resources to identify who has the duty to renegotiate the burdens. Next, I consider which moral criteria are most relevant for assuring both just distributors and a just distribution of resources, including a constructive proposal for allocating the burdens as well as the benefits of health care. In the conclusion, I discuss two ways to implement this proposal. One is a procedure to assure that all parties will be represented when health care resources are reallocated. The other is a change in personal and social habits, what might be called the burdens of conversion.

The natural environment—air, soil, and water—is the greatest influence on human health. Formerly, one's natural environment was thought to be beyond one's control. Now, though individuals can take few actions to improve the quality of their environment, persons who direct businesses and industries and government regulators have greater influence on the environment. It follows that they also have greater responsibility for its impact on health.

Social environment is nearly as influential as natural environment in its impact on human health. Social environments that affect human health include places, such as one's home and workplace, schools, and public buildings, as well as social institutions that provide fire and police protection, and businesses that make basic material goods like food, shelter, and clothing available. Like natural environments, social environments are largely beyond the control of individuals since they are more affected by persons who shape government and social policy. These persons have proportionately greater responsibilities to avert social practices that threaten the public health.

The next-ranking influence on human health, life-style, does not mean only one's personal preferences about housing or clothing, but also the plan of life by which one cultivates one's physical and mental capacities by morally justifiable means. Such a plan would include rest and exercise, nutrition, and appropriate education. An individual usually has control over the elements of this plan, including behaviors that risk illness or injury, such as abusing sedatives or engaging in skydiving. As the Declaration of Alma-Ata notes, whether individuals can obtain the elements of a healthy life-style may depend on the cooperation of others or on the availability of institutions, such as medical clinics, in the society. Therefore, arranging a healthful life-style may not always be primarily one's own responsibility.

Until recently, people had no control over the next most important influence on health, heredity. Now, because of advances in diagnosing and predicting genetic disorders, for example, couples considering parenthood have greater responsibilities, but for such sophisticated resources they must have the cooperation of medical professionals and institutions. Therefore, assigning responsibility for the burdens in matters of heredity is complex but clearly to be shared.

Last and least significant of the influences on human health is conventional health care. Broader than medical care, health care includes nursing and other professional services; public-health measures like vaccination programs, sanitation, and industrial health and safety inspections; and some of the supporting activities in the Alma-Ata definition of primary health care and the first-contact care described by Pellegrino and Thomasma. Health care should be understood as a form of cooperation with the other, more important, influences on human health.

Who is responsible for which resource depends on how health care is understood. In the conventional sense of health care, the resources are the medical ones provided by licensed professionals and institutions. Individual professionals have little independence and are constrained by the policies of their profession and institution, as well as by insurers and government agencies that, for example, issue licenses or fund research. Therefore, identifying who is responsible for allocating health care, understood in the narrow sense, involves discovering links between several actors.

Moral Standards

Thus far, my aim is to clarify the social goods that influence human health. I also make some inferences about responsibility for allocating these social goods and their burdens. Now I discuss some criteria for moral actions and decisions. The customary and legal standards that pertain to health care can be helpful, but they must be subordinate to impartial moral standards. Almost every moral principle can find an application in health care, but let us begin with the most general principle, respect for persons. From this principle, we infer that whatever resources or influences on health can be controlled by humans should be apportioned with respect for the worth and dignity of the persons receiving them. Respect for persons includes respect for self as a person (self-cultivation) and respect for others as persons (beneficence). Since one's life-style is a major influence on one's health, to respect one's self as a person one should consider how one's life-style can develop one's capacities, allocating the benefits and risks in morally justifiable ways and excluding morally unjustifiable harms to oneself. Similarly, to respect other persons, those who control or affect our natural or social environment, use genetic information, or provide health care should promote their well-being in morally justified ways without unjustifiably harming themselves or others. From respect for self and respect for others follow two specific moral inferences. The first is that, to respect and cultivate self, each person has a right to be involved in selecting health care resources and deciding how to use them. The second is that the overriding consideration in planning a person's health care is that person's needs, rather than, for example, commercial interests.

It may seem that I have not yet mentioned justice. As explained in the tripodal theory in chapter 1, justice can be understood as the right ordering of relations between an individual and his or her objects of desire or aversion. To respect self and others requires rightly ordered relations between persons, just principles, and just social arrangements. In rightly ordered or just relationships, health care professionals and others who apportion health care resources must speak truthfully, keep promises, and practice beneficence toward persons who seek health care, mindful that they have little or no control over its quality and accessibility. Respecting oneself and others requires distributive justice in apportioning the burdens of health care. As noted earlier, most accounts of meeting people's health care needs overlook the burdens of health care. Pellegrino and Thomasma allude to problems their program would cause, but they do not indicate who is to bear those burdens, how much they are to bear, or what principles will direct the allocation. Beauchamp and Childress are more explicit but, as mentioned, their position is not satisfactory because it applies both Marxist and libertarian interpretations. Being able to pay entails some burdens, but being unable to pay creates more serious ones. Beauchamp and Childress seem to have failed to recognize that allocating the burdens of health care according to ability to pay can create disproportionate burdens. They have a well-developed position on nonmaleficence, but they do not relate it systematically to justice.

In summary, most discussions of meeting people's needs for health care do not sufficiently treat the burdens. As I argue throughout this book, how the burdens of health care are allocated measures the justice of the distributors and the social arrangements they create. Therefore, we should try to identify the burdens, who bears them and how much, and which ones are decisive measures of justice.

Whoever decides, allocating the four greatest influences on health can be a grave burden. Because some deleterious effects cannot be averted, some persons may bear disproportionate burdens or harms. It is then a question of what criteria should be used to decide who bears these more serious harms. Deciding who should bear these harms should begin by considering how much control individuals have over the influences on health. For example, we must accept any deficits in our natural and social environment and heredity (burdens we have not bargained for) and accommodate them as best we can to serve our development. How we do reveals the justice in our moral characters. After natural and social environment, the greatest influence on health is life-style. The burdens of life-style are our responsibilities by the principle of self-cultivation and avoiding harm to self.

The burdens and responsibilities of health care professionals are complex. These persons should oblige themselves to perform some services pro bono publico (as lawyers call their unpaid services contributed for the public good)[31] and reciprocate for burdens borne for their sake by those who subsidized their training. The principle of beneficence arguably requires pro bono work by health care professionals in addition to the duties of nonmaleficence and no-harm. Accepting from the state a license to practice confers some social privileges that may imply a commitment to perform such public service.

The most complex responsibilities of health care belong to those who make decisions that affect social environments. These persons include officers of corporations in industry and agriculture, community leaders in education and civic affairs, directors of medical institutions and professional associations, and government officials who regulate commerce, business, or professions. Their responsibilities are commensurate with the power they exert over the four major influences on human health.

For example, many professionals and their associations, health care institutions, private insurers, governmental agencies and other payers, manufacturers of drugs and medical equipment, and government regulators are responsible for providing the benefits of the least important influence on health, conventional health care. Therefore, its burdens need to be broadly shared and in proportion to the control these persons have over access to health care. *Securing Access to Health Care* emphasizes that access to health care is a "societal" responsibility, one shared proportionally by all sectors of society, private and public. Unfortunately, the report of the President's Commission did not indicate how this responsibility should be proportioned (1983).

A Proposal

With so many persons and groups using so many criteria for apportioning the benefits and burdens of conventional health care, we desperately need to find some consensus about the moral criteria. I propose the following: Our shared understanding of health care is that we supported its development to meet the health needs of the members of our communities, not to create a commodity for sale or exchange in competitive markets. A set of basic health care needs is well established and recounted in the Declaration of Alma-Ata and in the definition of first-contact care given by Pellegrino and Thomasma. Therefore, to benefit and not to harm persons and to assist them to do the same for themselves as persons, a just health care system would make primary care (including Pellegrino and Thomasma's second and third priorities, treatment to cure or prevent illness and treatment for incurable diseases) accessible to every member of the community.

Payments, efforts, and other contributions made by patients are relevant considerations in allocating health care, but a system that allocates health care entirely on this basis does not respect our shared understanding of health care as a social good to meet the needs of our people. Contribution or achievement criteria would be more appropriate for Pellegrino and Thomasma's fourth priority, expensive, high-technology treatment of uncertain benefit, and their fifth priority, treatment of disorders that are not incapacitating and require only relief of symptoms or self-care (1981, 237–38, 242). Therefore, a health care system might make some levels of health care, corresponding to Pellegrino and Thomasma's fourth and fifth priorities, available on the basis of ability to pay (as with insurance) or on the basis of merit or rewardable productivity or perhaps even on the basis of freedom of choice alone, provided the choices are morally justified and not arbitrary preferences.[32]

In allocating the burdens of conventional health care, the pertinent principles are to benefit and not harm persons and to enable them to do the same for themselves. The burdens of health care should be allocated mainly in accord with the three harm principles. Some suggest that, to be fair, burdens be distributed according to some arithmetical formula, but this approach overlooks two features of health care resources. One is that control over all resources is shared and the other is that some persons may be less able to bear the burdens. I contend that the three harm principles better address these issues.

According to the principle of degree of harm to fundamental goods, whatever the resource and whoever distributes it, to apportion its burdens in ways that harm one's own or another's life or opportunities for a developed and happy existence is almost never justifiable. It might be justifiable if the harms affect instrumental goods like physical and mental health, and it would be more readily justifiable if they affect extrinsic goods like possessions. The financial burdens of health care affect extrinsic goods; the burdens of ordinary illnesses affect intermediate goods; and life-threatening illnesses and disabling injuries are harms to fundamental goods. Whether apportioned by oneself or others, one should recognize that these harms can affect the providers as well as the recipients of health care, and also that some harms are inevitable.

According to the principle of proportionate harm, even the less serious harms may be unjustifiable if they fall on persons (or certain classes of persons) who cannot well sustain or mitigate them. For example, genetic defects or serious illness can create severe disabilities, from which some persons may not recover. When allocating resources, persons should be guided by such morally relevant circumstances and by the principle of proportionate harms. Similarly, groups of persons—professional associations, families, institutions—should try to anticipate whether the risks created by their decisions are justifiable.

According to the principle of systemic harm, harms that affect entire classes of persons or several generations of persons, especially grave harms to fundamental human goods, are difficult to justify and should be prohibited in principle. If the classes of persons affected also suffer perduring injustices, the consequences can be tragic, as, for example, if no research and no therapies were being developed for conditions, like menopausal complications or sickle-cell anemia, that affect an ethnic, age, or sex group. It would also be tragically unjust if only hospital employees were expected to bear the cost of nonpayment of hospital services or if conditions in workplaces maximize productivity and profit but endanger employees' health.

Entire classes of persons can be doubly disadvantaged, first, by burdens they cannot bear or for which they have not bargained and, second, through inescapable systemic harms. Like other harms, these are apportioned by many persons, including the one harmed, and they affect the providers as well as the recipients of health care. The principle of systemic harm can guide decision makers toward more just arrangements.

As an example, consider contemporary financing of medical care. To economists who study our health care system, it is axiomatic that how the medical bills are paid largely determines the extent and type of treatment the patient receives. They are not claiming that money talks or that disputes end when one party exhausts its finances. Rather, as economist Karen Davis has demonstrated, this axiom relates accessibility of health care services to their cost, quantity, and incentives (1976). For example, economists have demonstrated that if patients share costs they do not abuse services and that incentives for providers to increase productivity and to assure quality effectively improve their services.

Effective financing can drive the expansion of one health care system and inadequate financing can threaten the existence of another. In the 1960s, federal programs tried to make quality health care accessible to more people. In one experiment, neighborhood health centers provided primary care and first-contact medical care. These centers were unreliably financed by piecemeal grants rather than by appropriations included in the budgets of existing programs. Despite their success, most centers closed for lack of funding. By contrast, the Medicare program was designed to subsidize conventional forms of curative rather than preventive care through conventional institutions and was financed by amendments to the Social Security Act. Although less effective than neighborhood health centers, Medicare has flourished.

Financing our health care system by insurance also stands to harm some classes of persons. Because having at least some insurance is a prerequisite for getting attention, much less attentive care, our health care system is inaccessible to an estimated thirty-three million uninsured persons, who bear unusually heavy burdens. They undoubtedly face serious risks to intrinsic human goods (their health). They probably are uninsured because they are unemployed or are employed irregularly or employed in businesses that provide no insurance benefits. Therefore, they are less able to protect themselves against harms from which they might not recover. Because it is financed through insurance, our health care system raises these harms to the level of systemic and institutionalized neglect of some classes of our population. The children of uninsured adults will also probably be neglected.

Thus, the assignment of the fiscal burdens of conventional health care—not to mention the burdens of the other influences on human health—may be harmful to people's intrinsic goods. The way our system assigns its burdens determines its degree of justice because it selects some persons to receive benefits needed by all, because the harms to some persons are disproportionate, and because some harms are systemic. In sum, when any system of assigning medical resources or the influences on human health regularly and systematically violates the prohibition "above all, do no harm," we have decisive evidence that it is not a just system and stands to be renegotiated.

Conclusion

Several ways of renegotiating the concepts and norms associated with primary health care have been proposed. In addition, I judge two conditions necessary for effective renegotiations: formal procedures to assure that all persons who receive health care and all those who provide or have control over it will be represented,[33] and some changes in personal and social habits that I call the burdens of conversion.

Although procedures cannot guarantee the substantive justice we need, they can keep policymakers focused on the correct goals, can help them clarify shared understandings about the concepts and norms applied, and can require that key people meet periodically to review how the four major influences interact to affect human health in our communities.

Individuals can independently make some decisions about how the major influences on health affect them, but often only in cooperation with others like family members, friends, or health professionals. Making choices that create a more healthful life-style have already been mentioned. In addition, one can consider the natural and social environments when choosing housing or seeking employment. Because individuals and their circumstances differ, few practices will be applicable to everyone, except perhaps an annual physical examination.

Some personal health decisions affect other persons, for example, the decision to have children. Because genetic defects can be serious, and because humans now have more knowledge about heredity and control over their reproduction, it would seem a moral obligation for couples to be informed about their own genetic endowment, about how likely a weak trait is to be transmitted to their children, and about available interventions or remedies. Any decisions should be made collaboratively by the couple and qualified professionals and reviewed as knowledge about genetics advances or family circumstances change.

Health care policymaking, however, encounters some serious problems. As Lester Thurow suggested in *The Zero Sum Society*, one of the greatest difficulties is that our society has no sensible criteria for assigning economic and political losses (1980, 11–12, 21–22, 206). Perhaps there are really only two ways to remedy this deficiency. One already mentioned (cited in the Declaration of Alma-Ata) is to create formal procedures that require those communities of persons that stand to be affected by a policy—especially a group that would be harmed— to have a voice in making the policy. Without a formal agreement that substantive, common human standards will be the ruling consideration, struggles among special-interest groups and political action committees could result.

Persuaded as I am that it is far less important to know who decides than to know their guidelines and convinced that the criteria must be shared and endemic to the community rather than foreign or imposed, I think we need most of all public dialog on the criteria. By this I do not mean that a token ethicist should be appointed to a commission, as if including one more expert, prone to impose norms rather than uncover them, might guarantee that a community's shared moral criteria will be articulated. What I do mean is that all the parties need to meet regularly and be committed to approximating justice in allocating their resources. Robert S. Morison observed that the equitable distribution of health care is a promising new endeavor in bioethics because its quandaries "require a societal rather than an individual frame of reference" and foster reflection on "the equitable distribution of other sources" (1981, 11–12) of basic human securities.

Renegotiating the burdens of justice in health care may require communities and individuals to revise their ways of thinking. One of the lighter burdens may be to take full account of the four major influences on health, their relative impact, and their implications for designing social environments, life-styles, and health care systems, for improving the natural environment, and for making decisions about reproduction. One of the more onerous burdens may be rethinking the concepts and principles people in a community share about health care policy and practice. Habits can be morally good or bad, but when they become troublesome—as I have shown they can be in a people's understandings about standards for allocating health care resources—to renegotiate the burdens of justice in health care, communities and individuals must accept the burdens of changing their habits of thinking.[34]

One's perceptions about health care can be misled by the understandings of one's culture. For example, in the United States people seem eager to take up the latest food fad or seek out practitioners of nontraditional modalities, like herbal medicine or acupuncture. Another fallacy arising from faulty habits of mind is inferring that health care resources are scarce because experimental, life-saving procedures are infrequently performed. These habits of thinking prevent many people from obtaining correct information about health and promote conventional but incorrect concepts of health care and justice. This chapter describes some of the gaps, confusions, and ambiguities in our popular understandings of health care in the United States. Examining popular understandings critically deserves more effort.

In public discussions about people's concepts of justice regarding health care some red herrings and some deep-seated cultural notions arise. Among the red herrings drawn across our path are the perception that egalitarian concepts are socialistic, the cynical identification of health care with business services and commodities, and the notion that people bring most of their health problems on themselves. Some of the deep-seated cultural notions about justice that become stumbling blocks in discussions are notions of rights, liberties, and impartiality, as well as the belief that all human goods are rewards for productivity and should be apportioned according to desert.

The problems with these notions about justice are plain but not readily overcome. Rights most often connote liberties or exercise rights rather than entitlements. But even when understood as entitlements, rights are not correctly related to their duties. In our democratic society, we are often reminded that for every right we have a corresponding duty. (For example, we have a right to vote and a duty to exercise it.) However, the rights and duties of health care are different because in health care someone bears the responsibility to make good on someone else's right. Therefore, rights-based approaches to health care must be complemented with duty-based approaches. Our culture embraces such concepts but we must rehabilitate them. We must break contemporary habits of reasoning that judge by results, that understand equal liberty as freedom from interference, and that believe that the best one can hope for in life is fair play, suggesting that justice is only a matter of impartial procedures. The difficulty is more than intellectual. It is a problem of the moral habits of both individuals and communities.

Decisions about one's own health or the health of others can be misguided by cultural norms used to allocate the resources and burdens of health care. Persons and communities that rely on conventional practices and accept only law as the source of norms continually risk serious errors in judgment and decision making. So too do those who elevate the norms of commercial competition and conflicting interests to the status of moral principles for making judgments and decisions about health care. So do those who focus on benefits and opportunities without recognizing the burdens they bring, particularly those that decisively reveal the justice of the health care system.

The intellectual and moral habits of individuals and communities are deep-seated and strengthened by innumerable cultural notions and mores. The conversions required to surmount them will be difficult but they will better enable persons and their communities to apportion the burdens as well as the benefits of health care justly.

In Contract Law

The role of law in assigning benefits and burdens in families, education, and health care has already been mentioned. Practitioners of law both reflect and shape cultural beliefs when they fashion or interpret laws that apportion the benefits or burdens of social goods. For example, public defender programs aim to assure that all defendants have the benefit of legal counsel, and funding such programs becomes the public's burden. The major areas of law—contracts and torts, evidence, and criminal, constitutional, and administrative law—make allocations of burdens that have subtle but profound effects on a society's beliefs and values.[1] For example, legal scholars and practitioners call on common morality to interpret or revise legal doctrines which, in turn, instruct the public about which moral values are legally enforceable. How clients are selected and which services are provided may have important consequences.[2]

This chapter selects the law of contracts to investigate interactions among law, culture, and society, and the social and cultural effects of allocating burdens.[3] Our inquiries again are factual, conceptual, and normative. We wish to determine whether the ways contract law allocates burdens determines the quality of distributive justice in a society and whether or not contracts work morally justifiable harms to fundamental human goods, harms disproportionate to people's capacity to sustain them, or harms that affect classes of persons for generations.

Case studies of contracts in nineteenth-century and twentieth-century United States law serve for factual inquiries. The nineteenth-century case illustrates the problems of apportioning monopolistic franchise advantages without disproportionately disadvantaging the public. In the twentieth-century case, merchants dictated the terms of sales contracts, allocating the advantages to themselves and the disadvantages to the buyers. In both cases, the one-sided contracts were questionable on legal as well as moral grounds. Before making our factual inquiry, we review some moral assumptions for making contracts justifiable and for claiming damages when they have been violated.

Most contracting parties arrange their bargains informally, according to whatever standards they have, but all parties assume they are free, that is, free from interference, to make the agreement as they see fit. Because some contracts have come to litigation, legal doctrines and rules have developed. These rules require some types of contract and prohibit others. Although they provide sanctions or remedies for breach of contract and resulting harms,[4] how to apply moral standards to the rules of contract law and to the behavior of legal practitioners is vehemently debated.[5]

Extreme libertarians hold that law and government have no role in agreements, implying that liberty in the negative sense is the only applicable moral standard. At the other extreme, some religious groups hold that human law should obey their version of divine law. In between lies a range of persons seeking to apply economic, moral, social, political, or cultural criteria to contract law. Most moderate positions include moral criteria but disagree on the standards and on who should enforce them, for example, whether a contract should be voided because its purposes are "bad" or whether certain terms should be required or prohibited to protect communities as well as contracting parties.[6]

In contract law, the most fundamental moral considerations frequently are those associated with distributive justice. How the burdens fall has moral consequences. For example, the case studies in this chapter illustrate the distributive effects of law. I hope to make clear that the moral value of freedom in making contracts and of the duty to keep promises rests on the presumption that the terms of contracts are fair, that is, that they distribute advantages and disadvantages justly and do no harm to the parties who depend on the fulfillment of the agreement.[7]

The purposes of contract law are usually said to be (*a*) to specify which agreements are legally binding, (*b*) to define rights and duties, and (*c*) to set penalties for an unexcused breach (Kronman 1980, 472).[8] However, until the middle of this century, the courts had only indirect remedies, such as interpreting the language of the contract, determining that certain terms were contrary to public policy, and manipulating the rules of offer and acceptance and the doctrine of consideration (which deals with the inducements for a party to agree to the contract).[9] Recent developments in contract law reflect the traditional strategies of equity courts, but have been criticized as paternalistic, restraining the freedom of the parties to set terms, and giving moral values undue weight (Farnsworth and Young 1980, 366; Kronman 1983, 763ff.).[10] For example, under contemporary equity methods in rules of contract law, a court may determine that a contract is unenforceable on any of three grounds: the capacity of the parties to commit themselves,[11] fraud or deception that would create an unequal exchange, and an unequal advantage that enables one party to overpower the other in negotiations (Farnsworth and Young 1980, 350–440).[12] This chapter is concerned with the third kind of fatal flaw.

Boston Elevated Railway Company Franchise

In an address at Boston University's School of Law in 1897, Justice Oliver Wendell Holmes, of the Supreme Judicial Court of Massachusetts, argued that law ought to be kept distinct from morality. He explored several areas in which the confusion of the two seemed particularly troublesome, but he believed contract law was the strongest example. In his view, "the duty to keep a contract at common law means a prediction that you must pay damages if you do not keep it—and nothing else." For those who find moral obligations in contracts, he added, "such a mode of looking at the matter stinks in the nostrils of those who think it advantageous to get as much ethics into the law as they can" (1897, 457, 462; 1881, 235–36).[13]

The same year in the same city, Louis Dembitz Brandeis became the public's champion in a dispute over a Boston transportation franchise, an enterprise that would demonstrate that Holmes was right about the source of the stench but not about its nature. Brandeis realized that the elegant and persuasive Holmesian doctrine on contracts could be exploited by economic and political interests to ends that Holmes would not have found acceptable.[14]

If franchises involving public properties are interpreted as gifts, the grantee has no obligation to the grantor. Thus, the public is liable to substantial, possibly systemic, harm. If franchises are regarded as contracts, corporations that hold franchises from a city are accountable to the public. In representing the public in franchise agreements made with utilities, transportation companies, and industries, Brandeis saw economic and political interests at work. He believed that the formal bargaining principles of contractual justice alone should not govern franchises because franchises create material problems in distributive justice. The test of justice in franchises is not whether public benefits are distributed evenly but whether public burdens, costs, and losses are distributed justly.

Although Brandeis was not a member of a Jewish congregation, his passionate commitment to justice and his embrace of key elements in Jewish tradition make the Boston franchise case a study of the relationships between law, religion, and morality. Louis Dembitz Brandeis was born in the United States of Bohemian Jewish parents who immigrated to the Midwest in the nineteenth century and settled in Louisville, Kentucky. By the age of forty, Louis Brandeis was a successful Boston lawyer well on his way to becoming a millionaire (Goldmark 1930). Though a leading advocate of free enterprise and competition in law and business, he understood that competition is not just unless the competitors stand on an equal footing. Brandeis found that free enterprise and competition did not prevail when powerful corporations crushed competitors and imposed terms on labor. The public, represented poorly or not at all, was helpless against the able lawyers of private interests.[15]

When he became financially secure, Brandeis volunteered to represent the public in disputes that he believed undermined the ideal of justice and liberty for all. His early opponents were corporations that improperly influenced government officials, for example, by bribing legislators in Massachusetts in the 1880s (Mason 1946, 89). In 1893, in what he called his "first important work," Brandeis helped prevent the West End Railway from getting a franchise to extend its trolley line across Boston Common (ibid., 106).[16]

While some other cities virtually gave away valuable franchises for the use of public streets,[17] Massachusetts taxed the franchisee, charged street rentals, and regulated fares. But in 1897 the newly organized Boston Elevated Railway Company stealthily pushed through the Massachusetts House of Representatives Bill 784, which expanded the Boston transit system and granted the company unusually liberal privileges at public expense.

On practically the eve of its passage, Brandeis learned about some of the bill's provisions. To rally immediate public opposition, he wrote to the editor of the *Boston Evening Transcript* arguing that the bill should be defeated. He cited two provisions that would "sacrifice the interests of the public to that of a single corporation" (ibid., 107). Brandeis described the two provisions: "The absolute right for thirty years to charge . . . a full five-cent fare for each passenger, regardless of the age of the passenger or of the distance carried . . . (and) immunity for thirty years from all franchise taxes or street rentals, except the trifling and inadequate compensation provided for by the bill" (April 30, 1897, letter to the *Boston Evening Transcript*).[18]

Brandeis argued that the bill would set an undesirable precedent, inviting other railroad, gas, and electric companies to demand similar privileges. Furthermore, because the costs of transportation were decreasing, fixing the fare for thirty years would undercut the company's incentive to manage efficiently and reduce fares when costs decreased (ibid., 316).

Brandeis analyzed how the franchise agreement would allocate the costs of the Elevated's privileges. The Elevated would pay the city of Boston a franchise fee equal to 0.5% of its gross annual earnings, or, in more profitable years, a higher rate as provided by an escalator clause: In any year in which the Elevated paid a 5% dividend (the prevailing rate at the time was 4%), the company would pay the city 1.5% of its gross earnings for the year.

After estimating the Elevated's annual revenue at $8.5 million, Brandeis calculated that the company would pay $42,500 in an ordinary year. If, say, annual earnings of $9 million were high enough for the company to pay the 5% dividend, then the company would pay the city $135,000 in franchise fees. Brandeis pointed out that even $135,000, the higher fee, was much less than transit companies were paying other cities. Citing New York, he reported that, under the franchise agreement made in April 1897, the Third Avenue Railway agreed to pay the city of New York a $1 million initial fee in addition to annual fees, and that the annual rates were higher than in Boston (in later years of the New York franchise, exactly ten times higher): 3% of the railway's annual gross earnings for three years, and 5% in subsequent years.

Applying the New York rate, 5%, to the Elevated's estimated annual earnings in an ordinary year, Brandeis calculated the revenue as $425,000 each year—ten times as much as the company would pay the city of Boston in an ordinary year and more than three times as much as in a more profitable year, not to mention the $1 million initial fee. Brandeis also noted that in some cities transit fares were falling to less than five cents. He calculated that, had fares in 1896 been only four cents, the people of Boston would have saved $1,666,662.

Because of the thirty-year fixed fare and the minuscule annual fee, the Boston public would lose twice—substantially in both instances: It would pay more than $1.5 million in fare overcharges for every cent the fare might have been reduced during the thirty-year period, and, compared to the New York public, Boston would lose the $1 million initial fee and nearly a half million dollars in annual fees. The terms of the franchise would make the public bear costs incommensurate with the benefits of an expanded transit system. The Elevated and its stockholders, not the commuters of Boston, would have been the principal beneficiaries.

Were it not for Brandeis's careful research and astute reasoning, most citizens would not have learned of the injustice to be done to them by the proposed agreement. Brandeis, acting as the people's attorney, lost the Boston Elevated franchise case, the first battle in a conflict called the Boston Traction Contest (1897–1911), but won the war. By his efforts in this case and in other struggles with corporations that had little regard for logic or morality and during his tenure on the United States Supreme Court, Brandeis averted systemic disadvantages for communities in contracts with powerful public utilities, industries, or financial corporations.

Jones v. *Star Credit Corporation*

Since judicial policing of contracts is no longer a specialty of equity courts, decisions in contract cases are made in the light of recent statutory and administrative law as well as common law. However, legal issues in contract cases still arise from three defects, that, if found in contracts, can invalidate them; namely, the status or capacity of the parties, their behavior, and the substance of their bargains (Farnsworth and Young 1980, 350ff.).

Status or capacity of a party refers to the ability of minors and other classes of persons called incompetent (that is, persons who stand to be disadvantaged or harmed) to enter into binding contracts. Matters of behavior or substance include sharp or misleading practices, like physical duress and intimidation, and coercion.[19] Such practices prompt courts to manipulate the doctrine of consideration in favor of fairness. The doctrine of consideration recommends that, after the parties have accepted some consideration, contracts be enforced whether or not the consideration accepted was commensurate with the promise made (ibid., 365). One-sided contracts are invalidated when courts find inadequate consideration, or that the contract assigned the aggrieved party only a small benefit, or that the bargain was struck under oppressive conditions. Sometimes, by employing the doctrine of overreaching, courts rescind or void contracts in which advantage was gained through gross unfairness, as by fraud, duress, or mistakes (innocent misrepresentations).[20] Courts examine the substance of the bargain as well as the behavior of the contracting parties (ibid., 350ff.).

Since the middle of this century, courts have construed the clauses in contracts in novel ways, reemphasizing the concept of good faith, and setting compulsory terms for certain contracts (Patterson 1964, 858–59). For example, the new concept of unconscionability, which builds on the legal concept of an equitable contract, has been applied to adhesion contracts,[21] those in which a more powerful party dictates terms to entire classes of persons (Farnsworth and Young 1980, 451, 468). According to the fifth edition of *Black's Law Dictionary*, the test of unconscionability is "whether under circumstances existing at the time of making of (a) contract and in light of (the) general commercial background and (the) commercial needs of (a) particular trade or case, (the) clauses involved are so one-sided as to oppress or unfairly surprise (a) party" (1979, 1367). Unconscionable contracts "involve gross overall one-sidedness or gross one-sidedness of a term disclaiming a warranty, limiting damages, or granting procedural advantages . . . coupled with the fact that the imbalance is buried in small print and often couched in language unintelligible to even a person of moderate education . . . (as occurs often when sellers are dealing with) a particularly susceptible party" (ibid.).

The contemporary concept of unconscionability tends to merge the older considerations of capacity, behavior, and substance (Farnsworth and Young 1980, 441). In tandem with the development of these recent concepts in contract law, legislation like the Uniform Commercial Code, the Consumer Protection Act, and the Truth-in-Lending Act was intended to redress the inequality of parties bargaining in the twentieth-century commercial environment. In the *Henningsen* case, the court described an environment of "standardized mass contracts" being used by enterprises "with strong bargaining power and position" against weaker parties who are "in need of the goods or services" but are "frequently not in a position to shop around for better terms" either because the drafter of the contract had a monopoly or because all competing businesses include the same clauses in their contracts (ibid., 441, 459, 470–73). The ruling in *Henningsen* stated that such monopolistic privilege is not justifiable under freedom of contract, for that traditional doctrine does not absolve parties from responsibility for negligence. In the last few decades, many one-sided contracts have been rescinded, voided, or declared unenforceable by courts following the *Henningsen* ruling.[22]

Although Justice Holmes did not believe in mixing legal and ethical considerations, debate about the relation between law and morality and about the role of distributive justice in contracts has continued. In a 1941 New Hampshire case involving overreaching, the court stated that, while it "is not practical that the law should adopt all precepts of moral conduct . . . it is desirable that its rules and principles should not run counter to them in the important conduct and transactions of life" (ibid., 394, 397). As recently as 1980, in Farnsworth and Young's text on contract law, one finds legal scholars distinguishing between the requirements of the law and those of conscience, while worrying that "in allowing bargaining advantages to be secured by persons of little scruple, the law may attach a competitive disadvantage to conscientious conduct" (ibid., 413). Clearly the relationship between law and morality remains open to discussion. In particular, the relationship between contract law and the moral standards of distributive justice also should remain open to debate, perhaps even more so today, when the distributive effects of contract law are being discussed more vigorously.[23]

Cases of unconscionability are a particularly rich vein to mine when inquiring about the role of morality and distributive justice in contract law. As Charles Fried observes, unconscionability focuses on the substantive unfairness of the agreement itself and thus is a far-reaching notion suggesting that even contracts knowingly and freely made (that is, not under blatant duress but perhaps under some economic coercion) may be judged so unfair as not to be binding (1981, 92–93). Fried concludes that the doctrine of unconscionability arose as a recent development in statutory and case law and suggests "we may have in the not too distant future a more candid set of principles to determine which promises should be enforceable in terms of the fairness of each type" (ibid., 39).[24]

Jones v. *Star Credit Corporation,* decided by the New York Supreme Court in 1969, anticipated that future.[25] Clifton and Cora Jones were welfare recipients who agreed in 1965 to pay $900 for a home freezer whose fair market value was no more than $300. The Joneses were offered the sales contract by a door-to-door salesman representing Your Shop at Home

Services, Inc. The purchase was financed by the Star Credit Corporation for a total cost of $1,234.80, including sales tax, credit, and life and property insurance. When the case was heard, in 1969, the Joneses had paid more than $600. Because of charges for extending the period of the loan, their total cost was now $1,439.69, of which they still owed $819.81.

The issue was whether this contract could be considered unconscionable under Section 2–302 of the Uniform Commercial Code. Holding that it indeed was unconscionable and that the contract should be amended, the New York Supreme Court made several telling points. The justices noted that the slogan *caveat emptor* (let the buyer beware) often protected the most unscrupulous in the marketplace and that efforts to eliminate exploitative practices raised difficult legal questions. How should the law balance the rights of parties to make agreements freely and the need to protect uneducated and poor members of communities? Since credit and installment sales are indispensable and merchants need to protect themselves against buyers who are poor risks, how can the law prevent unconscionable contracts from seeming respectable?

The justices concluded that the developing body of common and statutory law on unconscionability both respected the free enterprise system and safeguarded buyers. They claimed that the Universal Commercial Code enacted the "moral sense of the community into the law of commercial transactions" and authorized courts to refuse to enforce a contract they found unconscionable. Thus, the advantage-taking formerly adjudicated on grounds of fraud—which the court did not find in this case—was adjudicated under the Uniform Commercial Code. The justices concluded that "knowing advantage was taken" of the Joneses, who had no real choice because of their grossly weaker bargaining position. In sum, the way the court construed UCC Sec. 2–302 and their views about just prices and usurious loans implied that distributive justice is at stake in every contract. In the view of the justices, contemporary commerce creates disproportionate advantages and benefits for the unscrupulous and assigns disadvantages and harms to the already disadvantaged.[26]

The court used procedural considerations in saying that judges and attorneys, through adjudication, are responsible for policing the bargains made in contracts. Since *Jones*, legislators and government administrators also bear some responsibility because statutory and administrative law has expanded. As for the substantive grounds for enforcing, rescinding, or reforming a contract, the court considered defects of status, behavior, and substance. The court's decision in *Jones* affirms that these procedural and substantive matters entail moral issues, including those of distributive justice.

The Morality Contracts Suppose

In the nineteenth century, as in ours, philosophies of life lay beneath all legal reasoning and decision making. Like other people, the lawyers who become legislators, judges, and legal scholars invariably subscribe—even if unconsciously—to some philosophy of life.[27] They show their convictions when they invoke their senses of justice in legal matters. That their legal intuitions should be scrutinized is evident, for example, when a legal scholar asserts that most of the rules governing contracts promote efficiency, that people strive to maximize their own welfare in bargains, and that contract regulations should be designed accordingly (Gross 1980, 867–77).

These dubious assertions, like all philosophies of life embedded in legal reasoning, should be examined carefully. Here we consider some philosophies entailed in the Boston franchise and the *Jones* case. Our inquiries are conceptual and normative, bent on uncovering the logic in positions people take about contracts, not to judge but to observe their beliefs empathetically.

Brandeis and the Boston Franchise

Brandeis saw the industrialists, employers, bankers, and utility stockholders allied against the citizens of Boston, but their relationships with other powerful parties reached further than he had suspected. He found that his struggle was not only with the Boston Elevated Railway Company and the banks, but also with the press, which was controlled by the banks, and with the lawyers and clergy who had uncritically allied themselves with monopolistic power.[28] He found that actual social conditions did not allow some parties the freedom assumed in the free-dom-of-contract doctrine. He discovered that one must keep an eye on the future, for the public faced long-lasting harms other than the economic burden of paying needlessly high fares for thirty years. The Boston franchise would set a prece-dent for other cities and encourage other utilities to adopt the inefficient management methods prevalent in transportation (Mason 1946, 181, n. 14). Brandeis believed the managers of the Elevated were not committed to the public interest, that legislators could be bribed by lobbyists, and that the people of Boston did not have political power or legal representation equal to that of their affluent opponents.

The moral principles implied in the franchise agreement Brandeis proposed were grounded in these beliefs. According to one of his principles, equal liberty, the public and the rail-way should have equal freedom in competitive bargaining. According to another, an allocation principle, the benefits and costs of public transportation should be shared equitably by the public and the railway. Therefore, Brandeis's proposed contract aimed to place the public and the Elevated on an even footing and arranged a more equitable distribution by linking the privileges of the franchise to taxes and rentals paid by the company, relating profit margins to fares, and using an escalator clause to require periodic review of the terms.

The Jones Case

In *Jones,* the justices of the Supreme Court of New York out-lined "environmental and structural factors" in the relation-ship between the parties to the sale. The court described a marketplace of exploitive and callous practices that systemati-cally advantaged sellers. The court described the buyers in this case as a solitary, defenseless, and financially dependent cou-ple on welfare, burdened by a sales contract for a freezer which required them to pay nearly five times its fair market value. The court described the far better advantaged seller as an aggregate of persons who owned and sold the freezer. Also included were those who took a financial risk by making the loan but protected themselves by setting a high interest rate and insuring the buyer's life and property. Thus, it is difficult to identify who is bargaining on the seller's side. Moreover, since the contract was drafted by the seller and contained monopolistic terms, did the unfettered bargaining presumed by the doctrine of freedom of contract actually take place? Because it was unlikely that the buyer could have bargained effectively to protect his interest and because the contracting parties were plainly not on an equal footing, the court questioned the capacity of the buyer, the behavior of the seller, and the substance of the contract.

In addition to the notoriously vague UCC clause, the court cited both moral and legal principles as guides to fairness, chiefly one it called the moral sense of the community represented in Sec. 2–302. As they construed this section, if a contracting party has no meaningful choice or if one party takes knowing advantage of the other, the contract should not be enforced. We note that the court, without citing them, applied two standards of no-harm. One holds that the law should not assign contractual advantages to the unconscientious, thereby furthering their mischief and perpetrating social harms. The other is that the law should protect contracting parties who are vulnerable to such harms.

This argument runs counter to formal and abstract versions of the freedom-of-contract doctrine. The *Jones* decision demonstrates a realistic perception of the marketplace and its political entanglements. It seems to recognize that, although the marketplace is presumed apolitical, it often is a political instrument in the hands of the powerful to sustain their own social and cultural advantages.[29]

These untoward consequences may result not so much from deliberate mischief as from the legal reasoning endorsed by formal and strict compliance theories of justice. The New York justices countered this reasoning with their less formal, partial-compliance style of jurisprudence. These styles of reasoning should be scrutinized because they embody legal concepts or other assumptions that legal practitioners apply to contracts.

Two Forms of Jurisprudence

The legal controversies in the *Jones* case and in the Boston franchise dispute reflect different patterns of legal thinking. United States law embraces two fundamentally different ways of accounting for the logic of the law. One is formal jurisprudence, which presumes that the science of the law is objective and rational and separate from ethical, moral, and legislative questions.[30] The other form, called equity jurisprudence, recognizes ambiguity, irrationality, and inconsistency in the law and in the social conditions it was established to regulate. According to *Black's Law Dictionary,* equity jurisprudence arises in the effort to achieve fairness, right dealing, and, often, remedial justice. Unlike the formulations of common law, it does not strictly apply rules but seeks fairness. Black characterizes equity jurisprudence as a tradition independent of theories of common law (1979, 484–85, 767).[31] The legal reasoning found in our cases accords best with equity jurisprudence and contrasts sharply with formal jurisprudence. It also accords well with philosophical and theological theories of justice that emphasize partial rather than full compliance with the law and that seek to approximate justice in actual communities.

A lawyer characteristically uses one or the other form of jurisprudence largely because of his or her training and the legal issues that dominate his or her practice.[32] Law schools fall into two kinds, the night schools, which emphasize technical training, and the day schools, which are associated with universities and are perceived as more scholarly. The night schools are sometimes regarded as vocational schools, but some of the day schools, which are more prestigious, provide little more than technical training. As Chief Justice Warren Burger remarked, many graduates of the night schools feel socially inferior to the graduates of the day schools. Burger did not find that the graduates of the day schools were invariably better lawyers. Though he did not say so, the day schools may be so parochial that their professional value to society is questionable (Friedman 1973, 536). Narrowly conceived training in the science of the law can be as detrimental as narrow technical training. To form the intellectual and moral habits of just lawyers, legal education needs a broader perspective.

In addition, a lawyer may be morally handicapped if, because he nearly always represents individuals, he habitually overlooks the interests of communities. Lawyers can be affected adversely by what Jerome H. Skolnick calls the "subtle, sometimes unarticulate, yet discernible norms" that operate throughout the legal system (1975, iii) and which, I believe, establish presumptions favoring some persons more than others and conceal substantive forms of injustice under the wraps of procedural niceties.

In the 1960s a study of the criteria law firms used to determine whether poor persons were eligible for free legal services revealed that lawyers somewhat arbitrarily excluded some classes of poor persons. Asked whether all those whose income falls below a certain figure or only those who "deserve" it should receive free legal assistance, no lawyer would make an unqualified answer. The study demonstrated that, even when not articulated, the criteria the firms used prized merit more than need, and that, when articulated, they were expressed in morally invidious and unjustifiably discriminatory ways (Silverstein 1967). For example, for many years legal aid offices did not handle divorce or bankruptcy cases. They distinguished the deserving poor from the indigent, considering poverty the result of the poor person's own immorality. Recent guidelines for eligibility have given income more weight, but, like some presumptions in common law about criminal justice and welfare, they continue to reflect prejudices prevalent among lawyers and their principal clients.[33]

These judgments, which most legal professionals admit pervade the profession, become incorporated into laws and legal doctrines. Although many lawyers acknowledge that their education makes them blind to broad social issues, few recognize that these prejudices also color the law they interpret and the contracts they make. Appealing to legal precedents and their sometimes mistaken policies can blunt sensitivity to morally unjustifiable decisions and make what were de facto cultural beliefs de jure. By controlling access to legal services and by selecting both paying clients and pro bono clients, lawyers often promote their own cultural beliefs.

Furthermore, because of their training, lawyers may hold some beliefs not widely held by members of their society. For example, most people understand that form is not substance and that procedures are not results. But, because of their predilection for pursuing justice by formal procedures, lawyers may come to believe that the law can do no more than assure fair play, which often overlooks the advantages enjoyed by some players.

Thick and Thin Theories of Contracts

Some say that, to be scientific, the law must ignore the social status of persons, yet theories of other scientific disciplines do not make this demand. In contracts, these scientific but thin theories of law are tempting because they seem to simplify the issues[34] or assign them to other disciplines. Denser theories of law reckon with the actual society and expect that a well-ordered society will take time to achieve and will only partially comply with the rules. Thin theories describe a well-ordered society in ideal terms and envision strict compliance with the rules. They do not recognize how a community's history, institutions, or cultural understandings inform contract law and what contractual terms parties consider fair. Thin theories stipulate rather than discover what is just and set out formal procedures to attain it; thick theories rely on discovery and on substantive principles.[35]

Whether thick or thin, assumptions in theories of law acquire the status of unquestionable articles of faith. Constructing a theory of law resembles the process medieval theologians described as "faith seeking to understand itself without calling one's beliefs into question" (*fides quaerens intellectum*). Three classes of beliefs, whether stated or unstated, provide foundations for legal theories—beliefs about business practices and social conditions, beliefs about human nature, and beliefs about what the rules of human interaction should be. Thin theories of contract law rely on hypothetical models. For example, in an ideal market, parties would meet on an equal footing and freely enter an unbiased agreement that is morally and legally binding.[36] In this market, which exists only in the tales of social progress and economic liberalism created by Adam Smith and Jeremy Bentham, market exchanges are the only legitimate way to distribute goods and services. The ideal free market, now an enshrined concept in economics, supposes what it cannot demonstrate. It believes that real markets are unfettered by previous transactions, that actual practices are morally justifiable, that only the contracting parties are affected, and that the parties are equally free (Scanlon 1977, 43ff.).

From these assumptions, one might conclude that all contracts entered in such a market should be enforced. But courts sometimes overturn such assumptions, as in *Jones,* and declare a contract unenforceable. That they do will little comfort communities unless courts make realistic inquiries about whether the market and the parties are truly free or whether the terms in the contracts are just. Thicker theories of contract law would not rely on the invisible hand of market forces to guide transactions toward the greatest good for the greatest number. Such was the case in *Jones,* where the court employed a thick theory of law and considered how free the contracting parties actually were and which other parties had stakes in the contract.[37]

Thus, major differences between thick and thin theories lie in which aspect of contract law they apply and how they view the circumstances of the contract when it was made. Thin theories tend to accept customary business practices and legal precedents without attending to the conditions under which these practices and precedents were adopted. Thin theories are also reductionistic in that they favor choosing a single consideration, such as freedom from interference, the intention of the parties, fidelity to promises, or efficiency, on which to decide. In addition, thin theories fail to consider how previous allocations of property and power affect current contracts but thick theories make such considerations prominent (Scanlon 1977, 47, 60–62). As a result, thick theories resist serving vested interests better than thin theories.

Thick theories appeal to multiple rules that are stated like moral principles. For example, thick theories of contract law would apply a principle stating that it is not permissible for anyone to break a freely made promise to do something that is morally permissible (Donagan 1977, 92–93). The conditions *freely made* and morally *permissible* indicate grounds for holding some promises morally unjustifiable and therefore not binding. Just as this moral principle sets conditions for keeping promises, thick theories recognize that legal principles should be formulated with qualifiers and applied with discretion.

By presuming that customary contract terms are just, thin theories focus on technical problems in enforcing the contracts, but thick theories of equity jurisprudence critically examine those customs. Although *Black's Law Dictionary* suggests otherwise, business conditions and practices are central issues when contracts are being scrutinized, for a freely given promise may be held invalid if it was made in an unjust business climate (Scanlon 1977, 45–57).

Izhak England's analysis of tort law theory also illuminates some of the differences in contract law theories (1980). England, an Israeli legal scholar, wonders at contemporary theories of United States law, which, compared to traditional and pragmatic theories, are more abstract and formal and purport to make logical, scientific, and apolitical interpretations of tort law.[38] England identifies mythic assumptions modern theorists make, namely, an exalted view of rationality, understood as an abstract, formal science; the notion of humankind as basically economic beings; and an exalted view of reasoning based on results.[39] Because modern theories aim at largely economic goals, they may overlook the political agenda and become accomplices in aggravating unjust distributions (1980, 51).

Richard A. Posner's economic theory of contract law illustrates England's points about tort theory. According to Posner, the logic of the law is economics and humans are merely instrumental forces in the economy. They exist for economic ends and act to maximize their satisfactions (1981, 1–2, 64). By claiming that those intuitions about human nature are normative (ibid., 84), Posner risks basing legal decisions on a dubious practical insight.

As rational persons seek to maximize their own wealth, social institutions should maximize the society's wealth. Individual rights are merely transaction costs as the society maximizes its wealth. The public interest is nothing more than the aggregated interests of groups struggling for power (ibid., 71, 115, 381). Posner would give power only to people able to minimize transaction costs, because, as the early meritarians sought to use the Calvinist virtues of hard work, discipline, and thrift to make economic progress, these people would honestly and diligently maximize the society's wealth (ibid., 67–69, 71, 76). As England observes, Posner's theory depreciates the law's function of upholding the ideals of personal responsibility, communal care, and human compassion, ideals which transcend cost-benefit analyses (England 1980, 50). In addition, Posner's theory fails to reckon with the role of distributive justice in contracts.

The three most common legal misreadings of distributive justice are equating distributive justice with redistribution, confusing it with results, and misunderstanding what is being distributed. The first error pervades legal scholarship, and the second, although found in even the most traditional theories, is even more common in contemporary theories that would have the law take a larger role in distributions. For example, noting that contract law, through warranties on products, legal limits on interest rates, and minimum wage laws, already redistributes wealth, some legal scholars suggest that contract law should be designed to redistribute wealth fairly (Kronman 1980, 473; Kennedy 1976; Michelman 1978; Leff 1967). They equate distributive justice with certain results (Kennedy 1976, 1685, 1776; Michelman 1978, 1015–37 as cited in Kronman 1980, 472, n. 4). As I have argued, results do not represent the whole of distributive justice.

Perhaps the most serious error in legal scholarship is its misunderstanding about what is being distributed. For example, Posner claims that envy, rather than a desire to redress inequities, motivates redistribution and that the principle of maximizing wealth is superior to some other utilitarian principles because it more effectively protects property rights (1981, 80–83). Posner contends that "ethically proper principles by which rights are assigned" (ibid., 65) aim at distributive justice. By *rights* Posner evidently means property rights, but he does not define *ethically proper principles,* and, although he does not describe the wealth-maximization principle as ethically proper, it seems reasonable to infer that he perceives it so. Likewise, Posner accepts the principle that a distribution is just "unless costs equal or exceed benefits" (ibid., 56). Whatever Posner means by ethically proper principles, they would not call for redistributing property or raising aggregate costs, or create the excessive transaction costs that he identified with enforcing the equal-protection clause of the Fourteenth Amendment (ibid., 351–407).

As examples, Posner presents two contracts. In one, *A* sells himself as a slave to *B;* in the other, *C* borrows money from *D* and agrees that *D* may break *C*'s knees if he defaults. Posner, reasoning from the wealth-maximization principle, sees "no economic basis for refusing to enforce either contract unless some element of fraud or duress is present" (ibid., 86). Clearly the wealth-maximization principle cannot provide a solid moral basis for contract law.

More satisfactory is Kronman's argument. After opposing conventional libertarian theories of contracts, such as Robert Nozick's, he argues that "considerations of distributive justice not only *ought* to be taken into account in designing rules for exchange, but *must* be taken into account if the law of contracts is to have even minimum moral acceptability." The "idea of voluntary agreement . . . cannot be understood except as a distributional concept," one that needs guidance to determine which of the many forms of advantage-taking render an agreement involuntary and therefore unenforceable (1980, 473–97, n. 8).[40] Thus, Kronman implicitly acknowledges that the common law should respect the moral values considered in the next section.

Renegotiating the Burdens of Justice in Contract Law

Common law should respect the moral values that seek to protect the human goods of persons and communities and to stringently prohibit harms to these goods. As I argue in the factual, conceptual, and normative inquiries in this chapter, thick theories of contract law and partial-compliance theories of morality better respect these moral values. Now I propose to reinterpret the purposes of contract law by considering its effect on the fundamental human goods of persons and communities. I contend that the burdens are more important than the benefits when deciding whether contracts are just and that prohibiting harm should be the guiding principle in renegotiating those burdens.

Equity jurisprudence better answers empirical, conceptual, and normative questions like: What is being allocated in a contract? By which of the contracting parties? Under what terms? Equity jurisprudence also better addresses these related moral questions: When is a contract morally unjustifiable? Who is responsible for correcting it? What moral principles should guide these persons to approximate justice? (Smurl 1985, 1.12, 1.14).

Partial-compliance theories of law and morality recognize that social conditions shape current business conditions and practices and that, if they become incorporated into legislation and judicial decisions, they will continue to shape future conditions. Thus these models encourage better factual inquiries. Similarly, thick theories of contract law are better at conceptual inquiries because they recognize that legal concepts may entail political endorsements of past injustices. Thick theories are more likely to lead to inquiries regarding morally justifiable norms. However, most contemporary thick theories flounder when they equate distributive justice with remedial justice, confuse it with results, or misunderstand what is being distributed. Therefore their inquiries do not always lead to good criteria for allocations.

Achieving distributive justice requires more than thick theories of law or partial-compliance models of morality. It must take into account persons' human goods and the common good of the community and it must accept the principle of no-harm as controlling when justice can only be approximated.

Douglas Sturm puts it this way:

> Meanings of justice vary. But whether justice is understood as promoting liberty, equality, or mutuality, it signifies respect for the dignity of human life. It is a judgment against offensive bargaining [that is, bargaining with uneven advantages]. It is a declaration that some forms of compromise are intolerable. It is a directive that each and every person should be granted those rights and resources needed for full membership in the nation.

> Justice within the context of modern industrial society
> mandates a form of "affirmative constitutionalism" for all
> large organizational structures, political and economic.
> As Carl Friedrich, an American political scientist, has
> rightly argued, the roots of Western constitutionalism
> have their beginnings in the Judaic-Christian idea of tran-
> scendent justice. . . . [Thus] justice, as a distributive
> principle, is only one side of a public ethic. The other
> side is a holistic principle: the common good . . . the
> good of the whole (Sturm 1984, 23).

The chief moral considerations in contract law are how persons and communities and their fundamental human goods
will be affected. Ronald Dworkin (1986) proposes that a community should treat all its members in a principled and
coherent manner. That takes persons seriously enough but
does not also state that the principles employed must protect
the fundamental goods of persons and communities. Neither
does Dworkin's proposal identify which goods are most critical
for persons and communities. However, Dworkin's proposal
represents a substantial improvement over those that hold
that, to be objective, jurisprudence must set aside ethical and
political considerations.

Because thin theories of jurisprudence assume that the distributions contracts make are generally just, they implicitly
support my proposals and thus paradoxically demonstrate that
achieving a just distribution outweighs enforcing the contract.[41] Thick theories of jurisprudence, because they cannot
avoid asking whether a particular contract is just, whether the
parties behaved justly, or whether one party enjoyed an unfair
advantage, also demonstrate that ethical and political considerations cannot be entirely set aside.[42] More importantly, thick
theories show why the apportioning of advantages and disadvantages in contracts is more decisive and outweighs considerations of the parties' freedom from interference.

It is not reductionist or consequentialist to claim that distributive justice is the decisive value. It does not seek to
subsume contractual justice under distributive justice, nor to
focus solely on the effects of a contract.[43] Rather, distributive
justice in contracts is far more fundamental than contractual

justice, which works only when institutions and practices are distributively just.[44]

Formal, procedural, and mechanistic methods of legal reasoning cannot assure that parties will contract in a fair environment, especially if that environment is harmful to fundamental human goods of existence or developed existence. Under such circumstances, parties are not effectively free. Until theories recognize that creating a just marketplace is part of the purpose of contract law, we can reasonably expect damage to fundamental human goods. To avoid such harms, jurisprudence must help provide equal opportunity and effective freedom to achieve a developed existence. Lawyers, judges, and legal administrators, ostensibly committed by their licenses to a just and free society, must express that commitment in their activities in contract law.

In a just society, which protects at least fundamental human goods, contract law must do the same by respecting moral principles as much as formal legal rules. The controlling principles are that advantages and disadvantages must be justly apportioned, respecting peoples' differences in capacity and status. This principle must accompany the principle of equal opportunity, because long-standing privileges and inequalities in a community may preclude equal opportunity.[45]

In contrast to our cultural emphasis on benefits, achieving justice requires a new emphasis on how a contract or social arrangement allocates harms and costs. The stringent moral obligation against harming persons must be respected. If contracts harm persons' fundamental human goods or harm persons beyond their ability to sustain the harm or recover from it, or if these harms are passed along to new generations like a cultural inheritance, then the harms contracts create are intolerable and morally outrageous.[46] It would be unreasonable to hold contract law and its practitioners accountable for long-standing contract practices that harm persons but it is not unreasonable to hold them accountable for statutes, judicial decisions, and legal training that perpetuate those practices.

Distributive justice does not always call for specific allocations of basic human goods, commodities, or political power, but rather for fact-finding about how legal systems and entrenched practices distribute social and cultural goods, costs, and harms to persons and communities.[47] Whenever it is established that present allocations are working harms to fundamental goods of persons and communities or that present allocations stand to work systematic harms for generations, then a community needs to reconfigure these allotments to distribute their burdens more justly.

Conclusion

The franchise and sales contracts discussed in this chapter illustrate that fact-finding and renegotiation are warranted. They demonstrate how laws, morality, religion, and politics interact in a legal system. They highlight two points not adequately expressed by the doctrine of freedom of contract. First, by drawing attention to the conditions for bargaining, they reveal the interactions of law and morality. (This interaction is not recognized by those who perceive morality as subjective and law as objective, who perceive praise and blame as the whole of morality, or who believe that legal reasoning admits only formal interpretations.) Second, these contracts demonstrate that justice (both in the promise and in distribution) is more pertinent than freedom from interference. Finally, they point out the error of confusing distributive justice with consequences or with redistribution.[48]

Legislators, judges, lawyers, and educators of lawyers urgently need to rethink distributive justice as a moral and legal standard. These persons must understand human goods and harms and employ correctly formulated moral principles. Their legal education should be informed by appropriate cultural notions and should cultivate moral character. Lawyers are human beings formed by legal beliefs, evaluations, and loyalties who apply legal reasoning. They cannot reasonably disclaim responsibility for deleterious, if unintended, social and cultural consequences of legal actions rooted in those convictions and commitments. Yet it seems that the professional education lawyers receive advises them that ethical and political values are unrelated to jurisprudence. Thus, more adequate notions of liberty and justice need to be established in legal educations and in the legal culture fostered by professional associations. Legal professionals need to acknowledge that "communal commitment and individual fulfillment rise or fall together" (Fox 1987, 10) and that freedom brings responsibility. Only those practiced in the law can implement the concept that the human and social burdens assigned by the law are linked to social, cultural, and political conditions. As these conditions often require substantial reworking, so does the legal culture that both mirrors and shapes them.

Conclusion

As the United States' influence in world affairs diminishes and the postwar economic boom fades, our dominant social groups may seek their own interest under the guise of social stability, prosperity, or security. "Philosophic liberalism, for all its rhetoric of freedom, provides few resources for avoiding such an outcome . . . [giving] urgency to the conceptual and philosophic task of formulating a genuine public philosophy that can provide a reasoned basis for a new ethic of equity and cooperation" (Sullivan 1986, xiii).

The United States is undergoing a profound cultural, political, and social transformation, marked by social distrust and widespread disagreement about public values. Will the country attempt to revive outmoded ideas of the public good? The question is not so much whether we are on the verge of a new world as whether we have the courage to face the future. Public dialog about a just distribution of the social goods associated with achieving fundamental human goods can ensure that our future understanding of the common good will be more adequate than our present understanding. Throughout this book I have suggested how ethicists might help people lacking a common vision articulate their cultural notions and concepts and understand principles of justice. I have sought to focus on how communities can harm people by the ways they distribute urgent human goods in families, public education, health care, and contract law.

The chief good of a community is distributive justice. How the harms are apportioned is the decisive gauge of how the community distributes justice. In four areas of human goods, I have examined how the harms and costs are distributed and have suggested some policies. However, I have made more suggestions about the means to sustain public dialog by recommending topics and approaches, and especially by encouraging ethicists in the debate to be self-critical. Throughout, I have contended that all parties should be attentive, perceptive, intelligent, reasonable, and responsible.

The introduction suggests examining cultural concepts of distributive justice in the United States in the late nineteenth and late twentieth century to help us think clearly about contemporary concepts. Scholars should acknowledge being influenced by earlier notions and accept responsibility for forming present and future ones. Later chapters investigate the foundations for what people say is morally right or wrong in the allocation of four kinds of social goods.

When claims about distributive justice do not consider all the pertinent data, they rely on practical insights that are not attentive, perceptive, and intelligent. By comparison, our empirical inquiries uncovered more complete data about public financing for education, basic health care, and the social contexts of franchise and adhesion contracts. A thoroughgoing empirical inquiry attends to substantive as well as procedural issues and rejects reductionist views. The tripodal character of justice focuses attention on the moral state of situations as well as that of persons and principles and shows why improving the virtue of persons, the reasonableness of principles, and the justice of social relationships go together.

After empirical inquiries, conceptual inquiries should ask what justice in social relationships means. When we reflect on our cultural notions, the foundation of our concepts, we may discover some mistaken definitions, such as the negative concept of liberty or the numerical concept of equality. Other examples are restricting the meaning of health care to what is merely medical care, perceiving only the material obligations of one generation to another and emphasizing promise keeping over the bargaining power of contracting parties.

Another common notion that cries out to be tested for reasonableness is that of neighbor and stranger.[1] In the discussion of public education I remarked that, although public school children are vulnerable to us all, they are regarded as strangers who have no claim on us because they are not our own. This is to say that, if charity begins at home, justice too may begin and end there. If such a concept governs the relationship between persons and social goods, it must be found reasonable upon reflection. When ethicists scrutinize such concepts, they, to be reasonable and responsible, must examine the mixture of rational and nonrational cultural notions that justify misleading moral principles, some of which may prove indefensible. They must be mindful that a culture's prevalent understandings of social goods develop as their history unfolds and are rooted in cherished traditions and political interests.

Reflecting on moral principles such as beneficence, avoiding harm, or contractual justice must include questioning the norms, beginning with determining whether they are general and impartial. Moral standards are more general and impartial than legal or customary ones, but probing them requires probing the concepts they employ. For example, the principle that human rights should be respected must be scrutinized in terms of the concepts of these rights. Inquiries into norms test for the reasonableness of their foundations and the reasonableness of the actions they direct. They also evaluate moral principles to decide which should override others when not all can be observed. For example, I explain why principles of justice that apply to contracts represent only one form of distributive justice and should not be the overriding ones. Justice in allocating social goods is not merely a matter of fair dealing in selling and acquiring property and the worry that these ideas will call for forcibly redistributing social goods. More important is how an allocation promotes or damages persons' fundamental human goods. That is why I have related justice, beneficence, and nonmaleficence to normative inquiries and contended that the principles of fundamental harm, disproportionate harm, and systemic harm should determine the moral justifiability of most allocations. Justice is tripodal; it considers the authenticity and consistency of persons; the moral qualities of situations, such as social, work, and family situations; and the reasonableness of statements of moral principles and how they are applied.

Scholars and policymakers cannot make critical inquiries unless they are self-critical. The scholarly stance recommended in the introduction requires that, while remaining empathetic, one keep loyalty to one's cultural tradition at arm's length. To be consistent and responsible and to assure that public debate is authentic and appropriate, both the scholars and those to whom they address their findings must embrace justice and prudence, and recognize that the good of others and their own good lie in the same place.

Making empirical, conceptual, and normative inquiries helps one develop prudence in reasoning, but improving one's awareness of the metaphors that scholars and others live by is more effective. Moral concepts are like second-order metaphors, but are even further removed from people's personal experiences because they are built on cultural notions. In her account of Friedrich Nietzsche's theory of metaphor and the genealogy of morals, Sarah Kofman says:

> Beginning with *The Birth of Tragedy,* then, Nietzsche's generalized theory of metaphor rests on the loss of the self. . . . There is no metaphor without the stripping away of individuality, without masquerade, without metamorphosis. . . . One must be able to transpose oneself, to have conquered the limits of individuality; the same must partake of the other, it must become the other. . . . Metaphor is founded on the ontological unity of life . . . [which] is already parceled out and can only be reconstituted through . . . art [without which there can be no metaphor at all] (1977, 206).

To transcend one's metaphors, one must recognize that they inform both one's morals and one's intellectual habits and that they govern one's actions by tacitly approving some behaviors and prohibiting others, as Lakoff and Johnson have argued (1980). Some troublesome metaphors are embedded in our concepts of family and relations between generations; liberty and equality; the acquisition, transfer, and redistribution of property; neighbor and stranger; health; power; education, and taxation. Uncovering the meaning of these metaphors, transforming oneself, and becoming one with others in the unity of life can be a burden, part of the personal and social conversion that we undertake for the sake of liberating our consciousness, all of which renegotiation presumes. Scholars bear part of this burden because their metaphors influence, for example, what approach they choose for an inquiry and the habits of reasoning they employ during renegotiations.

Renegotiating the public covenant also demands social trust, the willingness of persons to share the burdens of the common good rather than to shift them onto others in harmful ways. Social trust largely depends on whether people have equal opportunity in, for example, education and the legal system and on whether people perceive that fundamentally unequal conditions are being rectified. Since Tocqueville's time, equality of conditions has been recognized as critical to democracy in the United States (Sullivan 1986, 210–14, 222–23).

When opportunities for upward mobility decrease, people become disillusioned. Without social trust, renegotiating the burdens of justice may be thwarted by powerful special interests. Encouraging social cooperation and improving opportunities for all persons to participate in the renegotiations may require, as William Sullivan has argued, a new understanding of freedom (ibid.). Lest one become too sanguine about transforming the social notion of freedom, one should remember that at best it can only approximate the goal. As John G. Bennett counsels,

> it is not difficult to describe ideal institutions for ideal people, but the more useful task is to describe good institutions for people as they are, or as they might reasonably be expected to become (1985, 203).

Similarly, Michael Walzer advises that social critics construct "stories about a society more just than, though never entirely different from, our own" (1987, 65). Bennett and Walzer seem more prudent than Amy Gutmann, who contends that communitarian critics of liberalism

> avoid discussing how morally to resolve our conflicts and therefore fail to provide us with a political theory relevant to our world. They also may overlook the extent to which some of their own moral commitments presuppose the defense of liberal rights [and] tend to look toward the future with nostalgia. We would be better off, by both Aristotelian and liberal democratic standards, if we tried

to shape it according to our present moral understandings (1985, 319–22).

As I seek to demonstrate throughout this book, if present moral understandings are mistaken, then we would be ill-advised to follow them in allocating society's benefits and burdens in the future. Better advice recommends finding an adequate account of distributive justice that addresses not only the cause of injustice but what a just society would be. We will take actions of one sort if our aim is to harmonize relationships among imperfect or contentious persons. We will take actions of a distinctly different sort if we seek to prevent some groups of persons from shifting their burdens onto other groups. To make lasting corrections, we must count on people's willingness to revise their moral concepts, judgments, and decisions, as well as their actions and the situations in which they encounter each other. However we encounter each other, we always encounter one another's moral understandings about allocating social goods. Distributive justice aims to design and maintain more common understandings of just workplaces, families, school systems, tax structures, legal theories, contracts, and health care systems, and to promote justice in the people who encounter each other in these systems.

The ideal of justice will differ in each sphere, for example, in education and in legal systems. Moreover, the ideal can be only approximated. Even so, all allocations of social goods achieved by public renegotiations and individual revision of moral concepts, judgments, and decisions will be more enduring than those achieved by coerced or voluntary redistributions of property. Attending to justice in persons, their principles, and their situations will, as I have argued, require a critique of the cultural notions and practices that people follow in distributing the benefits and burdens of common life in more just and less harmful ways.

Notes

Introduction

1. See Hume's essay "The Dignity and Meanness of Man." Hume's influence on Madison is demonstrated by Ketcham (1958) and by Lovejoy (1961).

2. Contemporaries like Tom Beauchamp and James Childress adopt Joel Feinberg's identification of distributive concerns with economic issues (1973, 107) and his understanding of distributive justice as fundamentally comparative (1979, 169–70).

3. Hume and Smith substituted "progress" for "divine providence," while George argued that God is not to blame for the social ills humans bring upon themselves but that individuals need to acknowledge and act upon the rules governing fairness in the acquisition and transfer of holdings. Some say George is a typical United States evangelical, a freewheeling, nondenominational, self-taught, and highly individualistic social reformer, the likes of which John Dewey found admirable (Geiger 1933 [Dewey's introduction]; see also Lawson-Peebles 1976; Faulkner 1931, 81).

4. Anticipating Nozick's position, the physician Robert M. Sade pointed out that if physicians' services were entitlements, then, like bakers' bread, they could be stolen from their owner (1971). Nozick argued that whatever the market will bear in earnings for a basketball star like Wilt Chamberlain, however disproportionate to ordinary wages, is the star's legitimate holding and ought not be taken from him and redistributed, say, by taxation (1974, 161–63).

5. For the view that political philosophizing has usually been undertaken in response to particular political events, especially threats and challenges, see Peter Laslett's "History of Political Philosophy"

in the *Encyclopedia of Philosophy* (1972, vol. 6, 370). For the view that systematic theological work on political justice has been equally "intermittent," see Walzer (1987, 86).

6. These narratives both reflect and shape cultural beliefs more than do more reflective and formalized rules and principles. The religious impulses, as expressed in ritual and music, paintings, and other depictions in art and literature also shape cultural beliefs (Ignatieff 1986, 135–42).

7. For example, Ryan distinguished between legal and moral, presumptive and strict titles to earnings, property, and other holdings. He claimed that the basis for distinguishing between different kinds of moral titles rested upon the different sorts of efforts and contributions people put forth as well as upon the different kinds of rights claimed on the basis of need or desert. Using traditional and comparative moral criteria for discriminating between claims (titles) based on merits, equality, and needs, he argued the priority of needs in some categories (wages) and the superiority of claims about deserts or merits in others (profits and rents). He offered reasons why and how one set of claims ought to override others in certain situations (1916).

8. The dialectical opposition between theories based on the right or human rights and those based on the good or human goods is characteristic of the differences between liberals or libertarians and communitarians in social philosophy (Gutmann 1985, 308).

9. In her account of this correlation between love and justice, Lebacqz draws upon theologian Emil Brunner's understanding of the phrase "to do justice is to know God" (1986, 105, 106).

10. One should note that the concept of justice as equal opportunity is, finally, more procedural than substantive. While it may be less results-oriented than positions that regard justice as a mere technique, it is still imperfect with respect to the substance of rightly ordered situations, persons, and actions. By holding that equal opportunity is the opportunity of citizens to compete in economic society, it seems not substantially different from other procedural conceptions of justice (Bellah 1985, 264).

11. Those espousing the liberal welfare position have had to become more concerned with a fair sharing of burdens and sacrifices,

but even writers who make this point still define distributive justice, as does Bellah in his glossary, as "a matter of the fairness of the society's system of rewards, of its distribution of goods and opportunities," without mentioning fair allocations of disadvantages, burdens, and harms (1985, 265, 334). It would seem that all such positions are like almsgiving: distributive justice is a good, old-fashioned form of benevolence, even when administered by bureaucratic governments.

12. Note also that Rawls's theory seems to require an equally strong state, as compared with Nozick's call for a minimal state. However, those who emphasize charity rather than justice count too heavily on the compassion of one individual for another, a moral strength not commonly found (Bellah 1985, 265).

13. For the origins of the term *gospel of wealth,* see Russell H. Conwell's *Acres of Diamonds* (1915), which influenced Andrew Carnegie and other philanthropists.

14. This tradition is represented also in the movement for voluntary legal aid services promoted by its founder, Reginald Heber Smith, in the first part of this century. However, as envisioned in the Legal Services Corporation and in the experiments with neighborhood law offices in the last few decades (Smurl 1978) legal aid is a matter of justice and entitlement. This tradition accords with the rise of hospitals but not with neighborhood health centers (Stevens 1989). Bellah's confidence in social movements shows the appeal of voluntarism (1985, 212ff., 240–43, 249). In addition, both communitarian altruism and the mediating structures created by voluntary associations can become tyrannical if political practices and structures do not restrain less altruistic tendencies (Gutmann 1985, 319, 321).

15. Some earlier forms of these positions were more communitarian than some present forms. For example, Andrew Carnegie and Harry Lee Higginson of Boston were persuaded that property was essentially communitarian and that the holders of property had responsibilities to use it for the benefit of the community as a whole (Bellah 1985, 260, 264, 289–90). Contemporary forms seem far less communitarian, especially in their conviction that the private sector is best suited to do what the older philanthropists and governments used to do. These positions are less in agreement with voluntary and philanthropic associations

and more in agreement with for-profit corporations and private worlds of professionals, the companionship of "the competent," and a society administered by gifted, expert elites (Haskell 1977).

16. In fairness to Rawls, however, one should note his interest in the comparative study of well-ordered societies. The moral conceptions needed in such societies must meet five requirements: generality, universality, ordering, finality, and publicity (Rawls 1975, 10–11; see also 1971, 130–36). The latter requirement in particular seems to be an especially strong condition in Rawls's argument. It requires that political principles acknowledge that legal power has shaped the character and aims of the members of society. Political principles must include a culture's moral principles for relationships between persons (1975, 12). Thus, moral arguments in such societies must appeal publicly accepted forms of social cooperation (ibid., 13). To that degree, then, Rawls's *publicity* strongly resembles Walzer's concept of shared understandings.

17. Brian Barry (1973) has made comparable points, but Galston's point that different bases for claims about distributive justice (such as need, desert, and freedom) are required by different kinds of human and social goods is an important supplement (1986).

18. Walzer, like Galston (see note 17 above), makes a case that multiple criteria of distributive justice are required but, in Walzer's account, they are to accommodate a people's shared concept of the nature of different social goods. He argues that, since people understand some goods as basic securities, the criterion for distributing them should be need, but since people understand some other social goods as luxuries, the criterion should be freedom (1983).

19. Similar points are made about just structures in David Miller's *Social Justice* (1976). Note, however, Lebacqz's awareness of the potential for institutional and coercive violence in all social systems, including the capitalist system (1986, 105).

20. Notable among the influential figures in this period of time have been most especially my colleagues in the department of religious studies, but also some important colleagues in the schools of law, medicine, and nursing.

Chapter 1

1. Adherents to David Hume's view of social justice regularly overlook this point (Galston 1980, 112–13, 115).

2. Some of our deepest and most important obligations are involuntary, as in families. They are less like the consensual relationships created by promises and contracts (which can entail limited commitments) and more like the membership relationships in families and communities in which people become vulnerable to each other because they depend or rely upon each other (Selznick 1987, 36–38; Goodin 1985).

3. Valid claims can be cleverly averted (Galston 1980, 5, 102, 105, 109–10).

4. These paradigms may be beyond cognition in that they go directly from insight to decision, action, and life-stance, while bypassing reflective and self-critical judgments. But, as noted later in this chapter, they should not be spared the latter kinds of scrutiny.

5. See James Sellers's account of the capacity media coverage has to underscore experiences that hurt, cause psychic loss, sap resolve, and undermine hope. These, he explains, are akin to the symbolic, ritual, and defensive measures people take against crises. Sellers cites the popularity of stringent gun control measures following the deaths of Martin Luther King, Jr., and John and Robert Kennedy (1970, 16, 17). Similarly, Gandhi, Nehru, and King believed suffering creates character and keeps revolution within moral bounds, thus engendering leniency in those required by law to administer the sufferings.

6. Among other schemes, narratives can be classified according to whether they promote social trust and cooperation, whether they are based on duties, rights, or results. Narratives that treat social trust may emphasize *praxis* or *technis*. According to Bellah et al., only the former help us understand that "shared activities . . . [should] not [be] undertaken as means to an end but . . . [rather because they are] ethically good in themselves . . . [thus] close to *praxis* in Aristotle's sense. . . ." Only the latter practices give rise to the habits of heart that keep communities together (1985, 335).

7. Some nationalistic stories may create problems (Elshtain 1986). Reinhold Niebuhr made similar warnings in the first half of this century .

8. See especially the essay "A Kantian Conception of Equality" (Rawls 1975; see also 1971, 504–12).

9. Such beliefs seem to animate the irrational and anti-intellectual frame of mind in theological ethics in the United States over the last decade or so.

10. This caution should be applied to recommendations made by Bellah (1975, 1985), MacIntyre (1981), and others.

11. This section draws upon the ideas of Clifford Geertz (1983, 161), Jürgen Habermas (1984), and David Tracy (1986).

12. See Lonergan about civilizational decline because of community conflict (1958, 619–22, 627; 1972, 52–55, 121–22, 240). For its application to religious communities, see Lonergan (1958, 729–30), and H. Richard Niebuhr's analysis of the cultural, economic, political, and social factors that restrict the freedom of religious communities (1975, 108–11). For the civil realm, see Bellah (1985), Dewey (1954, 1971), and Lovin (1986, 7–28). For an explanation of how what Niebuhr calls bourgeois individualism becomes bootstrap entrepreneurialism and status politics in some religions in the United States, see Liebman, Simpson, and Heinz (Liebman and Wuthnow 1983, 66, 68, 187–205, 133–48).

13. A theory of justice cannot stand independently of a theory of morality and a theory of morality must clearly identify its basis (duties, results, or rights, for example) and recognize the relation between the bases (as when rights make little or no sense apart from duties and obligations). Furthermore, moral principles (and principles of justice) are generally more reliable than are moral rules if they are stated in ways that make them universally true for humans. Finally, a theory of morality, like a theory of justice, must address three issues: why one ought to be moral (or just) and what characterizes moral persons, how to determine what is morally right or wrong (just or unjust), and how to evaluate the justice of situations and institutions.

14. MacIntyre alludes to disputed interpretations of desert but gives no clear definition. He contends that his concept of desert is dis-

tinguishable from Nozick's concept of entitlements, but contributions to community tasks could generate entitlements of several kinds. MacIntyre's point appears to be ideological, for his notion of desert defines one's interests in terms of one's community. MacIntyre is in accord with older Aristotelian traditions that should be revived (1981, 232–34). The meritarian concepts of Nozick and Rawls are equally ideological. They attempt to unite societies to make rules but neglect the historical influences.

15. Surprisingly, although the premises of position *A* and position *B* are not well demonstrated, MacIntyre does not challenge them, and chooses instead to emphasize the "internal coherence" of the positions (1981, 230–31, 236). One reason is that there well may be more consensus about first principles than about the secondary or derived principles that MacIntyre emphasizes to make his point about unalterable conflict. The other is Haskell's contention that professionals may become blind to matters that are clear to others (1977).

16. Nozick finds nothing to justify the involuntary transfer of justly acquired property, not even for the sake of preserving a human life (1974, 179, 238).

17. Lonergan interprets contemplated courses of action, motives, and obligations in the light of consistency between knowing and doing. In his account, objects of desire and aversion are the ethical counterparts of metaphysical potency. Practical insights give the form, and values, the objects of choice, represent the metaphysical act (1958, 605, 610–11, 614). James Sellers makes a similar point about responsible decision-making and action when he says that authenticity—in revolutionaries, for example—is critically important (1970, 257).

18. The tripodal theory stems from the link between the character of social situations and the virtue of persons in the society, including their standards and their habits (Lebacqz 1985, 152ff.). Thus, this theory is considerably more circumspect than theories that overemphasize habits and neglect the situations in which people live and the principles that guide their actions.

19. This line of reasoning builds on Aristotle's *Nicomachean Ethics* (4, 44), and on contemporary neo-Aristotelian interpretations by Troels Engberg-Pedersen (1983, 44, 47–48) and H. H. Joachim (1962). For a fuller discussion of disinterestedness and its

egocentric contraries, see Pieper (1965, 19–22) and MacIntyre (1981, 175–189). Related habits in social communications are discussed by Habermas (1984, 311, 325–6, 334, 336).

20. This position builds on Aristotle (*Politics* 1, 2, 1253a—18), and on more recent work by Engberg-Pedersen (1983, 53–62), Josef Pieper (1965, 17–21, 66, 68), and William Galston (1980, 101).

    In the *Nicomachean Ethics,* Aristotle calls justice a form of complete excellence, more wonderful than even the morning and the evening stars "because he who possesses it can exercise his excellence toward others too and not merely by himself" and because "the best man is not he who exercises his excellence towards himself but he who exercises it towards another." Justice and excellence are the same because "justice is, as a certain kind of state without qualification, excellence" (5, 1, 1129b30—1130a13; Barnes trans. 1984a: 1783). I contend that Aristotle implies that the personal rectitude or integrity we call justice incorporates social responsibilities to qualify as the full excellence of justice. In short, "the rule will show the man" (*Nicomachean Ethics* 5, 1, 1130a1) or, in Joachim's rendering, "office will find the man out" (1962, 131; see also Engberg-Pedersen 1983, 56).

    I argue that Aristotle is doing more than merely affirming the unity of the virtues (MacIntyre 1981, 166–68; Meilander 1983, 117 and 1984, 20). Rather, his point is that justice is the only virtue (Engberg-Pedersen 1983, 53–62). Of all reciprocals of prudence, justice is preeminent in social as well as personal conduct for the reasons given by Galston; namely, that justice, unlike other virtues, is essentially comparative; it orders the relations of other individuals as well as of one's self to the same objects (1980, 100–101).

21. Lonergan argues that the time required for reflection is a function of several factors, such as the character of the choices and the motives and habits of the chooser (1958, 610–11). He applies this argument to speakers, narrators, communicators, and political persuaders (ibid., 532–43), but not as fully as does Jürgen Habermas (1984).

22. Root paradigms that prompt us to view contractual justice as distinct from distributive justice or to consider contractual justice as the principal form of justice should be revised. Contrary to Nozick's entitlement theory, contractual justice is not really dis-

tinct from distributive justice but rather is a form of distributive justice in which the allotment of harms is decisive. See also chapter 5.

23. To paraphrase Lonergan, neither good will nor bad will is either better or worse than the intelligence and reasonableness it activates (1958, 629). Or, as R. G. Collingwood once observed, false consciousness rather than bad will is the real *radix malorum* (1938).

24. This account builds upon one by Bernard Lonergan (1958, 612–16).

25. This is a variation on Bernard Lonergan's thirty-one-point sketch of a solution to the problem of liberating rational consciousness from the problem of evil and enlarging effective freedom (1958, 696–726).

26. Other helpful classics can be found in the writings of Thomas Jefferson, James Madison, and Abraham Lincoln as well as in the Puritan-style public conversations carried on since John Winthrop by Ralph Waldo Emerson, William James, John Dewey, and Josiah Royce (see Bellah et al. 1985; Tracy 1986, 127–28). David Tracy cites the recent United States classics that arose from the experiences of Blacks, Catholics, feminists, Jews, Native Americans, and people south of the Mason-Dixon line (ibid., 128).

Chapter 2

1. In their recent social history of family life in the United States, Mintz and Kellogg offer further support for this finding. They argue that since the Puritans wrung their hands over changes in family life, the agonizing continues but the family as an institution has demonstrated stubborn persistence. While recognizing that families have changed and while acknowledging that, for the future, they will be small, not extended, families, characterized by late marriages and low birthrates, Mintz and Kellogg do not expect the family to change substantially (1988).

2. Most commentators on the family note that some social goods are specific to families, such as kinship, affection, parental concern, and filial respect (Walzer 1983, 227ff.). But families also generate social goods that are economic and educational, as well

as religious and cultural. Indeed, within the more private cultural and social life of the family one finds the entire range of social goods William Galston lists as candidates for invoking distributive justice. That list includes opportunities for development, economic goods, political goods like membership and citizenship and full protection of the laws, policymaking leadership in formulating, justifying, and executing community policies, and public honors like praise and recognition based on excellence and actions of behalf of the community (1980, 195–275).

3. At one end of the spectrum, we find what until recently were conventional definitions of the family as either a group of persons of common ancestry, a group of individuals living under one roof and under one head, or a social group composed of parents and their children. At the other end we find definitions that tell us that a family is "a community composed of a child and one or more adults in a close affective and physical relation which is expected to endure at least through childhood" (Fishkin 1983, 36). The adults need not be of opposite sex, in Fishkin's view, and above all must have a consensual and autonomous relationship, that is, free from state interference in raising their children (ibid., 36-38).

   Fishkin's definition, like so many others recently, emphasizes the autonomy of the family. His definition becomes a necessary premise in his argument for the primacy of negative liberty (that is, freedom from interference). It is "directed at cases where the state might wish to interfere in a family that preserves consensual relations—[that is] where there is not sustained and intense disagreement about its basic terms of cooperation . . . [thereby providing] parents considerable latitude in influencing the development of their children, in a manner preserving consensus within the family, as long as provision of the essential prerequisites for adult participation in the society were not endangered" (1983, 37).

4. This premise is all the more puzzling because Walzer presents points that are relevant to distributive issues in families but fails to mention them in the chapter on the family. See his discussion of hard work (1983, 173–75, 177, 179, 240). Furthermore, his list of the four requirements of distributive justice seems eminently pertinent to family life: a shared infrastructure, communal provision, equality of opportunity, and strong democracy (including resistance to being dominated by other spheres of social goods) (ibid., 240–41).

5. For a nuanced discussion of reproductive and genetic responsibilities toward prospective children and to others in the community, in other words, the burdens of procreation, see Bayles's *Reproductive Ethics* (1984, 93, 97–98, 99, 110, 128). Bruce Ackerman presents similar points in terms of birthrights but relies heavily on both a liberal theory of consensual or contractual agreements as the basis for such responsibilities and on the premise that these obligations occur in the context of a struggle for power (1980, 107ff., 201–11).

6. The recent contention that marriage is becoming less central in women's lives (at least in certain socioeconomic classes) is also worth investigating. With the passing of former divisions of labor, many of the advantages of marriage may have begun to disappear for women. As a consequence, some contend that contemporary women may come to rely more on other women for friendship and continue to be disappointed in men's ability to communicate.

7. Children seem invisible in conventional political analyses of the family, but Elshtain argues that children are the central consideration in a political theory of the family (1982, 29, 288).

8. According to Elshtain, at least three types of ideology can be instruments of oppression (1982, 297–300), as when shifts in the understanding shared by members of important social movements can make the members unwittingly oppressive. For a recent example from the feminist movement, consider the following:

> [The earlier feminists'] understanding of the role that socialization, economics and politics played in the oppression of women, in fact, tempered their anger against men with considerable sympathy. Feminists argued that men paid a high price for their dominant position. They forfeited their ability to lead a life that can bring both personal and professional fulfillment. . . . This means that men, as well as women, should share domestic tasks, explore and express both the so-called feminine and masculine sides of the human personality and raise children to do the same. Feminism's promise, then, was a life that balanced love, friendship and work for both sexes.

Unfortunately, almost as soon as feminism began to make some progress, its edge was dulled. What happened, not surprisingly in a consumer-oriented society, was that mainstream America quickly turned a powerful social movement into a vast and lucrative new market . . . [for] clothes, magazines . . . (Gordon 1987, A18).

Krouse makes similar points (1982, 171).

9. One of the unintended consequences of no-fault divorce is that courts consider a man's career assets *his* (even though they may be the product of efforts by both spouses). For this and other unintended consequences of no-fault divorce, see Lenore Weitzman (1985, xv, xvi, 368, 374–76).

10. Syphilis and gonorrhea and, more recently, chlamydia and AIDS are examples of such diseases.

11. A related point could be made about the personal and systemic harms associated with contemporary mortgages and consumer debt. If couples adopt contemporary views of the good life uncritically, they may take on fiscal burdens beyond their means.

12. See also the thoughtful, and sometimes prescient, analyses of Sen. Daniel Patrick Moynihan (1965, 1986).

13. Equally valid inquiries include obligations to past generations, such as the preservation of cultural traditions, expiation for past injustices (wrought by, say, the Holocaust, slavery, sexual discrimination, and the like). Obligations to future generations also merit attention, such as the preservation of our physical, social, and cultural environments. Because of the legacy of genetic defects and nuclear threats, contemporary generations may make existence itself or developed existence impossible for future generations.

   Mary Ann Warren contends that "the source of our moral obligations to future generations is the simple fact that we are in a position to materially affect their well-being." Thus, "the question of moral responsibility [like the moral responsibility for culpably causing foreseeable death or injury] turns on the predictability (and avoidability) of the fatal result, not on when, where or to whom it occurs. Anyone who acts in the knowledge that someday some innocent person or persons will probably be severely and unnecessarily harmed as a result of that action may be held to be morally responsible for those harms" (1982, 148, 165). For comparable arguments, see Barry (1977).

14. The emphasis on proximate generations encouraged by Moody (1985) and Barry (1978) does not ignore related and important responsibilities between the living and those who have died or may be born, and does not intend to downplay responsibilities between contemporaries, such as between rich and poor or between the sexes within the same generation. Attention to the latter is especially important because 70% of the elderly poor are female (Hayes 1986, 4).

15. Studies that echo this emphasis include Callahan (1987), Greenhouse (1986), and Longman (1987). The declining incomes of younger families over the last twenty years is even more serious because young families with children, poor families, and younger women who are heads of households have experienced sharper declines than have other young families (Danzinger and Gottschalk 1986).

16. Mary Ann Glendon argues that while employment relationships became more stable, marital relationships became less so. Work, rather than family, and career assets, rather than property, are now the principal sources of social standing and security (1981).

17. For example, in Bexar County, Texas (which includes San Antonio), up to $60,000 of the appraised value of property owned by persons over age 65 is tax-exempt. Because of its climate, ambience, cost of living, and medical centers—especially major military hospitals which attract the country's third-largest retired military population—the county has a large population of retired persons. However, the population of Bexar County overall is 60% minority and the county has little industry. Because much of the property of Bexar County is excluded from its tax base, local school districts have severe financial liabilities. See the next chapter for more on this point.

18. Not only is tax revenue lost because persons over age fifty-five are exempt from capital gains tax on the sale of their homes (Longman 1985). Younger citizens also pay disproportionately larger social security taxes (Moody 1985, 3).

19. These emphases mirror those suggested by Callahan (1987) and Moody (1985), who are more circumspect in their analyses of generational issues.

20. This seems to be the concept behind not only some versions of affirmative action and comparable pay but also, with some untoward consequences, behind no-fault divorce. Weitzman finds some are convinced that equality can be created through legislation but they also rely on erroneous beliefs about sexual equality in marriages and ignore the disproportionate opportunities marriage creates (1985, xi, 364, 365).

21. Requiring persons who apply for social security benefits to demonstrate need and taxing the benefits of higher-income recipients has been suggested to achieve equity between generations. Furthermore, though there are some significant tax differences between proximate generations, intragenerational inequities in taxes are more morally significant (Danzinger and Gottschalk 1986, 42). The difference between the percentages of incomes spent on taxes at the top and at the bottom of the income ladder is also morally significant (see Papke 1987 and the Indiana statistics in note 14 of chapter 3).

22. The academic success of Asian-American children is widely attributed to Confucian teachings that emphasize debts owed to one's parents. Children of Chinese, Japanese, Korean, and Vietnamese backgrounds demonstrate a discipline not shown by Laotians and Cambodians, who are more likely to be Buddhist, or by United States children from strongly individualistic backgrounds (*Time* 130:9 [Aug. 31, 1987], 45).

23. In the introduction this point of view was attributed to David Hume and his philosophical heirs. As Virginia Held observes, the problems in affirming responsibilities for future generations may stem from past traditions (like that of Hume) that too tightly link obligations of justice to property rights, rely too much on economic models, and believe that these obligations are best understood in terms of debts to a particular individual (1984, 242).

24. That not all senior citizens are blind to this injustice is evident from the following letter to *Time* magazine (January 25, 1988) in

response to a January 4, 1988, essay on the political influence of the American Association of Retired Persons: "I am an 87-year-old member of AARP, but I do not share or approve of the hog-it-all attitude held by many oldsters. To help reduce the deficit and balance the budget, the affluent aged should be willing to sacrifice cost of living increases in their Social Security payments, and senior adults should have their incomes taxed at the same rate as those of other people. I've been well paid for my services throughout my lifetime and do not feel society owes me any special privileges. (signed) Joseph H. Smart, Salt Lake City."

25. Recall also comments made earlier in this chapter that in many states divorced fathers have no legal responsibility for supporting their children after age eighteen, when most young people would be entering college.

26. This may not be true if one is attending a state-subsidized institution of higher education or a private one that has a substantial endowment. In both cases, however, others willy-nilly contribute to the costs of education.

27. Private-sector initiatives like Action Center for Educational Services and Scholarships, a consortium of twenty-five Boston companies, including the New England Mutual Life Insurance Company, assures high school graduates some financial aid in completing college and preference for jobs afterward in Boston. Similar initiatives have been established in Dallas, Chicago, Los Angeles, and New York City, by persons who contribute more than $250,000 each to underwrite the education of disadvantaged youth. Note, however, that these persons may be motivated by tax incentives as well as altruism. Therefore, such initiatives may be vulnerable to changes in tax laws.

28. Lest this interpretation of systemic harms be perceived as consequentialist, I emphasize that I am not discussing only equality or inequality of results (although advantages and disadvantages are, of course, results). Furthermore, I most assuredly am not claiming that results are the decisive moral issues of these harms. Rather, my point is that the harms that result to fundamental goods are not justifiable because we have a duty to respect and not harm human goods, that they are disproportionate to

persons' capacities to sustain or to recover from them, and that the cultural notions that sustain them are incorrect. The accepted practices often represent mistakes in the common sense of a community that undercut a community's willingness to act differently. Its members become instruments for transmitting harm to future generations because their mistaken common sense fosters injustice in persons, errors in principles of justice, and precarious institutions of justice.

29. Other alternatives include the softer, less competitive metaphor of compacts. Although compacts have a long and rich history in the United States, we read them as simple bilateral compacts. Also worth mentioning are local voluntary organizations, religious and otherwise, that mediate between families and community institutions as a major way to enhance the "family's capacity to take care of its children, its sick and handicapped, and its aged . . . [all of whose] needs are best taken care of within the family . . . [with public policy designed to] provide support for the family to discharge these caring tasks, rather than to relieve the family of these tasks . . . [say, through] special allowances . . . [rather than delegating tasks to] . . . outside agencies" (Berger and Berger 1984, 198–214).

   The Bergers' point, for all its wisdom, applies only to relatives, not to other members of proximate generations. The Bergers do not exclude this larger community from consideration. They argue that our public policy on families should emphasize the plurality of classes, races, ethnic groups, and religions in the United States, but they focus too heavily on ethnic, economic, sex, and racial groups (ibid., 208–9). The major weakness in their discussion is that voluntary organizations may be short-lived.

30. Classic statements about those outside the family, such as Plato's on the guardians, Orwell's on the Anti-Sex League, and Engels's on the family and capitalism support this contention (Walzer 1983, 229–33).

Chapter 3

1. Similar points are made by Callahan (1986, 247–67), Preston (1984, 44–49), and Warren (1982, 139–68).

2. Other important matters related to this discussion are admission policies, instruments to assess levels of competency and achieve-

ment, and inequalities in the public standards and procedures employed to decide such matters. This chapter is principally concerned with what Galston calls development opportunities, but we consider how these opportunities are financed. We consider economic goods and property because the issue in the case study in this chapter is the property tax method of financing public education (1980, 261–65, 195–260, 225ff.).

3. A legal case was selected because it demonstrates both the socio-cultural importance of education and the need for renegotiating its forms, because the courts are a powerful means of enforcement, and because court decisions clearly state the imperative to renegotiate our social arrangements.

4. Taxation policies shape social policies. By making some rather than other practices possible, they create the public perception that what is being done should be done. The way to implement one's preferred social policy is to fund it rather than its alternatives. Once implemented, a social policy acquires the status of tradition.

5. See, for example, the October 24, 1986, decision of Judge Hull in the United States District Court (Hawkins County, Tennessee), in which, on the basis of the free-exercise clause of the First Amendment, he gave curriculum exemptions to children whose parents were offended by textbooks that the parents contended promoted witchcraft, feminism, globalism, equivalence among religions, pacifism, situational ethics, and secular humanism. See also the 1987 Alabama District Court decision by Judge W. Brevard Hand defining secular humanism as a religion subject to the establishment clause of the First Amendment. The Tennessee decision was overturned unanimously by the Sixth Circuit Court of Appeals in Cincinnati in 1987 on the grounds that having children read and discuss ideas is not tantamount to forcing them to practice them. The Alabama decision was overturned unanimously by the eleventh Circuit Court of Appeals in Atlanta in 1987 on the grounds that instilling "such values as independent thought, tolerance of diverse views, self-respect, maturity, self-reliance and logical decision-making" was "entirely appropriate."

Judge Hand had already ruled that prayer in public schools is constitutional. In Judge Hand's opinion, the establishment clause did not apply to the individual states. For the United

States Supreme Court's interpretation of the First Amendment regarding free exercise and the establishment clause, see A. James Reichley (1985).

6. Texas, for example, made wide reforms under Gov. Mark White in the period 1984–1986, reportedly at the urging of financier J. Ross Perot. The reforms set student achievement standards, require that students meet academic standards to participate in extracurricular activities, define teacher competency, and raise salaries and establish merit raises for teachers, but make less progress in finance reform. Under the formula for per-pupil expenditures, the state pays a greater portion, reducing the disparity between property-rich and property-poor districts (see note 11 for recent decisions). But district property taxes continue to fund merit raises for teachers, and sales and luxury taxes, which are not adjusted for the purchaser's ability to pay, provided the initial funds to make salaries competitive. For how progressive and regressive taxes affect educational opportunities, see Justice Marshall's analysis in the court record of *Rodriguez* (at 77–79).

7. For demographic trends and their implications, see Callahan (1986) and Preston (1984). For financing trends and their effects on state public school systems, see Lehnen and Johnson (1984). For a telling summary of the impact of fiscal policies on poor children, see the 1979 West Virginia case *Pauley* v. *Kelley* (255 SE2d 859).

8. In *Rodriguez,* the Court cited *Brown* v. *The Board of Education* (347 US 483), decided by the Supreme Court in 1954, to the effect that education is one of the principal functions of local and state governments (411 US at 29). The Court seems to have interpreted the First and Fourteenth amendments together.

9. The legal precedent was the 1972 New York decision in *Committee for Public Education* v. *Nyquist* (413 US 794ff.). For the constitutional context of Supreme Court cases immediately before *Rodriguez,* see Reichley (1985, 115–67), Kurland (1961), and Lehnen and Johnson (1984, 44, 58).

10. Victor Turner (1976) uses the root paradigm. Robert Nozick (1974) presents the principal contemporary theory of justice that radically subordinates all forms of justice to transactional justice.

11. This result was unexpected because the Court drew analogies between basic provisions and securities (like food and shelter) and the intelligent exercise of free speech and the right to vote, considering both categories as outcomes of quality education. As Virginia Held observes, "instead of seeing this as an argument for substantive rights to food, shelter, and so on . . . the Court took it as an argument against a right to equal education" (1980, 16–17). Federal courts have been reluctant to interpret entitlement rights protected by the Constitution to include economic claims. They repeatedly have held that governmental classifications based on wealth or poverty are not inherently suspect and do not require the same degree of scrutiny as do classifications based on race (at 37 and 54).

    However, other legislation and decisions seem to imply a right to basic needs. Federal courts may make shelter a right, since some cases claim that the homeless are victims of state and local laws regarding zoning, real estate, and residency requirements for welfare. The language in many state constitutions implies that people have a right to basic needs. At least eight state constitutions have defined education as a fundamental right (Lehnen and Johnson 1984, 43–60). In 1987, Judge Harley Clark of the 250th Judicial District Court ruled that the revised 1984 Texas financing formula (see note 2 above) was discriminatory and unconstitutional. His decision was unanimously upheld by the Texas Supreme Court in 1989. Funding legislation in Texas in 1990 reflected this decision.

12. Before *Rodriguez,* only three cases challenged state methods of school finance, but at least sixteen have followed. In twenty decisions by 1984, the Supreme Court or the highest state court upheld the finance structures of twelve school systems, citing local fiscal control of education (although some states, like Indiana, demonstrated little local control), but ruled against eight others, declaring education a fundamental right (Lehnen and Johnson 1984, 43–60). Decisions in Kentucky in 1989 and in New Jersey in 1981 and 1990 have either set a limit on expenditures for each district or have turned to income and other taxes to increase their tax base.

13. For a cogent account of equal liberty, see Held (1984). See also notes 8 and 11.

14. Because property and sales taxes are levied as a fixed percentage of assessed value or purchase price, they do not respect the taxpayer's ability to pay or recognize that some taxpayers are already disadvantaged by tax structures. Thus, property and sales taxes disproportionately harm those less able to bear the burdens. Income taxes are more progressive and just than sales taxes because they are proportioned to one's ability to pay. States that rely on sales taxes rather than income taxes create an obvious and unjustifiable disparity. For example, in Indiana, income taxes account for less than a third of total state revenues. Taxpayers in Indiana at the lowest income levels carry a tax burden that is more than 9% greater than those at the highest income levels, while those in the middle group carry a third more than those in the highest group, which bears about one third less of the burden than those in the lowest group (Papke 1987).

15. Regarding deficiencies in our collective sense of responsibility for others' children, see Callahan (1986) and Preston (1984, 48). See also chapter 2 for the discussion of Bexar County, Texas, where the education of disadvantaged children depends on taxpayers who are largely tax-privileged retirees without school-age children.

16. The procedural criteria employed below were suggested by David Tracy (1986) and Jürgen Habermas (1984).

17. Religious traditions can be helpful in these public renegotiations, but they must be carefully handled. Some advocate negative freedom, a minimalist state, or a form of social organization with little responsibility for public affairs. Such communities invite people to act unilaterally, to perceive justice in terms of exchanges, and to use power politics (Tracy 1986, 119, 121, 127; Bellah et al. 1985). Even the less troublesome religious groups may prefer to wait for outside intervention rather than participate in public affairs (Hauerwas 1981, 128).

18. Some of these classical expressions can be found in note 26 in chapter 1.

19. As A. T. Mason noted in his biography of Louis D. Brandeis, both lawyers and judges can become "lieges of monopolists" and are poorly trained for holding elite power (1946, 101–2).

20. This may not be easy to achieve. Members of separatist traditions may not recognize that they share some experiences with other groups. For example, a group may be devoted to what Reinhold Niebuhr called American forms of "culture religion" or what his brother, H. Richard Niebuhr, described as an accommodation of religious, moral, and social values to middle-class concepts of liberty that does not recognize the importance of equality. Religious groups should call their members to greater public activities and recognize that the burdens of teaching and promoting religious and cultural values of children in public schools belong primarily to their parents.

21. At the time of *Rodriguez*, the population of Texas, like the population of some other coastal states, was moving from small, mainly rural centers to industrial and commercial ones. However, Texas exhibited more wisdom than its counterparts when it established its method of financing public schools in the late nineteenth century (411 US at 7–8).

22. Although the majority on the Court believed that present financing systems provided greater freedom for state and local governments (411 US at 41), Justice White noted in his dissenting opinion that freedom for the Edgewood district was curtailed because it had "no meaningful option" (at 64–65 and 67) since, as Justice Marshall's rebuttal of the majority's interpretation of freedom pointed out, the financing system made property taxes the sole source of revenue and limited the tax rates (note 75 at 116).

23. See the definition of indigency used by the majority in *Rodriguez* (at 20ff. and in the example described in note 60 at 25).

24. See also Justice Marshall's rebuttal of this claim (at 88 and 89) and note the importance of determining how and by whom the minimum is defined.

25. This interpretation differs sharply from the conceptually ambiguous claims found in the majority's conclusions regarding the "heaviest burdens" (411 US at 10), "proportionate local burdens" (at 14), "great but not insurmountable" burdens (at 21), and "disproportionate" burdens (at 22), and is closer to the more adequate concepts presented in the dissenting opinions of Justices White and Marshall (at 65, 75, and 78).

Chapter 4

1. Purtilo and Sorrell cite Shore and Levinson (1985) on defining health care as a commodity. Purtilo and Sorrel's study of rural health care discovered that conflicts of interest between patients and hospitals are common. They also observed neighbors helping those in need. They noted that public health problems are a heavier burden in rural areas because physicians have fewer professional colleagues (Purtilo and Sorrel, 26–27).

2. As reported in an article titled "Health Group Decries Unequal Access" in *The Boston Sunday Globe,* June 8, 1986, 17.

3. However, only 52% agreed that everyone should be entitled to equal access to health care, and only 28% agreed that everyone should be entitled to the same level of health care.

4. The ideal that the costs of providing charity care should be shared by all sectors of society is underscored by the President's Commission. If only one class of persons or institutions, for example, the American Medical Association or the American Hospital Association, were required to absorb the cost, that class would be assigned a disproportionate burden.

5. Unlike other industrialized nations, the United States does not assure basic health care to all its citizens.

6. See, for example, the United Nation's Declaration of Alma-Ata (cosponsored by WHO and UNICEF) or the United States Public Health Association's disavowal of the 1987 draft of *A Health Policy Agenda for the American People.*

7. But, as argued in chapter 1, justice is the only moral value and virtue, for it embraces and measures all others.

8. The need for such information seems to have escaped the notice of several prominent commentators on medical ethics. Their claims about the meaning of justice or how it should be applied prompt one to ask about the experiences their judgments reflect. Walzer reminds us, "different experiences and different conceptions lead to different patterns of provision" (1983, 65).

9. For the story of union efforts, see Stevens (1971). For the counterattack by the AMA, see Burrow (1963). For an account of the

United States Catholic bishops' promotion of social insurance against illness and other contingencies, see Abell (1968, 341). For the social and cultural contexts of new developments in tort law, see G. Edward White. Besides industrialization and three other trends, White notes that it was becoming more common that litigants were strangers to each other (1977, 672).

10. Federally insured programs are funded through deductions for social security rather than from general revenues. Daniel Callahan and others note that cost increases in Medicare and Medicaid have prompted some politicians to urge that families take financial responsibility for aged parents (1986, 255). Furthermore, Callahan notes our contemporary persuasion that "the very meaning of medicine includes a perpetual effort at improvement, obsessively persistent experimentation, and the constant fueling of hope that suffering can be reduced and death somehow pacified" (1986, 261). A result of acting on this persuasion is that, although in the 1950s and 1960s the United States found funds for health and welfare programs that benefit all age groups, since 1979 many programs for children have been reduced and programs for older people have expanded (Callahan 1986, 263; Preston 1984, 44).

11. For an insightful account of related trends since 1965, see Stevens's history of United States hospitals in the twentieth century (1989, 284ff.). For a discussion of the tension between the supporters of free-enterprise medicine and supporters of community medicine, see Walzer (1983, 87–90).

12. Pellegrino and Thomasma call recognizing that health care is a form of personal security the "moral center" of arguments about health care. They contend that the anxiety created by illness evokes the ability to relieve it, "to transfer it, and [that] to know what is happening is to begin the process of healing or adaptation essential to the reconstruction of the individual's existence" (1981, 237, 242).

13. It may be more accurately described as an ideal right which brings the holder a duty to make health care more widely available. Joel Feinberg argues that a "deprived claimant in conditions of scarcity remains in a position morally to make a claim, even when there is no one in the corresponding position to do anything about it, but should circumstances change so that the corresponding position finds an occupant, then that person

instantly assumes a duty to help. Another consequence of the view that all persons have human rights even to goods in short supply is that it provides a basis for ascribing duties to governments and responsible agencies to work for the alleviation of shortages, so that the valid claims of other human beings in the future will not go unanswered" (Feinberg 1978, 1510).

14. Beauchamp and Childress, for example, do not mention all these factors, but their emphasis on scarcity and competition suggests an ideological bias. They also moralize about life-styles, especially in the earlier works of Childress (1970) and in Outka (1974).

15. These positions confuse ordinary medical services with costly, high-technology, life-saving procedures applied in extreme cases. For another view, see Feinberg's point about ideal rights in note 13.

16. See, for example, Beauchamp and Childress, whose treatment of justice assumes competition and leads to a skewed conclusion favoring procedural comparative justice (1979, 18–19, 192).

17. Beauchamp and Childress accord too much prestige to common law. They seem unaware that the law embodies and promotes undeserved privileges and therefore needs reform. See Feinberg about injustice in the general rules of law (1973, 104).

18. Thus, it is not enough to assert, as do Beauchamp and Childress, that "moral principles are not disembodied rules, cut off from their cultural settings" (1979, 61), unless one also provides a discriminating principle to identify biased cultural presumptions.

19. Though Pellegrino and Thomasma seem to acknowledge some of these factors (ibid., 240), their emphasis on human vulnerability to illness results in an illness-based model of health care.

20. In Galston's view, a "theory of justice has two essential elements: a specification of what is beneficial for individuals; and principles of rational entitlement to govern cases in which (*a*) individual benefits come into conflict with or exclude one another or (*b*) there is a conflict between the desired benefit and some characteristic of the individual who desires it" (1980, 92).

21. Galston classifies needs as "natural, social, [and] luxurious," defining natural needs as those "means required to secure, not

only existence, but also the development of existence" (ibid., 164). Walzer adds that needed goods are not commodities but rather only those goods that are sought after needs are met might be considered commodities (1983, 90).

22. Except for mentioning some obstacles to making primary health care accessible to everyone, Pellegrino and Thomasma do not mention the burdens.

23. That Beauchamp and Childress state productivity before need suggests a mercantilist perspective on social goods.

24. Beauchamp and Childress seem to equate ordinary discourse with that of "the respectable part of contemporary culture" which they then make normative.

25. The way Beauchamp and Childress present their argument suggests that one must apply either a Marxist or libertarian concept of justice in allocating health care. It would be more pertinent to ask who controls the social goods for which society established and sustains the professions.

26. Beauchamp and Childress's concept of comparative justice relies on Feinberg's (1973, 107ff.) and derives from David Hume and Adam Smith, as recounted in the introduction.

27. Commercialization of elective procedures, expensive treatment of doubtful benefit, and treatment for disorders that are not disabling (Pellegrino and Thomasma's lowest priorities) might be justifiable.

28. What Pellegrino and Thomasma have in mind is called a positive entitlement right, as distinguished from a negative or liberty right. A positive entitlement right establishes a claim to some good or service. A liberty right warrants a negative claim, for example, not to be interfered with. Pellegrino and Thomasma seem to emphasize entitlement rights, while Beauchamp and Childress seem to emphasize liberty rights.

29. Observe, for example, the habit of appealing to "our senses of justice," as in Charles Fried's statements that "my guess is that the American people would not want to . . ." and that certain arguments "would be found strange and repellent in the United States" or that they represent a "political philosophy which I take

is not the dominant one in our society" (1976a, 30–32). Our ethos sets many of the terms in our discussions of justice but they need to be employed critically.

30. This argument derives from the theological paradigm advanced by the well-known Christian ethicist Paul Ramsey (and acknowledged by Childress, Fried, and Camenisch). However, that paradigm can be refuted (Goodin 1985).

31. Many health care professionals already do pro bono work among relatives and in their neighborhoods. This volunteer service might be extended and made more predictable if organized by religious institutions or neighborhood agencies.

32. Other options would be credits, allowances, copayments, and deductibles. But all such options should be cost-effective and ethically sound.

33. As Walzer notes, procedures should prevent wealthy or prominent persons from dominating the process (1983). Galston considers procedures important in discussions about financing health care because health care is politically entangled with provider organizations, interest groups, and governments (1980, 265–73).

34. Many commentators fail to mention changes in the judgments of communities and individuals. Beauchamp and Childress, for instance, mention forms of "bad conscience," that is, inconsistencies between the decisions and actions of individuals (1979, 238, 241), but do not mention the false consciousness that enables communities to rationalize their inconsistencies.

Chapter 5

1. See Lawrence Friedman on these influences throughout United States history (1973). For constitutional history, see Kelly and Harbison (1970).

2. When lawyers decide which cases or which clients to accept, the consequences may be serious. These decisions, especially the ones about clients, are ways of systematically allocating the costs of life in communities. See Auerbach (1976), Fletcher (1972), and Smigel (1964). See Stone (1934) regarding how judges reflect and shape public morality, thereby creating what Leon

Green calls "environmental facts" (1977, 1ff., esp. at 263). See Sadurski (1984) on social justice and legal justice, and G. Edward White (1977) on the intellectual underpinnings of tort law. Furthermore, economic and political goods—such as economic opportunities, political freedoms, the rights of citizenship, and offices of public trust and responsibility—are greatly influenced by the law (Walzer 1983, 265–75). Especially pertinent, finally, is Judith Shklar's point that legal theorists should regard law, along with morals and politics, not as a discrete entity but as part of a social continuum so that jurisprudence and other social theories should be correlated (1986b).

3. Much of our commentary on contract law also applies to criminal law, constitutional law, and the rules of evidence. Jurisprudence in contract law is analogous to jurisprudence in the other areas of law and many legal scholars, such as Roscoe Pound, Friedrich Kessler, and Charles Fried, came to jurisprudence by way of contract law.

4. The doctrine of freedom of contract has a long history. As recounted by Kelly and Harbison (1970, 276ff.), the drafters of the Constitution were concerned that the police powers of states could threaten private property rights. The first test (*Fletcher* v. *Peck*, decided in 1810 under Chief Justice John Marshall) forbade states from restricting the freedom of public or private contracts. The *Dartmouth College* case later applied Marshall's decision to college charters, but in *Charles River Bridge* v. *Warren Bridge* (1837) and other cases, the Court modified Marshall's contract doctrines to limit the inviolability of contracts. A more substantive form of due process prevailed in the judicial review of contracts after 1890, notably in the construction of the Fifth Amendment's due-process clause. For example, decisions in *Allgeyer* v. *Louisiana* (1897) and *Holden* v. *Hardy* (1909) invalidated state regulations for working conditions. Decisions regarding labor contracts limited the doctrine of freedom of contract but *Adkins* v. *Children's Hospital* (1923) gave the doctrine wider scope by declaring that minimum wage laws were unconstitutional. *Adkins* is often cited to identify laissez-faire economics with a constitutional right (ibid., 527ff.).

5. For an astute analysis of the debate between those arguing for moral accountability in contract law and those maintaining that contract law is merely an instrument of society and should be governed by efficiency, see George P. Fletcher (1972, 537–38).

6. For a discussion of the social relevance of moral standards in cases of contract, see Kronman (1980, 474–75). See Michelman (1978, 1026–1027) for the role of noneconomic community morality in tort decisions.

7. Selznick contends that social conditions are as much a part of a contract as the promise it records (1987). Walzer (1983) argues that the moral value of fulfilling the terms of a contract is as relevant as the political value of government officials' fulfilling their duties. Goodin (1985) discusses the moral issue of vulnerability of parties. Contract law decisions are regularly applied in tort cases in which a plaintiff claims he has been harmed by another's wrongful act. Some tort cases have considered how costs and other burdens should be distributed. See Keeton and Keeton (1977, 759ff.) and Kronman in Farnsworth and Young (1980, 414, 429). Although these writers on law are more advanced than most writers on ethics, to them the foundation of distributive justice is rights or results rather than duty. They do not address the attitudes that a just person would have.

8. The same wisdom holds that the purpose of tort law is to provide remedies for everyday hurts (Green 1960, 269), to distribute losses, and to protect those less able to help themselves (Kennedy 1982, 565). Kennedy notes that tort law and contract law overlap largely because, to avoid torts, some commercial contracts are required to include warranties (ibid., 591–92).

9. See the commentary on Sec. 2–302 in the Uniform Commercial Code (1982, 62). For the construction of *consideration,* see *Black's Law Dictionary* and Farnsworth and Young (1980, 349ff.).

10. The new methods represent moral constraints on the meaning of *consideration* in contracts or on the notion that a promise should be enforced whether or not something of equal value was given for it (Farnsworth and Young 1980, 365). For an argument that the new constraints rest on moral values, such as distributive justice, self-respect, and moral imagination, see Kronman (1983, 771ff.).

11. For some broader interpretations of incapacity in cultural terms, see Kronman (1983, 775, 786–97).

12. For example, legislative and judicial rules on contracts prohibit contracts that are racially discriminatory, those that are usurious,

and those that set wages below the legal minimum. For a summary of paternalistic restrictions on freedom of contract and of recent compulsory terms see Kronman (1980, 499; 1983, 798). See also Kennedy's account of compulsory terms like *good faith performance* under Sec. 2–203 of the Uniform Commercial Code and parallels with tort law, for example, warranties property owners must make for maintenance and repairs, warranties physicians make regarding malpractice, and warranties employers make regarding wrongfully discharging employees (1982, 590–91).

13. By ethics, Holmes meant what we now call morality. He did not distinguish first-order moral considerations (issues of justifiability of actions) and second-order moral considerations (issues of praise and blame). He seems to equate morality with the latter. For example, he was not interested in blaming or praising persons for their intentions (1897, 463). Calling blame and praise subjectivist, Holmes countered with an objectivist theory of contracts (ibid., 463–72).

    For an example of opposing approaches in tort law, see Duncan Kennedy's description of formalist and informalist doctrines (1976). Richard Posner's contemporary economic formalism is discussed later in this chapter. Note, however, that Posner cites Holmes's *Common Law* as an authoritative interpretation of the moral dimensions of contracts (1972, 31, n. 7).

14. Despite the elegant formalism and persuasive brilliance of the Holmesian doctrines of contracts and their analogs in contemporary reductionist economic theories of contracts and torts, these doctrines are seriously deficient in several respects. According to Henry Gross, economic theories of law are limited analytic tools because the foundations of the law of contracts and torts are not only economic but also social (1980, 877). According to Michelman, some noneconomic foundations of community morality are at work in the law. Michelman considers purely economic legal doctrines as reductionist in the extreme (1978, 1026–27, 1046). Leon Green claims that tort law would seem the simplest of all law because it merely provides remedies (payment of damages) for harms to persons, property, or relations with other persons. But, says Green, the public good is at stake in the decisions lawyers, juries, and judges make and thus lawyers, juries, and judges appropriately make wide-ranging inquiries before they decide, for tort law is "public law in disguise" (1960, 269).

15. The burdens of injuries and damages caused by early private industries were assigned to others through tort decisions and insurance. Shifting the costs this way is widely considered a public subsidy of those industries, but Richard Posner disagrees, offering a purely economic analysis rather than a moral inquiry into the justice of allocating the social costs of industry (1972, 29–30).

16. Lest Brandeis's phrase "first important public work" be misread, note that he had been defending the public interest as early as 1884, when he joined the Civil Service Reform Association. In 1887, he joined the Boston American Citizenship Committee. In 1891 he tried to dissuade a state legislative committee from recommending hastily drafted temperance legislation, in part because it would encourage distillers to bribe public officials. While he was preparing to give a series of lectures in business law at Massachusetts Institute of Technology, news of the Homestead Strike (July 1892) inspired him to consider whether the common law could deal adequately with modern relationships between labor and industry and the lectures he gave reflected a dramatic change in his thinking (Mason 1946, 87–91, 107–9; Goldmark 1930, 13).

17. As cities in the nineteenth century gave away franchises, some states now attract or hold industry by giving away tax benefits.

18. The typescript of this letter is in the Louis Dembitz Brandeis Papers at the University of Louisville, NMF series, folder 1–5a.

19. In assessing sharp or misleading business practices, courts recognize degrees of economic pressure. For example, employment contracts may provide inadequate consideration and be made under economic coercion (Farnsworth and Young 1980, 380, 384, 402, 471).

20. What constitutes a just allocation of risks in misrepresentations, not all of which are patently unjustifiable, is debatable. For example, when one party concealed facts to gain a bargaining advantage, some contracts were held enforceable because the concealment did not involve deceit and tortious liability (Farnsworth and Young 1980, 413–16, 421–22).

21. According to Patterson's historical review, the notion of unconscionability is not new but the term was coined early in this

century (1964, 856–58). Farnsworth and Young point out that it has expanded since midcentury (1980, 441).

22. The decision in *Henningsen* intimates that equal freedom is the ideal form of freedom of contract (Farnsworth and Young 1980, 462–63; see also Dworkin 1977). Note that courts have held that the doctrine of freedom of contract does not excuse parties from responsibility for negligence (Farnsworth and Young 1980, 443, 447, 453, 460 [the *O'Callaghan* case], 470).

23. On one side of this debate, Alan Schwartz calls the doctrine of unconscionability a cover for smuggling notions of distributive justice into the judicial process, which, because UCC Sec. 2–302 is vague, then becomes a value-laden process as courts determine whether the parties are on an equal footing. Schwartz advises courts to abandon the subjective concept of unequal bargaining power in favor of construing contracts in the terms in which they were written (1974, 367ff., esp. 392 and 396). On the other side, Anthony Kronman contends that courts are always engaged in assigning more or less equal advantages in interpreting contracts (1980, 473, n. 8, 474–97).

24. However, Fried fails to mention that status and behavior, as well as substance, may make a bargain unconscionable. Furthermore, his interpretation of unconscionability is of a piece with his misreading of distributive justice (1981, 103–11, esp. 106, 110). He not only confuses distributive justice in contracts with the economic reasoning based on results that many apply to distributive issues in torts today (Englard 1980, 27, n. 1, 28) but also confuses it with redistribution, thus evoking fears of forcible appropriation and redistribution of property, as in Robert Nozick's entitlement and exchange theory of justice (1974). By suggesting that some form of redistribution is unavoidable, Fried implies that the price of distributive or social justice may be too high or too unpopular to achieve.

25. *Jones* was tried under the Uniform Commercial Code in 1969 (59 Misc2d 189, 298 NYS2d 264). Other illustrative cases are *Campbell Soup*, also contested under the UCC, *Wilson Trading*, argued in terms of consumer remedies for unfair marketing practices, and *Williams* v. *Walker*, adjudicated according to its substance (Farnsworth and Young 1980, 489ff., 494ff., 504).

26. The moral concern about harm to persons may have informed concerns about the capacity of persons to enter a contract or about how much pressure a contracting party may legitimately exercise during bargaining and may have informed the argument in the *O'Callaghan* case, which held that the doctrine of freedom of contract does not absolve parties from their responsibilities not to harm others through negligence in the substance of the contract (Farnsworth and Young 1980, 381, 443). Even Holmes, who argued that law and morality should be separate, seems to concur with the reasoning in *O'Callaghan,* for he argued that there is no freedom to contract to commit a crime or to violate essential morality (*Adkins* v. *Children's Hospital of District of Columbia,* 261 U.S. 525ff., at 568; Farnsworth and Young 1980, 446).

27. The phrase *philosophy of life* can and should signify more than one's personally determined way of making sense of life. I use that phrase to include constructs, however inchoate, about the physical world, about human nature, about how humans know and understand, and about the values and habits people live by. In this broader sense, philosophies of life are social and political as well as personal.

28. In Brandeis's view, monopolistic power creates apathy, smugness, and greed, blocks human ingenuity and development, and creates social conditions that make coercion and overreaching in contracts seem inevitable.

29. For a comparable assessment of formalist tort theories, see England (1980, 31, 32).

30. Thus, the 1979 edition of *Black's Law Dictionary* gives only the formal definition of jurisprudence, as Justice Holmes would have defined it. Contemporary theorists like Richard A. Posner carry on this history, equating legal justice with objectivity and equating traditional doctrines of negligence with subjectivity and the interest of moralistic busybodies (1972, 31). That Black also excludes political considerations is even more puzzling, for he notes that when rules conflict, the task of the law is to choose the rule that produces the "greatest advantage to the community" and alludes to Aristotle's concept of justice as a political good (1979, 767).

31. Black's unqualified identification of common law with strictly formulated rules is surprising because, as Black himself notes, law and equity actions have merged in federal courts and most state courts since civil procedure and jurisdiction were reformed in the twentieth century (1979, 485; see also s.v. "Chancery" and "Court of Chancery").

32. For studies and commentary on these processes of acculturation and socialization, see Auerbach (1976), Carlin (1962, 1966), Friedman (1973), Hurst (1950), and Smigel (1964).

33. Because these cultural beliefs and judgments function throughout legal reasoning, what the law safeguards and enforces is a consequence of how lawyers apprehend conflicts and act upon them, how they apply the law (by advising and negotiating, as well as by litigating cases) and how they select clients, legal issues, and legal specialties. For early instances in the United States, see the Federalist Papers, particularly James Madison's discussion of the tensions between private interests and the public good (Bellah et al. 1985, 253–36, 270–71). For the views of Oliver Wendell Holmes and Louis Dembitz Brandeis on power, economics, and social progress and how their beliefs influenced their perceptions of labor contracts and judges who favored business interests, see Mason's biography of Brandeis (1946, 572–77). For how social and cultural beliefs of lawyers in business and government can significantly influence their recommendations to allocate the costs of community life, see Mason (1946, 329) and Calabresi (1970, 292, 304–6).

34. For a comparable assessment of United States tort theory, see England (1980). For an analysis of property, see Scanlon (1977, 60–62).

35. In defining justice, some legal scholars claim that these understandings are held "by people generally." For example, Henry Gross claims that most existing legal rules for contracts are consistent with efficiency and that people strive to maximize their own welfare in contracts (1980). Gross's assertion seems to stem from unexpressed beliefs that human nature is egoistic and inclined to pursue self-interest, a concept recounted by Jeremy Bentham, Thomas Hobbes, and Ayn Rand. Another recent example is Guido Calabresi's cost-benefit analysis of how liability

should be assigned in accidents. Note his claim that his analysis satisfies "our sense of justice" and represents a "political fact" about what the public will accept (1970, 291–92, 304, 306).

36. Scanlon calls this model "formal egalitarianism" (1977, 51ff.). It emphasizes fidelity to one's word and considers promise-keeping a distinct and compelling form of obligation, and is sometimes called a "will theory" of contracts (Fried 1981, 6). For a different view, emphasizing the vulnerability of persons who trust that the promise will be kept, see Goodin (1985).

37. Other parties in torts, if not in contracts, are the people we call the public (Green 1959, 1960; Englard 1980; Scanlon 1977, 43–44).

38. George P. Fletcher descries the technical virtuosity these theories employ and claims that in our technological age, traditional moral norms may not appear as rational as the techniques of the social sciences. For example, when legal scholars define risks, assess the consequences of risk, or analyze costs and benefits, the "respectability of precision and rationality" may lead them into a "spectacular lawyerly fallacy . . . of misplaced concreteness" (1972, 573).

39. In his analysis of modern scholarship on United States tort law, Englard finds a "desperate scholarly rear-guard action to preserve a traditional system of individualism in a changing world" or a nostalgic desire to return to an early nineteenth-century version of free enterprise (1980, 32, 57–58, 68). Neither the individualistic "economic liberalism" found in Calabresi (1970) and Posner (1972, 1973, 1978, 1980, 1981, 1986; Posner and Landes, 1987) and the individualistic social and political rights found in Epstein (1974) and Fletcher (1972) are realistic about contemporary social and economic conditions, but these theories are cited as arguments against redistribution (Englard 1980, 32). Posner's work at least seems to bear out Englard's thesis because it claims that the principle of wealth-maximization is a firmer foundation for distributive justice because, among other reasons, it is less hospitable to redistribution (Posner 1981, 80; 1979).

40. Although Kronman does not say that morality should guide contracts in making distributions, it seems reasonable that it should

because his conclusion to this section appeals to a moral test similar to Rawl's difference principle (1980, 474–75, 492).

41. Fried seems to acknowledge this point when he refers to unexpressed premises of contracts (1981, 88).

42. Although consciously set aside, ethical and political considerations nonetheless exert influence. Perhaps the reasons they are set aside is to avoid recognizing their power.

43. Gilmore also descried the consequentialist point of view in *The Death of Contract* (1974).

44. Friedman makes similar points about the historical and social ties between property and contract law before and after the nineteenth century (1973, 244–46, 464ff.) and Gilmore concurs (1974, 87ff.). Friedman traces the same ties in tort law (ibid., 261–62 and 409ff.), in the way the power to punish crimes is apportioned and how criminal law expands as the economy grows (ibid., 251–58, and 502ff.). In a 1954 criminal case, Judge David C. Bazelon expanded the definition of insanity to recognize that unjust social conditions cannot be corrected by punishing crimes (1988). In Posner's sharply contrasting view, punishment is better explained as a way of recovering economic costs from the persons who create them (1980).

45. A contrary view holds that equal opportunity is the proper model of distributive justice for our civilization. Although contemporary views invoke religious authority by applying the covenant metaphor, this concept has several weaknesses. First, it is related to certain concepts that have negative connotations, such as *promised land*, which has been used by many as a pretext to seize others' territory. Second, it says little about how advantages and disadvantages are apportioned and thus avoids, for example, the question of whether economic competition can be fair. Other religious metaphors, such as *sacred trust* and *stewardship*, may be more useful.

46. Fletcher's concept of the human good approximates this conclusion but is excessively individualistic and does not extend to the good of human communities. In his theory, tort laws protect the individual's fundamental human goods from harm by a

community pursuing its legitimate interests (1972, 568, 573). See also note 38 in this chapter.

47. This approach is precisely opposite to theories of contract law that claim to be objective. For example, Gilmore describes one objective theory as avoiding questions of fact (1974, 98) through a Euclidean rather than an experimental jurisprudence. Similarly, Lawrence Friedman describes Langdell's empirical method of jurisprudence as "a geology without rocks, an astronomy without stars, and a dry and arid logic divorced from society and life" (1973, 535).

48. Some writers strongly oppose all forms of redistribution, even those proposed to redress patent inequities (Hazard 1965, 2,10; 1970, 254–55; 1971, 48ff.). For example, Hazard does not distinguish commutative, corrective, and adjudicative justice; confuses distributive and social justice; and claims his interpretation builds on Aristotle's distinctions of commutative and distributive justice (1969, 705, n. 13 and 711). Englard confuses the corrective (and sometimes retributive) justice in tort law, which aims to restore the balance between victim and injurer, with Aristotle's concept of commutative justice. Seriously misreading Aristotle, Englard claims that distributive justice "transcends the mutual relationship [in commutative justice] by linking it to the totality of society . . . such that . . . the situation of the individual would be measured against the collectivity's resources and judged accordingly" (1980, 27, n. 1).

Conclusion

1. For an insightful account, see Michael Ignatieff's *The Needs of Strangers* (1986). For a thoughtful exposition of how we learn to relate to others, see Parker Palmer's *The Company of Strangers* (1988).

References

Abell, Aaron I. 1968. *American Catholic Thought on Social Questions.* Indianapolis, Ind.: Bobbs-Merrill.

Abbott, Philip. 1981. *The Family on Trial.* University Park, Penn.: Pennsylvania State University Press.

Ackerman, Bruce J. 1980. *Social Justice in the Liberal State.* New Haven, Conn.: Yale University Press.

————. 1984. *Reconstructing American Law.* Cambridge, Mass.: Harvard University Press.

Aiken, Henry David. 1962. *Reason and Conduct.* New York: Alfred A. Knopf.

Aquinas, S. Thomae. 1949. *In Decem Libros Ethicorum Aristotelis Ad Nicomachum Expositio.* Rome: Marietti.

————. 1952. *Summa Theologiae.* Pars IIa-IIae. Rome: Marietti.

Aristotle. 1962. *Nicomachean Ethics.* Translated by Martin Ostwald. Indianapolis, Ind.: Bobbs-Merrill.

————. 1958. *Politics.* Translated by Ernest Becker. New York: Oxford University Press.

————. 1984a. *The Complete Works of Aristotle.* Revised Oxford translation. Edited by Jonathan Barnes. 2 vols. Princeton, N.J.: Princeton University Press.

————. 1984b. *The Politics*. Translated with an introduction, notes, and glossary by Carnes Lord. Chicago: University of Chicago Press.

Auerbach, Jerold S. 1976. *Unequal Justice: Lawyers and Social Change in Modern America*. New York: Oxford University Press.

Barber, Benjamin R. 1974. "Justifying Justice: Problems of Psychology, Politics, and Measurement in Rawls." In *Reading Rawls*. Edited by Norman Daniels. New York: Basic Books.

————. 1985. *Strong Democracy: Participatory Politics for a New Age*. Berkeley and Los Angeles: University of California Press.

Barry, Brian. 1973. *The Liberal Theory of Justice: A Critical Examination of the Principal Doctrines in "A Theory of Justice" by John Rawls*. Oxford: Oxford University Press.

————. 1977. "Justice between Generations." In *Law, Morality, and Society: Essays in Honor of H. L. A. Hart*. Edited by P. M. S. Hacker and J. Raz. Oxford: Clarendon Press.

————. 1978. "Circumstances of Justice and Future Generations." In *Obligations to Future Generations*. Edited by R. I. Sikora and B. M. Barry. Philadelphia: Temple University Press.

Bayles, Michael D. 1984. *Reproductive Ethics*. Englewood Cliffs, N.J.: Prentice-Hall.

Bazelon, David L. 1988. *Questioning Authority: Justice and Criminal Law*. Foreword by Associate Justice William J. Brennan, Jr. New York: Alfred A. Knopf.

Beauchamp, Tom L., and James F. Childress. 1979. *Principles of Biomedical Ethics*. 2nd edition. 1983. New York: Oxford University Press.

Bellah, Robert. 1970. *Beyond Belief: Essays on Religion in a Post-Traditional World*. New York: Harper and Row.

————. 1975. *The Broken Covenant: American Civil Religion in a Time of Trial*. New York: Seabury.

————. 1982. "Social Science as Practical Reason." *The Hastings Center Report* 5 (December): 32–39.

Bellah, R., R. Madsen, W. M. Sullivan, A. Swidler, and S. M. Tipton. 1985. *Habits of the Heart: Individualism and Commitment in American Life.* Berkeley and Los Angeles: University of California Press.

Bennett, John G. 1985. "Ethics and Markets." *Philosophy and Public Affairs* 14:194–204.

Berger, Brigitte, and Peter L. Berger. 1984. *The War over the Family: Capturing the Middle Ground.* New York: Doubleday Anchor.

Berke, Joel S. 1974. *Answers to Inequity: An Analysis of the New School Finance.* Foreword by Arthur E. Wise. Berkeley, Calif.: McCutchan Publishing.

Berlin, Isaiah. 1958. *Two Concepts of Liberty.* Oxford: Clarendon Press.

Berman, Harold. 1974. *The Interaction of Law and Religion.* Nashville, Tenn.: Abingdon Press.

Black, Henry Campbell. 1979. *Black's Law Dictionary.* 5th ed. St. Paul, Minn.: West Publishing.

Bloom, Allan. 1986. "Rousseau on the Equality of the Sexes." In *Justice and Equality: Here and Now.* Edited by Frank S. Lucash. Ithaca, N.Y.: Cornell University Press.

Blum, Henrik L. 1976. *Expanding Health Care Horizons: From a Systems Concept of Health to a National Health Policy.* Oakland, Calif.: Third Party Associates.

Bombeck, Erma. 1987. *Family: The Ties That Bind—And Gag.* New York: McGraw-Hill.

Bowne, Borden Parker. 1892. *The Principles of Ethics.* New York: Harper and Row.

———. 1988. "The Syphilis Epidemic and Its Relation to AIDS." In *Science* 239/4838:375–80.

Broderick, Francis L. 1963. *Right Reverend New Dealer John A. Ryan.* New York: Macmillan.

Burrow, James Gordon. 1963. *The American Medical Association: Voice of American Medicine.* Baltimore: Johns Hopkins University Press.

Calabresi, Guido. 1970. *The Costs of Accidents: A Legal and Economic Analysis.* New Haven, Conn.: Yale University Press.

Callahan, Daniel. 1986. "Adequate Health Care and an Aging Society: Are They Compatible?" *Daedalus* 115/1:247–67.

———. 1987. *Setting Limits: Medical Goals in an Aging Society.* New York: Simon and Schuster.

Camenisch, Paul F. 1976. "Commentary: On the Professions." *The Hastings Center Report* 6 (October): 8–9.

Caplow, Theodore, Howard M. Bahr, Bruce A. Chadwick, Reuben Hill, and Margaret Holmes Williamson. 1982. *Middletown Families: Fifty Years of Change and Continuity.* St. Paul, Minn.: University of Minnesota Press.

Carlin, Jerome. 1962. *Lawyers On Their Own.* New Brunswick, N.J.: Rutgers University Press.

———. 1966. *Lawyers' Ethics: A Survey of the New York City Bar.* New York: Russell Sage Foundation Press.

Carlson, R. J., and R. Cunningham, eds. 1978. *Future Directions in Health Care: A New Public Policy.* Cambridge, Mass.: Ballinger Publishing Company.

Childress, James F. 1970. "Who Shall Live When Not All Can Live?" *Soundings* 43:339–55.

———. 1979. "Priorities in the Allocation of Health Care Resources." *Soundings* 62:256–74.

———. 1984. "Ensuring Care, Respect, and Fairness for the Elderly." *The Hastings Center Report* 14:27–31.

Churchill, Larry R. 1987. *Rationing Health Care in America: Perceptions and Principles of Justice.* Notre Dame, Ind.: University of Notre Dame Press.

Cohen, Morris. 1933. "The Basis of Contract Law." *Harvard Law Review* 46:553.

Coleman, Jules L. 1974. "On the Moral Argument for the Fault System." *Journal of Philosophy* 71:473–90.

Collingwood, R. G. 1938. *The Principles of Art.* Oxford: Clarendon Press.

Conwell, Russell H. 1915. *Acres of Diamonds.* New York: Harper and Brothers.

Cragg, Kenneth. 1975. *The House of Islam.* 2nd ed. Belmont, Calif.: Dickenson Press.

Dahl, Robert A. 1970. *After the Revolution.* New Haven, Conn.: Yale University Press.

———. 1983. "Justice Between Age Groups: Am I My Parents' Keeper?" *Millbank Memorial Fund Quarterly* 61:3.

———. 1985. *Just Health Care.* New York: Cambridge University Press.

Danzinger, Sheldon, and Peter Gottschalk. 1986. "Families with Children Have Fared Worst." *Challenge* (March-April), 40–65.

Davis, Karen. 1976. *National Health Insurance: Benefits, Costs, and Consequences.* Washington, D.C.: Brookings Institution.

Demos, John. 1979. "Images of the American Family: Then and Now." In *Changing Images of the Family.* Edited by Virginia Tufte and Barbara Myerhoff. New Haven, Conn.: Yale University Press.

Dewey, John. 1954. *The Public and Its Problems.* Chicago: Swallow Press.

———. 1971. *A Common Faith.* New Haven, Conn.: Yale University Press.

Dionne, E. J., Jr. 1987. "Tough Decisions Along a New Ethical Frontier." *The New York Times* (15 March), E–3.

Donagan, Alan. 1977. *The Theory of Morality.* Chicago: University of Chicago Press.

Dworkin, Ronald. 1977. *Taking Rights Seriously.* Cambridge, Mass.: Harvard University Press.

————. 1986. *Law's Empire.* Cambridge, Mass.: Harvard University Press.

Edwards, Paul, ed. 1967. *The Encyclopedia of Philosophy.* 8 vols. New York: Macmillan.

Ellinghaus, M. P. 1969. "In Defense of Unconscionability." *Yale Law Journal* 78:757.

Elshtain, Jane Bethke. 1982. "Thank Heaven for Little Girls: The Dialectics of Development." In *The Family in Political Thought.* Edited by Jean Bethke Elshtain. Amherst, Mass.: University of Massachusetts Press.

————. 1986. "Citizenship and Armed Civic Virtue: Some Critical Questions on the Commitment to Public Life." *Soundings* 49:99–110.

Engberg-Pedersen, Troels. 1983. *Aristotle's Theory of Moral Insight.* Oxford: Clarendon Press.

Englard, Izhak. 1980. "The System Builders: A Critical Appraisal of Modern Tort Theory." *The Journal of Legal Studies* 9:27–69.

Epstein, Richard A. 1973. "A Theory of Strict Liability." *The Journal of Legal Studies* 2:151.

————. 1974. "Defenses and Subsequent Pleas in a System of Strict Liability." *The Journal of Legal Studies* 3:1.

————. 1975a. "Intentional Harms." *The Journal of Legal Studies* 4:391.

————. 1975b. "Unconscionability: A Critical Reappraisal." *Journal of Law and Economics* 18:219–315.

————. 1976. "Medical Malpractice: The Case for Contract." *American Bar Foundation Research Journal* 1:87–149.

————. 1985. *Takings: Private Property and the Power of Eminent Domain.* Cambridge, Mass.: Harvard University Press.

Farnsworth, E. Allen, and William F. Young. 1980. *Cases and Materials on Contracts.* 3rd ed. Mineola, N.Y.: Foundation Press.

Faulkner, Harold U. 1931. *The Quest for Social Justice: 1898–1914.* Vol. 11 in the series *A History of American Life.* New York: Macmillan.

Fein, Rashi. 1986. *Medical Care, Medical Costs: The Search for a Health Insurance Policy.* Cambridge, Mass.: Harvard University Press.

Feinberg, Joel. 1970. *Doing and Deserving.* Princeton, N.J.: Princeton University Press.

―――. 1973. *Social Philosophy.* Englewood Cliffs, N.J.: Prentice-Hall.

―――. 1977. "Noncomparative Justice." In *Justice: Selected Readings.* Edited by J. Feinberg and H. Gross. Belmont, Calif.: Wadsworth.

―――. 1978. "Rights: Systematic Analysis." In *Encyclopedia of Bioethics.* New York: Macmillan and Free Press.

Fishkin, James S. 1983. *Justice, Equal Opportunity, and the Family.* New Haven, Conn.: Yale University Press.

―――. 1984. *Beyond Subjective Morality.* New Haven, Conn.: Yale University Press.

Fiske, Edward B. 1986. "Student Debt Reshaping Colleges and Careers." *The New York Times* (3 August).

Flax, Jane. 1982. "The Family in Contemporary Feminist Thought: A Critical Review." In *The Family in Political Thought.* Edited by Jean Bethke Elshtain. Amherst, Mass.: University of Massachusetts Press.

Fletcher, George P. 1972. "Fairness and Utility in Tort Theory." *Harvard Law Review* 85:537–73.

Foot, Philippa. 1978. *Virtues and Vices and Other Essays in Moral Philosophy.* Berkeley, Calif.: University of California Press.

Fox, Richard. 1987. "The Liberal Ethic and the Spirit of Protestantism." *The Center Magazine* 20:4–14.

Frankena, William. 1973. *Ethics.* 2nd ed. Englewood Cliffs, N.J.: Prentice-Hall.

―――. 1976. "Some Beliefs about Justice." In *Perspectives on Morality.* Edited by Kenneth E. Goodpaster. Notre Dame, Ind.: University of Notre Dame Press.

Fried, Charles. 1976a. "Equality and Rights in Medical Care." *The Hastings Center Report* 6/1:30–32.

————. 1976b. "The Lawyer as Friend: The Moral Foundation of the Lawyer-Client Relationship." *Yale Law Journal* 85:1060–89.

————. 1978. *Right and Wrong.* Cambridge, Mass.: Harvard University Press.

————. 1981. *Contract as Promise.* Cambridge, Mass.: Harvard University Press.

Friedman, Lawrence M. 1973. *A History of American Law.* New York: Simon and Schuster.

Fuchs, Victor. 1986. *The Health Economy.* Cambridge, Mass.: Harvard University Press.

Gal, Allon. 1980. *Brandeis of Boston.* Cambridge, Mass.: Harvard University Press.

Galston, William A. 1980. *Justice and the Human Good.* Chicago: University of Chicago Press.

————. 1986. "Equality of Opportunity and Liberal Theory." In *Justice and Equality: Here and Now.* Edited by Frank S. Lucash. Ithaca, N.Y.: Cornell University Press.

Gannon, Thomas M., ed. 1987. *The Catholic Challenge to the American Economy: Reflections on the U.S. Bishops' Pastoral Letter on Catholic Social Teaching and the U.S. Economy (with the complete text of the Bishops' Letter).* New York: Macmillan.

Geertz, Clifford. 1983. *Local Knowledge: Further Essays in Interpretive Anthropology.* New York: Basic Books.

————. 1988. *Works and Lives: The Anthropologist as Author.* Stanford, Calif.: Stanford University Press.

Geiger, George R. 1933. *The Philosophy of Henry George.* Introduction by John Dewey. New York: Macmillan.

George, Henry. 1879. *Progress and Poverty.* New York: Robert Schalkenbach Foundation.

————. 1891. *The Condition of Labor: An Open Letter to Pope Leo XIII.* New York: U.S. Book Co.

———. 1906. *Social Problems*. New York: Doubleday, Page and Co.

Gilmore, Grant. 1974. *The Death of Contract*. Columbus, Ohio: Ohio State University Press.

Glendon, Mary Ann. 1981. *The New Family and the New Property*. Toronto: Butterworths.

———. 1987. *Abortion and Divorce in Western Law*. Cambridge, Mass.: Harvard University Press.

Goldmark, Josephine. 1930. *Pilgrims of '48: One Man's Part in the Austrian Revolution of 1848 and a Family Migration to America*. Preface by Josef Redlich. New Haven, Conn.: Yale University Press.

Goodin, Robert E. 1985. *Protecting the Vulnerable: A Reanalysis of Our Social Responsibilities*. Chicago: University of Chicago Press.

———. 1988. *Reasons for Welfare: The Political Theory of the Welfare State*. Princeton, N.J.: Princeton University Press.

Gordon, Suzanne. 1987. "Feminism Goes to Market." *Boston Globe* (18 October), A17–18.

Green, Leon. 1959. "Tort Law Public Law in Disguise." Part I. *Texas Law Review* 38:1–13.

———. 1960. "Tort Law Public Law in Disguise." Part II. *Texas Law Review* 38:257–69.

———. 1977. *The Litigation Process in Tort Law: No Place to Stop in the Development of Tort Law*. 2nd ed. Indianapolis, Ind.: Bobbs-Merrill.

Green, Ronald M. 1988. *Religion and Moral Reason*. New York: Oxford University Press.

Greenhouse, Steven. 1986. "Passing the Buck from One Generation to the Next." *The New York Times* (17 August), E5.

Gross, Henry. 1980. Review of *The Economics of Contract Law* by Anthony T. Kronman and Richard A. Posner. *Columbia Law Review* 80:867–77.

Gunnemann, Jon P. 1985. "Capitalism and Commutative Justice." In *The Annual of the Society of Christian Ethics.* Edited by Alan B. Anderson. Washington D.C.: Georgetown University Press.

Gutmann, Amy. 1985. "Communitarian Critics of Liberalism." *Philosophy and Public Affairs* 14:308–22.

———. 1987. *Democratic Education.* Princeton, N.J.: Princeton University Press.

Habermas, Jürgen. 1984. *The Theory of Communicative Action.* Vol. 1. *Reason and the Rationalization of Society.* Translated by Thomas McCarthy. Boston: Beacon Press.

Harrington, Michael. 1985. *The Politics at God's Funeral.* New York: Penguin.

Hart, H. L. A. 1979. "Between Utility and Rights." In *The Idea of Freedom: Essays in Honor of Isaiah Berlin.* Edited by Alan Ryan. Oxford: Oxford University Press.

Haskell, Thomas L. 1977. *The Emergence of Professional Social Science: The American Social Science Association and the Nineteenth-Century Crisis of Authority.* Champaign, Ill.: University of Illinois Press.

Hauerwas, Stanley. 1981. *A Community of Character: Toward a Constructive Christian Social Ethic.* Notre Dame, Ind.: University of Notre Dame Press.

Hayes, Christopher L. 1986. "Challenging the Intergenerational Conflict." *American Family* 9 (January-February): 4.

Hazard, Geoffrey. 1965. "Rationing Justice." *The Journal of Law and Economics* 8:1–10.

———. 1969. "Social Justice through Civil Justice." *The University of Chicago Law Review* 36:699–712.

———. 1970. "Law-reforming in the Anti-poverty Effort." *The University of Chicago Law Review* 37:242–55.

———. 1971. "Legal Problems Peculiar to the Poor." *Journal of Social Issues* 26:47–58.

Heinz, Donald. 1983. "The Struggle to Define America." In *The New Christian Right*. Edited by R. C. Liebman and R. Wuthnow. New York: Aldine.

Held, Virginia. 1980. *Property, Profits, and Economic Justice*. Belmont, Calif.: Wadsworth.

———. 1984. *Rights and Goods: Justifying Social Action*. New York: Free Press.

Hite, Shere. 1987. *Women and Love: A Cultural Revolution in Progress*. New York: Alfred A. Knopf.

Hoffman, Elizabeth, and Matthew L. Spitzer. 1985. "Entitlements, Rights, and Fairness: An Experimental Examination of Subjects' Concepts of Distributive Justice." *Journal of Legal Studies* 14:259–97.

Hollenbach, David. 1977. "Modern Catholic Teaching Concerning Justice." In *The Faith That Does Justice*. Edited by John C. Haughey. New York: Paulist Press.

———. 1983. *Nuclear Ethics*. New York: Paulist Press.

Holmes, Oliver Wendell. 1881. *The Common Law*. Boston: Little, Brown and Co.

———. 1897. "The Path of the Law." *Harvard Law Review* 10:457.

Hume, David. 1741. "Of Commerce." In *Essays, Moral, Political and Literary*. Vol. 1. London: Longmans, Green.

———. 1751. "Of Justice." In *An Enquiry Concerning the Principles of Morals*. Reprinted in *Justice: Selected Readings*. Edited by J. Feinberg and H. Gross. Belmont, Calif.: Wadsworth, 1977.

———. 1777. *An Enquiry Concerning the Principles of Morals*. London: Cadell.

Hurst, James Willard. 1950. *The Growth of American Law: The Law Makers*. Boston: Little, Brown and Co.

———. 1977. *Law and Social Order in the United States*. Ithaca, N.Y.: Cornell University Press.

Ignatieff, Michael. 1986. *The Needs of Strangers*. New York: Viking Press.

Joachim, H. H. 1962. *Aristotle: The Nichomachean Ethics, A Commentary*. Edited by D. A. Rees. Oxford: Clarendon Press.

Johnson, Carlyn E. 1985. *A Generation at Risk*. Indianapolis, Ind.: Indiana State Teachers Association.

Jonas, Hans. 1984. *The Imperative of Responsibility: In Search of an Ethics for the Technological Age*. Translated by Hans Jonas with the collaboration of David Herr. Chicago: University of Chicago Press.

Keeton, W. Page, and Robert E. Keeton. 1977. *Cases and Materials on the Law of Torts*. 2nd ed. St. Paul, Minn.: West Publishing.

Kelly, Alfred H., and Winfred A. Harbison. 1970. *The American Constitution: Its Origins and Development*. 4th ed. New York: W. W. Norton.

Kennedy, Duncan. 1976. "Form and Substance in Private Law Adjudication." *Harvard Law Review* 89:1685.

———. 1982. "Distributive and Paternalist Motives in Contract and Tort Law, with Special Reference to Compulsory Terms and Unequal Bargaining Power." *Maryland Law Review* 41:563–658.

Kessler, Friedrich. 1943. "Contracts of Adhesion—Some Thoughts about Freedom of Contract." *Columbia Law Review* 43:629–42.

Ketcham, Ralph L. 1958. "James Madison and the Nature of Man." *Journal of the History of Ideas* 19:62–76.

Kingson, Eric, Barbara A. Hirschorn, and John M. Cornman. 1986. *Ties that Bind: The Interdependence of Generations*. Washington, D.C.: Seven Locks Press.

Kofman, Sarah. 1977. "Metaphor, Symbol, Metamorphosis." In *The New Nietzsche: Contemporary Styles of Interpretation*. Edited with an introduction by David B. Allison. New York: Dell Publishing.

Kronman, Anthony T. 1978. "Mistake, Disclosure, Information, and the Law of Contracts." *Journal of Legal Studies* 7:1–34.

————. 1980. "Contract Law and Distributive Justice." *Yale Law Journal* 89:472.

————. 1983. "Paternalism and the Law of Contracts." *Yale Law Journal* 92:763–98.

Krouse, Richard W. 1982. "Patriarchal Liberalism and Beyond: From John Stuart Mill to Harriet Taylor." In *The Family in Political Thought.* Edited by Jean Bethke Elshtain. Amherst, Mass.: University of Massachusetts Press.

Kurland, Philip B. 1961. *Religion and the Law: Of Church and State and the Supreme Court.* New York: Aldine.

Lakoff, George, and Mark Johnson. 1980. *Metaphors We Live By.* Chicago: University of Chicago Press.

Laslett, Peter. 1972. "History of Political Philosophy." In *Encyclopedia of Philosophy.* Vol. 6. Paul Edwards, ed. New York: Macmillan.

Lawson-Peebles, Bob. 1976. "Henry George the Prophet." *Journal of American Studies* 10 (April): 37–51.

Lebacqz, Karen. 1985. *Professional Ethics: Power and Paradox.* Nashville, Tenn.: Abingdon Press.

————. 1986. *Six Theories of Justice.* Minneapolis, Minn.: Augsburg.

————. 1987. *Justice in an Unjust World: Foundations for a Christian Approach to Justice.* Minneapolis, Minn.: Augsburg.

Lee, Philip R., and Carol Emmott. 1978. "Health Care: Health Care System." In *Encyclopedia of Bioethics* 2:613. New York: Macmillan and Free Press.

Leff, Arthur Allan. 1967. "Unconscionability and the Code: the Emperor's New Clause." *University of Pennsylvania Law Review* 115:485.

————. 1974. "Economic Analysis of Law: Some Realism about Nominalism." *Virginia Law Review* 60:451.

Lehnen, Robert G., and Carlyn E. Johnson. 1984. *Financing Indiana's Public Schools: An Analysis of the Past and Recommendations for the Future.* Indianapolis, Ind.: Indiana University School of Public and Environmental Affairs.

Lerner, Max. 1931. "The Social Thought of Mr. Justice Brandeis." *Yale Law Journal* 41:1–32.

Liebman, Robert C. 1983. "Mobilizing the Moral Majority." In *The New Christian Right.* R. C. Liebman and R. Wuthnow, eds. New York: Aldine.

Liebman, R. C., and R. Wuthnow. 1983. *The New Christian Right.* New York: Aldine.

Linzer, Peter. 1981. "On the Amorality of Contract Remedies— Efficiency, Equity, and the Second Restatement." *Columbia Law Review* 81:111–39.

Lonergan, Bernard J. F. 1958. *Insight: A Study of Human Understanding.* New York: Philosophical Library.

———. 1972. *Method in Theology.* New York: Herder and Herder.

Longman, Phillip. 1985. "Justice Between Generations." *The Atlantic Monthly* 255:73–81.

———. 1987. *Born to Pay: The New Politics of Aging in America.* Boston: Houghton Mifflin.

Lovejoy, Arthur O. 1961. *Reflections on Human Nature.* Baltimore: Johns Hopkins University Press.

Lovin, Robin W. 1986. "Religion and American Public Life: Three Relationships." In *Religion and American Public Life.* Edited by Robin W. Lovin, with a foreword by Martin E. Marty. New York: Paulist Press.

MacIntyre, Alasdair. 1981. *After Virtue.* Notre Dame, Ind.: Notre Dame University Press. 2nd ed. in 1984.

———. 1988. *Whose Justice? Which Rationality?* Notre Dame, Ind.: Notre Dame University Press.

Mason, Alpheus Thomas. 1946. *Brandeis: A Free Man's Life.* New York: Viking Press.

May, Henry F. 1967. *Protestant Churches and Industrial America.* New York: Harper and Row.

May, William F. 1983. *The Physician's Covenant.* Philadelphia: Westminster.

Meilander, Gilbert C. 1983. "Josef Pieper: Explorations in the Thought of a Philosopher of Virtue." *The Journal of Religious Ethics* 11/1:114–34.

———. 1984. *The Theory and Practice of Virtue.* Notre Dame, Ind.: University of Notre Dame Press.

Messinger, Sheldon L., and Philip Selznick. 1986. "Law, Society, and Education." *The Center Magazine* 19 (May-June): 33–41.

Michelman, Frank I. 1967. "Property, Utility, and Fairness: Comments on the Ethical Foundations of 'Just Compensation' Law." *Harvard Law Review* 80:1165–1258.

———. 1971. "Pollution as a Tort: a Non-Accidental Perspective on Calabresi's Costs." *Yale Law Journal* 80:647.

———. 1978. "Norms and Normativity in the Economic Theory of Law." *Minnesota Law Review* 62:105.

———. 1979. "A Comment on Some Uses and Abuses of Economics in Law." *The University of Chicago Law Review* 46:307.

Miller, David. 1976. *Social Justice.* Oxford: Clarendon Press.

Mintz, Steven, and Susan Kellogg. 1988. *Domestic Revolutions: A Social History of American Family Life.* New York: Free Press.

Moody, Harry R. 1985. "Inter-Generational Responsibilities: Aging and Social Policy in the 1980s and Beyond." A speech presented at the Conference on Social Policy and the Economics of Aging (Ohio State University, September 30, 1985).

Morison, Robert S. 1981. "Bioethics after Two Decades." *The Hastings Center Report* 11 (April): 8–12.

Moynihan, Daniel Patrick. 1965. *The Negro Family: The Case for National Action.* A report from the Office of the Secretary of Labor.

————. 1986. *Family and Nation.* San Diego, Calif.: Harcourt Brace Jovanovich.

Musto, David. 1973. *The American Disease: Origins of Narcotic Control.* New Haven, Conn.: Yale University Press.

National Conference of Catholic Bishops. 1986. *Economic Justice for All: Pastoral Letter on Catholic Social Teaching and the U.S. Economy.* Washington, D.C.: National Conference of Catholic Bishops/ United States Catholic Conference.

Niebuhr, H. Richard. 1960. *Radical Monotheism and Western Culture.* New York: Harper and Row.

————. 1975. The *Social Sources of Denominationalism.* New York: New American Library.

Niebuhr, Reinhold. 1932. *Moral Man and Immoral Society.* New York: Scribners.

————. 1943. *The Nature and Destiny of Man.* Vol. 1. New York: Scribners.

————. 1945. *The Children of Light and the Children of Darkness.* London: Nisbet.

————. 1964. *The Nature and Destiny of Man.* Vol. 2. New York: Scribners.

————. 1979. *An Interpretation of Christian Ethics.* New York: Seabury.

Nozick, Robert. 1974. *Anarchy, State, and Utopia.* New York: Basic Books.

O'Brien, David J. 1968. *American Catholics and Social Reform: The New Deal Years.* New York: Oxford University Press.

Okin, Susan Moller. 1989. *Justice, Gender, and the Family.* New York: Basic Books.

Outka, Gene. 1974. "Social Justice and Equal Access to Health Care." *The Journal of Religious Ethics* 2/1:11–32.

Palmer, Parker. 1988. *The Company of Strangers.* New York: Crossroad Publishing.

Papke, James A. 1987. *The Composition and Burden of Indiana's Tax System: Interstate Comparisons.* Indianapolis, Ind.: Indiana State Teachers Association.

Patterson, Edwin W. 1964. "The Interpretation and Construction of Contracts." *Columbia Law Review* 64:833.

Pellegrino, Edmund, and David Thomasma. 1981. *A Philosophical Basis of Medical Practice.* New York: Oxford University Press.

Pieper, Josef. 1965. *Four Cardinal Virtues.* Notre Dame, Ind.: University of Notre Dame.

Posner, Richard A. 1972. "A Theory of Negligence." *Journal of Legal Studies* 1:29–96.

———. 1973. "Strict Liability: A Comment." *Journal of Legal Studies* 2:205–21.

———. 1978. "Adjudication as a Private Good." *Journal of Legal Studies* 8:235.

———. 1979. *The Economics of Contract Law.* Boston: Little, Brown and Co.

———. 1980. "Retribution and Related Concepts of Punishment." *Journal of Legal Studies* 9:71–92.

———. 1981. *The Economics of Justice.* Cambridge, Mass.: Harvard University Press.

———. 1985. *The Federal Courts: Crisis and Reform.* Cambridge, Mass.: Harvard University Press.

———. 1986. *Economic Analysis of Law.* 3rd ed. Boston: Little, Brown and Co.

Posner, Richard A., and William M. Landes. 1987. *The Economic Structure of Tort Law.* Cambridge, Mass.: Harvard University Press.

President's Commission for the Study of Ethical Problems in Medicine and Biomedical and Behavioral Research. 1983. *Securing Access to*

Health Care: The Ethical Implications of Differences in the Availability of Health Services. Vol. 1: Report. Washington, D.C.: U.S. Government Printing Office.

President's Commission on Education. 1986. *A Nation at Risk.* Washington, D.C.: U.S. Government Printing Office.

Preston, Samuel H. 1984. "Children and the Elderly in the U.S." *Scientific American* 251:44–49.

Purtilo, Ruth, and James Sorrell. 1986. "The Ethical Dilemmas of a Rural Physician." *The Hastings Center Report* 16/4:24–28.

Rauschenbusch, Walter. 1912. *Christianizing the Social Order.* New York: Macmillan.

Rawls, John. 1971. *A Theory of Justice.* Cambridge, Mass.: Harvard University Press.

———. 1975. The Independence of Moral Theory. *Proceedings and Addresses of the American Philosophical Association* 48:5–22. Newark, Del.: American Philosophical Association/University of Delaware.

———. 1981. *The Basic Liberties and Their Priority.* The Tanner Lectures on Human Values, delivered at the University of Michigan, April 10, 1981.

———. 1985. "Justice as Fairness: Political not Metaphysical." *Philosophy and Public Affairs* 14:223–51.

Reichley, A. James. 1985. *Religion in American Public Life.* Washington, D.C.: Brookings Institution.

Ryan, John A. 1907. *A Living Wage.* New York: Macmillan.

———. 1916. *Distributive Justice.* New York: Macmillan.

———. 1931. "The Ethics of Public Utility Valuation." In *Questions of the Day.* New York: Books for Libraries Press.

Sade, Robert M. 1971. "Medical Care as a Right: A Refutation." *The New England Journal of Medicine* 285:1288–92.

Sadurski, Wojciech. 1984. "Social Justice and Legal Justice." *Law and Philosophy* 3:329–54.

Sandel, Michael J. 1982. *Liberalism and the Limits of Justice.* Cambridge: Cambridge University Press.

Scanlon, Thomas M. 1975. "Preference and Urgency." *Journal of Philosophy* 72:655–69.

———. 1977. "Liberty, Contract, and Contribution." In *Markets and Morals.* Edited by Gerald Dworkin, Gordon Bermant, and Peter G. Brown. New York: Wiley.

Schmookler, Andrew Bard. 1984. *The Parable of the Tribes: The Problem of Power in Social Evolution.* Boston: Houghton Mifflin.

Schwartz, Alan. 1974. "Seller, Unequal Bargaining Power and the Judicial Process." *Indiana Law Journal* 49:367–98.

Sellers, James. 1970. *Public Ethics: American Manners and Morals.* New York: Harper and Row.

———. 1975. *Warming Fires.* New York: Seabury Press.

———. 1979. "Human Rights and the American Tradition of Justice." *Soundings* 62:226–55.

Selznick, Philip. 1987. "The Demands of the Community." *The Center Magazine* 20:33–43.

Shklar, Judith N. 1986a. "Injustice, Injury, and Inequality: An Introduction." In *Justice and Equality: Here and Now.* Edited by Frank S. Lucash. Ithaca, N.Y.: Cornell University Press.

———. 1986b. *Legalism: Law, Morals, and Political Trials.* Cambridge, Mass.: Harvard University Press.

Shore, Miles F., and Harry Levinson. 1985. "On Business and Medicine," *New England Journal of Medicine* 313:5(1985), 319–21.

Silverstein, Lee. 1967. "Eligibility for Free Legal Services in Civil Cases." *Journal of Urban Law* 44:549.

Simpson, John H. 1983. "Moral Issues and Status Politics." In *The New Christian Right*. R.C. Liebman and R. Wuthnow, eds. New York: Aldine, 1977.

Skolnick, Jerome H. 1968. "Coercion to Virtue." *Southern California Law Review* 41:607.

———. 1975. *Justice Without Trial*. 2nd ed. New York: Wiley and Sons.

Smigel, Erwin O. 1964. *The Wall Street Lawyer: Professional Organization Man*. New York: Free Press.

Smurl, James F. 1978. "In the Public Interest: The Precedents and Standards of a Lawyer's Public Responsibility." *Indiana Law Review* 11:797–828.

———. 1979. "Eligibility for Legal Aid: Whom to Help When Unable to Help All." *Indiana Law Review* 12:519–51.

———. 1983. "Allocating Public Burdens: The Social Ethics Implied in Brandeis of Boston." *The Journal of Law and Religion* 1:59–78.

———. 1985. *A Primer in Ethics*. Bristol, Ind.: Wyndham Hall Press.

———. 1987. "Renegotiating the Burdens of Justice in Public Education." In *The Annual of the Society of Christian Ethics*. Washington, D.C.: Georgetown University Press.

Stannard, David E. 1979. "Changes in the American Family: Fiction and Reality." In *Changing Images of the Family*. Edited by Virginia Tufte and Barbara Myerhoff. New Haven, Conn.: Yale University Press.

Stevens, Rosemary. 1971. *American Medicine and the Public Interest*. New Haven, Conn.: Yale University Press.

———. 1989. *In Sickness and in Wealth: American Hospitals in the Twentieth Century*. New York: Basic Books.

Stone, Christopher. 1975. *Where the Law Ends: The Social Control of Corporate Behavior*. New York: Harper and Row.

Stone, Harlan Fiske. 1934. "The Public Influence of the Bar." *Harvard Law Review* 48:1–14.

Strong, Josiah. 1898. *The Twentieth Century City*. New York: Baker and Taylor.

Sturm, Douglas. 1984. "Crisis in the American Republic." A paper presented at a symposium on religion and the life of the nation at Indiana University in Indianapolis, Ind., March 1, 1984.

Sullivan, William M. 1986. *Reconstructing Public Philosophy*. Berkeley and Los Angeles: University of California Press.

Thurow, Lester C. 1980. *The Zero-Sum Society*. New York: Basic Books.

Trachtenberg, Alan. 1982. *The Incorporation of America: Culture and Society in the Gilded Age*. New York: Hill and Wang.

Tracy, David. 1986. "Particular Classics, Public Religion, and the American Tradition." In *Religion and American Public Life*. Edited by Robin W. Lovin, with a foreword by Martin E. Marty. New York: Paulist Press.

Turner, Victor. 1976. "Religious Paradigms and Political Action: The Murder in the Cathedral of Thomas Becket." In *The Biographical Process: Studies in the History and Psychology of Religion*. Edited by Frank E. Reynolds and Donald Capps. The Hague, Netherlands: Mouton.

Walzer, Michael. 1977. *Just and Unjust Wars: A Moral Argument with Historical Illustrations*. New York: Basic Books.

———. 1983. *Spheres of Justice: A Defense of Pluralism and Equality*. New York: Basic Books.

———. 1985. *Exodus and Revolution*. New York: Basic Books.

———. 1986. "Justice Here and Now." In *Justice and Equality: Here and Now*. Edited by Frank S. Lucash. Ithaca, N.Y.: Cornell University Press.

———. 1987. *Interpretation and Social Criticism*. Cambridge, Mass.: Harvard University Press.

Wang, K. S. 1982. "Reflections on Contract Law and Distributive Justice: A Reply to Kronman." *Hastings Law Journal* 34:513–27.

Warren, Mary Anne. 1982. "Future Generations." In *And Justice for All: New Introductory Essays in Ethics and Public Policy.* Edited by Tom Regan and Donald VandeVeer. Totowa, N.J.: Rowman and Littlefield.

Weitzman, Lenore. 1981. *The Marriage Contract: Spouses, Lovers, and the Law.* New York: Free Press.

————. 1985. *The Divorce Revolution: The Unexpected Social and Economic Consequences for Women and Children in America.* New York: Free Press.

White, G. Edward. 1977. "The Intellectual Origins of Torts in America." *The Yale Law Journal* 86:671-693.

Wilson, William Julius. 1987. *The Truly Disadvantaged: The Inner City, the Underclass, and Public Policy.* Chicago: University of Chicago Press.

World Health Organization. 1978. *Declaration of Alma-Ata.* New York: United Nations.

Index

Accountability for motives, 32
Action Center for Educational Services and Scholarships, 163
Adjustment to distribute justice, 2–3
Adkins v. *Children's Hospital of District of Columbia,* 175, 180
Affirmative action, 162
Allgeyer v. *Louisiana,* 175
Altruistic prudence, 15, 32
American College of Healthcare Executives, 94
Aquinas, Thomas
  intellectual heritage of, 10
  undue application of reason to justice described by, 23
Aristotelian tradition, 30–31, 45–46, 155
Aristotle
  central question of justice for, 15
  excellence of justice for, 156
  intellectual heritage of, 10
  regime described by, 20
Asian-American children, academic success of, 162

Barry, Brian, claims about distributive justice of, 152
Bazelon, David C., definition of insanity broadened by, 183
Beauchamp, Tom L.
  allocation of burdens for health care proposed by, 106
  "bad conscience" for, 174
  health care text by, 97
  identification of distributive concerns with economic issues by, 149
  view of health care of, 100–102, 172–73
Beecher, Henry Ward, view of equalizing wages of, 3, 6–7
Bellah, Robert
  confidence in social movements of, 151
  narratives that treat social trust described by, 153
Beneficence, 145
  in health care, 105–6
  as responsibility of married persons, 53
Bennett, John G., need to describe good institutions noted by, 147
Bentham, Jeremy, market described by, 132
Berger, Brigitte, 164
Berger, Peter L., 164

Bexar County, Texas, tax base for education of, 161, 168
Black Americans
  disproportionate benefits for better educated and better motivated, 60–61
  systemic disadvantaging practices toward, 39
Bloom, Allan, family described by, 50
Blue Cross, 95
Boston Elevated Railway Company franchise, 119–23, 127–28 Boston Traction Contest, 122
Bowne, Borden Parker, 4
Brandeis, Louis Dembitz
  arguments against Boston Elevated Railway Company of, 121–22
  biographical information about, 120, 178
  as public's champion in transportation franchise dispute, 120, 127–28
  results of monopolistic power according to, 180
Brown v. *The Board of Education,* 166
Burdens
  equitable allocation of common, 1, 33–34
  harms created from, 57
  of health care, 106
Burdens of justice, 1–48
  in basic health care, 93–115
  between generations, 61–75, 160, 162
  in contract law, 117–41
  in couples, 52–61
  in families, 49–76
  in financing public education, 77–91
  special interests and, 147
  unwillingness to accept, 43
Burger, Warren, graduates of day and night law schools compared by, 130

Calabresi, Guido, assignment of liability in accidents described by, 181–82
Callahan, Daniel, 63, 171
Campbell Soup case, 179
Carnegie, Andrew, property as communitarian according to, 151
Children
  collective sense of responsibility for others', 168
  decision to have, 112
  health and welfare programs for, 171
  neglect of, 62

principle of proportionate harm
applied to, 57
responsibilities toward prospective, 159
standard of living of, 62
systemic harm of poorly educating,
77–88
Childress, James F.
allocation of burdens for health care
proposed by, 106
"bad conscience" for, 174
health care text by, 97
identification of distributive concerns
with economic issues by, 149
view of health care of, 100–102, 172–73
Claims on property
based on need, 67
establishing, 173
noncompelling, 99
Clark, Harley, ruling about Texas school
financing formula by, 167
College expenses, 68–73
Collingwood, R. G., false consciousness
described by, 157
Committee for Public Education v. *Nyquist*, 166
Commodities, perceiving all goods as,
21–22, 173
Common law
identified with rules for Black, 181
moral values respected by, 136
prestige accorded by Beauchamp and
Childress to, 172
Communitarian position, 151–52
Communities
cooperation in, 47
disagreeable or strenuous work in, 33
distributive justice as chief good of, 143
effects of contract law on, 138
just allocation of social goods as chief
virtue of, 47
just persons in public affairs needed
in, 83
lawyers who overlook interests of, 131
participation in reforming public
education in, 89
religious, 46
social goods provided by, 100
Community expressions, 18
Community habits, 24
Compacts, 164
Comparative justice, 173
Compassion for the disadvantaged, 9
Competition
conflicts created by, 3

as force for Christianizing a people, 3
just, 120
Confucian teachings of filial duty, 162
Conjugal family defined, 51
Consent to unjust apportioning of
opportunities, 55
Contract law
burdens of justice in, 117–41
moral considerations in, 138, 175
nineteenth-century case of, 117–18
purposes of, 119
renegotiating burdens of justice in,
136–40
tort law overlapping with, 176
twentieth-century case of, 118
wealth distributed by, 135
Contracts
ability to enter, 123, 180
compulsory terms for, 123–24
consideration in, 176
deciding justness of, 136–37
defects that invalidate, 123
examining customs in, 134
moral value of freedom in making,
118, 129
morality supposed in, 127–36
policing the bargains made in,
126–27
prohibitions in, 176–77
reductionist economic theories of, 177
thick and thin theories of, 132–38
will theory of, 182
Contractual justice, 87
Conwell, Russell H., origins of term
gospel of wealth by, 151
Coughlin, Charles, 4
Couples, burdens of justice in, 52–61
Criteria
applied to contract law, 118
for assigning economic and political
losses, 112–13
for distributive justice, multiple, 152
for free legal services, 131
to identify solutions for human
decision making, 46
for moral habits or virtues, 32
for moral standards in pursuit of
justice, 24–25, 29, 32
shared and endemic, 113
Cultural domination, 60
Cultural practices, concepts and theories
of justice and equality in, 63–67
Culture religion, 169

Davis, Karen, accessibility of health care related to cost, quantity, and incentives according to, 110
Debt for college expenses, 68–73
Decisions
imperatives for making, 44–47
in marriages, 56
rightness and wrongness of, 40
Declaration of Alma-Ata, 98, 104, 108, 170
Development opportunities, 164
Disadvantaging practices, systemic, 38–39
of Black Americans, 39
for classes of persons, 62
for funding higher education, 68–72
in public education, 87
Disinterestedness to cultivate prudence and justice, 41, 155–56
Distributive justice, x–xii
as balance of competing claims for scarce resources, 101
calls for greater, 2–4
classification of desert as impacting theory of, 30
in contracts, fundamental nature of, 138–39
expressed in terms of voluntary altruism, 8
as form of love-based charity or welfare, 7–8
franchises creating material problems in, 120
legal misreadings of, 135
misunderstanding what is being distributed in, 135
as most urgent moral quality, 2
nature of social life and social goods as reason for invoking, 10
as problem of incomes, 4–7
purpose of investigation into, 1
Rawls' egalitarian and Nozick's meritarian views of, contrasting, 26–31
as redistribution, 135
results confused with, 135
Distributors of resources, accountability of, 11
Division of labor, Marxist narratives about, 19
Divorce
conflicts between those in stable marriage and those in, 63
financial impact of, 62, 163
Doctrine of freedom of contract, 118, 129, 140, 175, 179

Doubly disadvantaged classes of persons, 110
Dupree v. *Alma School District,* 82
Dworkin, Ronald, ethical and political considerations of, 138

Earnings, decline in yearly, 61–62
Economic coercion, 178
Economic hardships, recovery from, 71
Economic liberalism, 182
Edgewood Independent School District of San Antonio, Texas, 81, 86, 169. *See also* Texas school system
Education. *See* College expenses, Private schools, *and* Public education
Effective freedom, factors determining, 40
Egalitarianism, 26–27
Elderly people
affluent versus impoverished, 63
poverty percentages for, 161
reluctance to fund schools of, 63, 73
resources and programs for, 62, 68
taxing of, 73–74
Elshtain, Jane B., instruments of oppression listed by, 159–60
England, Izhak
analysis of tort law by, 134, 182
Aristotle misread by, 184
Entitlement rights, 173
Entitlements
basis for, 5–6
economic claims as rights of, 167
to health care, 93
putatively earned, 66–67
Environment
natural, 103–4, 112
social, 104, 112
Environmental facts, 175
Equal liberty, 83, 102, 167
Equal opportunity, 150, 183
Equality, popular concept of, 64
Equity jurisprudence, 130–31, 137

Families
burdens of justice in, 49–76
changes during last fifty years in, 49, 157
conditions and practices associated with hard work in, 38
cultural practices about, 63–67
declining incomes of younger, 161
definitions of, varied, 158

disproportionate harms learned in and passed on to later generations of, 59

public policy on, emphasis of, 164

social goods generated by, 157–58

theories of justice for, 65–67

Federal funding for higher education, reduction of, 69

Federalist Papers, 181

Fee-for-service medical practice, 95

Fein, Rashi, comprehensive health care program called for by, 93

Feinberg, Joel, 149, 171–72

Feminist movement, 58–59

Financial and industrial elites, assumption of stewardship for wealth of nation by, 9

Fishkin, James S., definition of family of, 158

Fiske, Edward B.
  privatist, instrumental values named by, 73
  student debt analyzed by, 68

Fletcher, George P.
  concept of the human good of, 183–84
  misplaced concreteness of legal scholars noted by, 182

Fletcher v. *Peck*, 175

Formal egalitarianism, 182

Formal jurisprudence, 130–32, 139

Frankena, William, competition for health care analyzed by, 102

Freedom-of-contract doctrine, 118, 129, 140, 175, 179

Fried, Charles
  appeals to sense of justice by, 173–74
  causes of unconscionability for, 179
  focus of unconscionability noted by, 125
  unexpressed premises of contracts for, 183

Friedman, Lawrence
  influences on law analyzed by, 174
  ties between property and tort law for, 183
  view of empirical method of jurisprudence of, 184

Full-compliance theory of justice, 66

Galston, William
  appeals to distributive justice examined by, 10, 152
  candidates for invoking distributive justice according to, 158

development opportunities described by, 165

essential elements of theory of justice for, 172

health care classified as social good by, 98–99

internal and external social goods distinguished by, 13

justice compared with other virtues by, 32–33, 156

natural needs defined by, 172–73

principles of entitlement of, 30–31

procedures in health care important to, 174

Geertz, Clifford, 17–18

Generations
  burdens of justice between, 61–75, 160
  equity between, 162
  proximate, 161–62

George, Henry
  redistributive response to allocation issues of, 6
  root of social ills according to, 149
  view of Leo XIII's call for rights of laborers of, 4

Gilmore, Grant
  consequentialist point of view of, 183
  theory of contract law of, 184

Glendon, Mary Ann, sources of social standing described by, 161

Golden Age of Athens, 77

Good
  of a community, moral, 33. *See also* Distributive justice
  cultural, 139
  fundamental, 58, 61, 75, 86, 140, 163
  human, 32, 52, 58, 60, 68–72, 75, 99, 111, 137–39
  personal long-term, 32, 53
  theories based on right versus, 150
  urgent basic, 99
  urgent social, 99–100

Good faith, 123

Goodin, Robert E., moral issue of vulnerability of parties discussed by, 176, 182

Gross, Henry, welfare maximized in contracts according to, 181

Gutiérrez, Gustavo, *x*

Gutmann, Amy
  communitarian critics of liberalism described by, 147–48
  critique of MacIntyre by, 26–27

Habermas, Jürgen, criteria of competence described by, 23–24
Habits of consciousness, 40–44
Habits of justice learned in family life, 50
Habitual justice, lack of, 40
Hand, W. Brevard
  prayer in public schools ruled as constitutional by, 165
  secular humanism defined as religion subject by, 165
Hard work, assigning, 33–37
  decisions and actions in, 42–43
  future generations in mind during, 39
Hard-work caste, creation of, 38
Harms
  community allocation of, 67–68, 84–88
  evaluating, 53
  to fundamental goods that become systemic, 72–73
  proportionate, principle of, 53, 55–58
  systemic, principle of, 53–54, 58–61, 85
  transmitted to future generations, 59–60, 85, 139
Harrington, Michael, trade unions examined by, 46
Hazard, Geoffrey, view of forms of justice of, 184
Health care
  access to, 96, 108, 110–11, 170
  burdens of justice in basic, 93–115
  as commodity or basic provision, 93, 170
  contemporary financing of, 110
  conventional, 104–5, 108, 111
  effective financing for, 110
  elective procedures in, 173
  moral issues in providing, 94
  moral standards for, 105–8
  norms for allocating, 101–2
  perceptions about, misled, 113
  primary, 97–98, 101, 105, 111, 173
  priorities for, 95–96, 108
  proposal for, 108–11
  red herrings and cultural notions about, 114–15
  right to, 95–96
Health care providers, 98
  pro bono publico services of, 107, 174
Health care resources, categories of, 103–5
Health insurance, number of Americans who lack, 94
Health maintenance organizations (HMOs), 95

Held, Virginia
  affirming responsibilities for future generations assessed by, 162
  governance of public policies described by, 24–25
  ways of changing public policy explored by, 88
Henningsen case, 124, 179
Heredity
  knowledge about, 112
  responsibility for burdens in matters of, 104
Hexeis, 21
Higginson, Harry Lee, property as communitarian for, 151
Holden v. *Hardy*, 175
Holmes, Oliver Wendell
  keeping law distinct from morality advocated by, 119, 125
  objectivist theory of contracts of, 177
Home ownership, 61
Hume, David, 2, 149
  Beauchamp and Childress's concept of comparative justice derived from, 173
  obligations of justice linked to property rights by, 162
  view of social justice of, 153

Ignatieff, Michael, public language called for by, 46
Income
  distributive justice as problem of, 4–6
  Galston's view of, 30
  titles to, 6
Income tax
  progressiveness of, 84, 168
  unions inspired by, 95
Indigency defined, 169
Industries
  burdens of injuries and damages caused by private, 178
  today's tax benefits to, 178
Infertility, 59
Insurance, health care, 95, 111
Interest on capital, titles to, 6–7
Intergenerational responsibilities, 39
Involuntary relationships in communities, 14

Jones, Clifton, 125–26
Jones, Cora, 125–26

Jones v. *Star Credit Corporation,* 123–27, 128–30, 133, 179

Judges, public morality reflected and shaped by, 174

Jurisprudence, two forms of, 130–32

Just arrangements as base of tripodal theory, 58

Just persons as base of tripodal theory, 58

Just situations and practices, 38–39

Justice. *See also* Distributive justice, Personal justice, *and* Principles of justice

  Aristotelian view of, 32–33

  as balance of benefits and burdens of common life, 24

  basis for theory of, 154

  cultivating, 41

  defined, 106, 180

  as equal opportunity, 150

  ideal of, 148

  as most urgent moral quality, 2, 47

  notions of, in cultural notions, 65

  notions of, in the legal culture, 140–41

  Nozick's view of, 66–67, 166

  patterns in human lives of, 1–2

  relations ordered by, 21–22

  resources for achieving, 45

  scope of, *ix*

  tensions between generosity and, 51

  tripodal character of, 144

  understanding, 47

  worth assigned to, 15

Kellogg, Susan, social history of family life by, 157

King, Martin Luther, Jr.

  gun control measures following death of, 153

  schizophrenia in America described by, *x–xi*

Kofman, Sarah, Nietzsche's theory of metaphors analyzed by, 146

Kronman, Anthony

  process of interpreting contracts according to, 179, 182–83

  rules of exchange analyzed by, 136

Labor

  division during times of crisis, 55–56

  relationships between industry and, 178

Laslett, Peter, causes of philosophizing according to, 149–50

Lasswell, Harold, *xi*

Law schools, two types of, 130

Lawyers

  cultural beliefs of, 131–32, 140–41

  decisions to accept cases by, 174–75

  training of, 130

Lebacqz, Karen

  correlation between love and justice for, 150

  tripodal account of justice by, 10

Legal aid, 151

Leo XIII, encyclical calling for rights of laborers by, 4, 7

Liberty

  establishing more adequate notions of, 140–41

  preserving, 38–39

Liberty right, 173

Life-style as influence on human health, 104, 112

Locke, John, intellectual heritage of, 10

Lonergan, Bernard

  civilizational decline described by, 154

  imperatives in fostering practical insights described by, 23

  means of enlarging effective freedom analyzed by, 157

  rightness of decisions examined by, 40

  time for reflection according to, 156

MacIntyre, Alasdair, 5–6

  concept of desert of, 154–55

  critiques of liberalism by, 11

  intellectual heritage of, 10

  mistakes in seeing moral history as dualistic by, 26–31

  secondary or derived principles emphasized by, 155

McPherson, Michael S.

  college expenses described by, 68

  new social contract between generations called for by, 75

Madison, James, 3, 149, 181

Market exchanges, 132–33

Marriage

  conflicts between those in divorce and in, 63

  decision making in, 56

  declining importance in women's lives of, 159

  degree of harm to fundamental goods in, 53–55

  opportunities of, 53

  proportionate harms in, 55–58, 60

  responsibilities not to harm their partners of, 53

systemic harms in, 58–61
unbargained-for responsibilities in, 65
Married persons, 52–62
Marshall, John, test of doctrine of freedom of contract decided by, 175
Mason, A. T., view of lawyers and judges of, 168
Medicare, 111
Meritarianism, 27
Metaethical inquiries, 12
Metaphors, 146, 164
Middletown study (Lynd), 49
Miller, David, just structures described by, 152
Mintz, Steven, social history of family life by, 157
Mistakes about principles of justice, 25
Moody, Harry R., 66
Moral accountability for harms, 43–44
Moral constraints, consideration of, 3
Moral principles
    applied to health care, 105
    for apportioning burdens of justice between generations, 67–75
    authority of, 25
    in contract law, 128
    multiple rules stated like, 133–34
    reliability of, 154
Moral standards
    for contract law, 118, 176
    for health care, 105–8
Morison, Robert S., 113
Moynihan, Daniel Patrick, view of social security of, 65
Mythic metaphors in decision making, 41–42

Narratives
    classifying, 153
    cultural, 19–20, 150
    defined, 18
    Marxist, 19
    for social goods, 20–22
National harmony, attainment of, 8
National proposal for allocating hard work, 37
Neighborhood health centers, 110–11
Neocapitalism, illusions of, 8–9
Niebuhr, H. Richard
    accommodation of values to liberty examined by, 169
    freedom of religious communities analyzed by, 154
Niebuhr, Reinhold

Christian realism promoted by, 7
culture religion defined by, 169
warnings about nationalistic stories issued by, 154
No-fault divorce, 160, 162
Noblesse oblige, 9
Nonmaleficence, 53, 84, 145
Norms for distributive justice, 13–48
Nozick, Robert
    acts of acquisition as basis for entitlements according to, 5, 7
    call for a minimal state by, 151
    position on distributive justice of, 26–29, 149, 156–57
    renewal of interest in distributive justice stimulated by work of, 11
    theory of justice of, 66–67, 166
    view of involuntary transfer of justly acquired property of, 155
Nyquist case, 79

O'Callaghan case, 180
Okin, Susan Moller, impact of family life described in, 50
Overreproductivity, 59

Parochial schools, 80. *See also* Private schools
Partial-compliance theories of law and morality, 137
Partial-compliance theory of justice, 66
Pastoral letter of U.S. Catholic bishops on economic life, 14
Pauley v. *Kelley*, 166
Payroll taxes for social security, 62
Pellegrino, Edmund
    allocation of burdens in health care ignored by, 106
    first-contact care described by, 105, 108
    right to health care advocated by, 95–98, 100–102, 171–72
Personal justice, work assignments by people lacking, 33
Philanthropic altruism, 9, 19
Philosophy of life, 180
Plato, argument of the *Republic* by, ix
Positive entitlement right, 173
Posner, Richard A.
    economic theory of contract law of, 134–36, 177, 182
    punishment for, 183
Potency, 17
Practical insights, 144
    communicated in cultural concepts, 64

correlations in data as function of, 96
in cultural narratives, 19–20
expressions of, 16–18
faulty, 19
for governing social goods, 22
in narratives, scrutinizing, 18–19
questioning correctness of, 26–32
role of mediation between experiences of social goods and expressions about them of, 15
tracing patterns of consciousness from, 39
Praxeis, 21
Praxis, 54, 153
Principle of beneficence, 107
Principle of degree of harm to fundamental goods, 53–55, 85, 109, 145
Principle of proportionate harm, 53, 55–58, 71, 85, 109, 145
Principle of equal rights, 64
Principle of systemic harm, 53–54, 58–61, 85, 110, 145
Principles of justice
    reasoning toward habits and, 25–39
    for special situations, 36
    understanding of, as base of tripodal theory, 58
Private schools
    direct maintenance grants to, 80
    public aid for, 79–88
Property
    approaches to, 4–9
    theories of justice that liken entitlements to, 74
Property tax
    ad valorem, 82
    malaproportioned, 84
    school items funded by, 166, 169
    system, U.S., mistaken cultural concepts and theories of justice reinforced by, 74
Protestant traditions of moral philosophy, 40
Prudence
    Aquinas's description of, 23
    cultivating, 41
Public aid for private schools, 79–88
Public education
    "adequate," 90
    allocation of harms in, 84–88
    financing, 77–91, 166, 169
    as function of local and state governments, 166
    as fundamental right, 167

kinds of harm perpetuated in, 87–88
promoting religious and cultural freedom in, 79
reforming, 79
renegotiating the burdens of justice in, 88–90
state Supreme Court rulings about finance structures of, 167
trends in, 166
types of questions about financing, 90
Public philosophy, call for new, *xiii*
Public properties, franchises involving, 120
Public schools, segregation in, 79
Purtilo, Ruth, 93, 170

Ramsey, Paul, theological paradigm of, 174
Rationality, exalted view of, 134
Rauschenbusch, Walter, 5
Rawls, John, *x, xiii*
    comparative study of well-ordered societies of, 152
    position on distributive justice of, 26–27, 29–30
    theory of justice of, 10–11, 20, 151
Redistributions
    arguments against, 182
    equating distributive justice with, 28
    theories of distributive justice overreliant on, 67
Regime defined, 20
Release-time programs, 79
Religious traditions as resource for achieving justice, 45, 168
Resources
    accountability of distributors of, 11
    for achieving justice, 45–46
    control over, 11
Respect for persons, 105
    moral inferences of, 106
Respect for self
    moral inferences of, 106
    as responsibility of married persons, 53
    self-cultivation as, 105
Responses to injustice, appropriate, 10
Risks
    community allocation of, 67–68
    just allocation of, 178
Rodriguez case, 77–88
    moral issues and harmful policies in, 83–88
Root paradigms, 17, 42, 156–57, 166

Ryan, John A., moral justifiability of titles examined by, 4–5, 7, 150

Sacrifice, gift giving and sacredness involved in, *xii–xiii*
Sade, Robert M., view of physicians' services of, 149
Sadurski, Wojciech, difference between justice and generosity noted by, 51–52
Sales taxes
   disparity caused by, 168
   unjust, 74
San Antonio Independent School District et al. v. *Rodriguez et al.,* 77–88
Sandel, Michael J., 11
Scanlon, Thomas M., formal egalitarianism of, 182
Scarcity, conflicts created by, 3
School districts, funding of, 62–63
Schwartz, Alan, courts' interpretation of contracts described by, 179
Sellers, James
   authenticity important to, 155
   governance of public policies examined by, 24–25
   internal moral standards described by, 46
   media coverage underscoring negative experiences according to, 153
   ways of changing public policy explored by, 88
Selznick, Philip, social conditions in contracts analyzed by, 176
Shklar, Judith, law viewed as part of social continuum by, 175
Skolnick, Jerome H., norms affecting lawyers noted by, 131
Smith, Adam, 3
   Beauchamp and Childress's concept of comparative justice derived from, 173
   insights about labor of, 20
   market described by, 132
   social ills according to, 149
Smith, Reginald Heber, movement for voluntary legal aid services promoted by, 151
Social goods
   internal versus external, 13–14
   just allocation of, as chief virtue of communities, 47
   as means to attain human goods, 14
   negative aspects of, 13–14

right provision of, 1
   sovereignty of separate spheres of, 22
   validity of narratives about, 20
Social security
   benefits paid by versus contributions to, 64–65
   burden of payroll taxes for, 62
   funding of federally insured programs through, 171
   intent of, 74
Social Security Act, 95, 111
Social Security Administration, 65
Solidarity with mutuality of sacrifice, *xii*
Sorrell, James, 93, 170
Standard of rationality, 82
Star Credit Corporation, 126
State aid for public schools, 79–88
Sturm, Douglas, *ix–xiii*
   meanings of justice described by, 137–38
Sullivan, William, new understanding of freedom called for by, 147
Symbols that enlarge effective freedom, 44
Systemic harm
   principle of, 35–36
   results of, 163

Tax structure, reforming, 87
Taxation policies, 165
Taxes
   exemptions of people over 55 from, 161
   income. *See* Income taxes
   justifiable, 84
   local, 86
   property. *See* Property tax
   regressive, 85
   revenue from, 161, 166
   sales. *See* Sales taxes
Technis, 54, 153
Telos, 30
Texas school system
   financing formula in, original, 169
   financing formula in, revised, 167
   reforms in, 166
   U.S. Supreme Court case about favoritism in, 77–88
Textbooks, religious objections to, 165
Theological ethics, 154
Theory of morality, 154
Thomasma, David
   allocation of burdens in health care ignored by, 106

first-contact care described by, 105, 108
right to health care advocated by,
95–98, 100–102, 171–72
Thurow, Lester, criteria for assigning
losses of, 112–13
Trade unions, 46
Tribal totem, family as, 49
Tripodal theory of the just distribution
of benefits and burdens, 50
base of, 57–58, 155
Turner, Victor, analysis of root paradigms by, 42, 166

Unconscionability
cases of, 125
coinage of the term, 178–79
concept of, 124
Uniform Commercial Code, 124, 126, 177
United States
approaches to distributive justice in, 2
forms of Hume's approach in, 2–3
schizophrenic character of, x–xi
social interpreters in, 6
transformation of thought patterns
and practices of society in, xiii
U.S. Public Health Association, 170
U.S. Supreme Court, 77. *See also*
Rodriguez case
Usman, Mike, college expenses of, 69, 72

Van Cott, Ann, college expenses of, 69, 72
Virtue
justice as, *ix*
link between character of social institutions and people's, 155
Voluntary creation of institutions to
benefit the public, 9
Voluntary organizations, 164

Walzer, Michael, *xii*, 152
allocations of social and political
power as necessary for, 10
commodities for, 173
domination of health care by the
wealthy or prominent feared by, 174
experiences linked with patterns of
provision by, 170
focus of social critics described by, 147
freedom as most appropriate distributive rule according to, 51
moral value of fulfilling terms of contract for, 176
multiple criteria required for distributive justice for, 152

national proposal for allocating hard
work by, 37
requirements of distributive justice
for, 158
work on political justice according to,
150
Warren, Mary Ann, source of moral
obligations to future generations
analyzed by, 160–61
Washakie County School District No. 1 v.
Herschler, 82
Weak classes, creation of, 14
Wealth-maximization principle, 135–36
Welfare liberalism, 8–9, 150–51
Welfare programs to support graduates
of poor education system, 87
Welfare system
government responsibility for administering, 19
as response to distributive problems,
7–8
West End Railway, 121–23
White, G. Edward, trends in tort law
analyzed by, 171
Will as the key to morality, 41
Williams v. *Walker,* 179
Wilson Trading case, 179
Wilson, William Julius
causes of economic hardships for the
poor studied by, 71
harm to lower socioeconomic classes
within ethnic group studied by, 60
Women
decline in standard of living after
divorce of, 62
declining importance of marriage to,
159
single-parent families headed by
Black American, 60
systemic harms for, 58–59
unequal division of labor for
employed married, 55–58
Work, assigning hard, 33–37
with future generations in mind, 39
World Health Organization, 97

Younger generations
inequities faced by, 61–62
social responsibilities to their elders
of, 74
Your Shop at Home Services, Inc., 125–26